THE PERSONAL SECURITY HANDBOOK

More related titles

Holiday Courses for Long Weekends and Short Breaks
A guide to the best holiday courses and workshops in the UK and Ireland

A unique guide full of fascinating and often unusual things you can do on your next holiday. Gain a new skill, pursue an exciting hobby, or develop an interest you already have.

The Home Security Handbook
How to keep your home and family safe from crime

Helps to identify a range of vulnerabilities, threats and risks and provides effective countermeasures to keep a home and family safe from crime.

Making a Will
A self-help guide

'If you want to save a lot of money on solicitors' bills, the self-help guide to *Making a Will* has just been published.' – *The Observer*

7 Ways to Beat the Pension Crisis

Explains clearly the new rules and outlines seven effective ways in which you can secure a more prosperous retirement.

howtobooks

Please send for a free copy of the latest catalogue to:
How To Books
3 Newtec Place, Magdalen Road
Oxford OX4 1RE, United Kingdom
Email: info@howtobooks.co.uk
www.howtobooks.co.uk

THE PERSONAL SECURITY HANDBOOK

How to keep yourself and your family safe from crime

D. G. CONWAY

howto**books**

OXFORDSHIRE COUNTY COUNCIL	
3200942872	
Bertrams	**20.10.05**
613.6 CON	**£12.99**

Published by How To Books Ltd
3 Newtec Place, Magdalen Road,
Oxford OX4 1RE, United Kingdom
Tel: (01865) 793806. Fax: (01865) 248780
email: info@howtobooks.co.uk
www.howtobooks.co.uk

All rights reserved. No part of this work may be reproduced or stored in an information retrieval system (other than for purposes of review) without the express permission of the publisher in writing.

© Copyright 2005 D. G. Conway

British Library Cataloguing in Publication Data
A catalogue record for this book is available from the British Library.

Produced for How To Books by Deer Park Productions, Tavistock
Cover design by Baseline Arts Ltd, Oxford
Typeset by Kestrel Data, Exeter
Printed and bound in Great Britain by Cromwell Press, Trowbridge, Wiltshire

NOTE: The material contained in this book is set out in good faith for general guidance and no liability can be accepted for loss or expense incurred as a result of relying in particular circumstances on statements made in this book. Laws and regulations are complex and liable to change, and readers should check the current position with the relevant authorities before making personal arrangements.

Contents

1 Introduction	1
Origins of this book	1
Lack of understanding and knowledge	2
Approach	2
Definitions	4
Security	4
Vulnerability	4
Threat	4
Risk	5
Countermeasures	5
Safety	7
Non-security problms	8
Review Method	8
Stage 1: Review Security	8
Stage 2: Prioritise problems	8
Stage 3: Define countermeasures	9
Stage 4: Adopt and prioritise countermeasures	9
Stage 5: Implement	10
Review Pace	10
What you will need	11
When to do it	12
It's your decision!	13
2 Theft	14
Credit cards	14
Lost credit/debit cards	15
Dishonest retail staff	16
Cash cards	18
Receipt left at cash point	19
Bogus phone survey/check	19
Cash point sleeve	20
Shoulder surfing	21
Skimming	22
Micro camera	23

v

The Personal Security Handbook

Man in a box	24
Cash point robbery	25
Forced withdrawal	26
Pickpockets	**27**
Other tricks and methods	**30**
Chain letters	30
Phoney foreign fines	31
Tricks and cons	32
'You've won a prize' letters	33
Counterfeit money	35

3 Everyone — 36

Mobile phones	**36**
IMEI number	27
If your mobile is stolen	37
Mobile Equipment National Database	38
Your keys	**38**
Copying keys	38
Looking after your keys	39
Keys hidden outside	42
Defending yourself	**43**
Handling conflict	44
Assault	**44**
Conflict management	**45**
Approches to violence	45
Underlying awareness	46
Actions and behaviour	47
Identify the signs	49
Impact factors	51
Recognise escalation	52
Identify escape routes	53
Personal space	53
Conscientious citizen	54
Internet Security	**54**
The criminals	54
Your equipment	55
Software updates and patches	55
Passwords	56
Illegal software	57
Spam	58
At work	58
Computer privacy	59
Shopping and on line theft	59
Ergonomics and health	60
General security	61
Identity theft	**62**
Taking your identity	63
Phishing	64
Junk mail avalanche	**67**

Contents

4	**Vehicle security review**	**69**
	Theft of and from cars	**69**
	Buying a car	70
	Your car told me!	70
	Additional security	**71**
	Steering wheel locks	71
	Immobilisation	72
	Key codes	72
	Alarms	73
	Stickers	73
	Etching	74
	Radio transmitters	74
	Mapping transmitters	75
	Stealing a car with the car key	**75**
	House breaking	75
	Leaving the keys in the ignition	76
	Selling your car	76
	Car jacking	**78**
	Accident	79
	Something wrong	79
	Assault/attack	79
	Stealing valuables from a car	**83**
	What they will take	**85**
	Where they will steal it	**87**
	Car parks	87
	Home – on-street parking	89
	Home – off-street parking	90
	Home – garage parking	90
	Cars at petrol stations	91
	Main road service areas	92
	Badly-managed leisure centre and hotel car parks	94
	Garage workshops	95
	Getting into a car	96
	Stopped at the lights	97
	'Lapping'	99
	'Spotting' in car parks	100
	Who is targeted	101
	Criminal damage	**104**
5	**Mostly men**	**106**
	Why young men?	**107**
	Excess alcohol	**108**
	Binge drinking	109
	Effects of alcohol	109
	Why it happens	111
6	**Mostly women**	**116**
	General	**117**
	At home	**120**

Bogus callers	121
Nuisance telephone calls	123
Travelling	**125**
Safety when walking	127
Using public transport	130
Cycling	135
Shopping	**137**
Bag theft	137
Shopping bag theft	138
Back at the car	139
Handbags	**141**
Running/jogging/cycling/riding	**143**
Attacks by strangers	**145**
If attacked	**147**
Sexual assault	**150**
How he gets control	151
Safe dating	**152**
Internet dating	155
Speed dating	156
Trusting	**157**
Offenders	**158**
Setting boundaries	**159**
Assumed consent	160
Drug-assisted sexual assault/'date rape'	165
Advice for victims	**169**
If you don't remember anything	170
If you have been raped	170
Safety at work	**173**
Working outside the office	176
Domestic violence	**181**
What the options are	183
Am I a victim of domestic violence?	183
Preparing to leave	186
When assault happens	187
What men can do	**188**

7	**Mostly your children**	**191**
	Not my child!	**192**
	Bullying	**193**
	What is bullying?	194
	How do I know?	194
	What can I do?	196
	My child is a bully	199
	Child abuse	**208**
	Possible signs	208
	General child protection advice	**210**
	Stranger danger	210
	Knowing who the abusers are	214

General advice to parents	**215**
Children and the Internet	**217**
You and the Internet	217
Email	218
Chat rooms	218
Children and mobile phones	**222**
Cycle helmets	**224**
Drugs	**224**
Signs of drug use	225
Widely-available drugs	227
Young adults	**232**

8 Mostly older people — 235
How vulnerable are you?	**235**
Driving and the elderly	**237**
Driving warning signs	239
Warning signs elsewhere	240
Driving assessment	240

9 Terrorism — 241
Terrorism – countermeasures	**241**
General	242
At home	243
Travelling	246
What to do after an attack	**247**

10 What now? — 252
Procedure	**252**
The real risk	**253**
When do I review security again?	**253**

Useful websites	**255**
Index	**258**

1 Introduction

We all know that society is less than perfect and that crime could easily touch us all, and most of us at least know somebody close to us who has been the victim of crime. That scares people and they feel helpless because they think that there is nothing they can do to protect themselves. They are wrong! There is a lot that the average person can do to protect themselves and their family. This security handbook will teach you how to perform a security review on various different aspects of your life to identify and resolve any threats, vulnerabilities and risks.

Origins of This Book

I first considered writing a security tutorial when I joined friends who were discussing what they would buy if they won millions on the lottery. Most people included the expected fast cars, luxury holidays and big houses, but there was one priority purchase that was common to most of them and which really surprised me. Almost all of them dreamed of using their fortune to buy a 'secure and safe lifestyle'!

They were ordinary people, leading ordinary lives, people who I thought would have no specific security worries. I investigated further because I wanted to know what additional security they thought they needed. I wanted to know what special threats they thought they faced and how they thought sudden wealth would help them to improve their security. Most of their concerns could be listed under two main classifications:

1. Aspects of their lifestyle that I thought were already within their control.
2. Headline-grabbing crimes, which they were very unlikely to encounter.

Basically, people were worrying about nothing, because with the right information and guidance they could make significant improvements to their personal security with minimal effort and at minimal cost.

This book will teach you how to look at your lifestyle to identify potential vulnerabilities, threats and risks. When you have identified them I will propose simple, affordable and achievable countermeasures that the average person can implement to increase their levels of security.

Lack of understanding and knowledge

Most people don't understand about real crime, or how they can take simple measures to help them to avoid becoming victims of crime. Some people are vaguely aware of some of the issues, but most of the knowledge on which they base their opinions about crime comes from lurid news stories and a smattering of 'information' from television police dramas, most of which are American! The bottom line is that they are really worried about crimes, which only actually affect one in fifty thousand people!

This was bad enough, but the biggest problem was that they don't understand the actual and common threats they face, or what they can easily do to avoid them. They have little concept of how real crime actually applies to them and they certainly don't recognise or understand the range of simple counter-measures that are available for them to protect themselves, their family and their unique lifestyle.

Approach

Crime statistics are rising, but that is due partly to the effect of new recording rules and procedures, and partly to a greater willingness to report crime. I want to apply a new understanding of crime and how to avoid it.

As a simple example, are you more like 'Sid Stupid' or 'Colin Careful'?

Sid Stupid gets his cash point card in his hand, with the scrap of paper he has written the PIN number on because he can't remember it. He walks up to the nearest cash machine and withdraws his maximum limit because he is going to buy a motorbike. Sid withdraws the cash then walks away from the machine as he counts his cash to make sure the cash machine hasn't cheated him. Shoving

Introduction

his wad of cash in the back pocket of his jeans Sid Stupid heads for the pub for a quick one before he goes to buy his motorbike.

Colin Careful knows he has to withdraw his maximum limit from the cash machine so he thinks safety. He keeps an eye out on his way to the bank, looking for suspicious activity – for example louts hiding their faces under hooded tops and hanging around the cash point with no apparent reason. He also looks out for drunks, aggressive beggars and other troublemakers who like to loiter around the cash point. When he gets to the bank, there are some people around but he has already decided to use the cash point inside. Colin Careful knows that inside the bank, CCTV cameras and bank staff make it a more secure location to withdraw that much cash. Colin checks the machine for unofficial criminal devices, hunches over it to make the transaction and then counts his cash in private. He puts the cash in an envelope he brought with him, seals it and wraps an elastic band or two around it. Then slides it into his inside jacket pocket. He uses a safety pin to secure that pocket and then closes his jacket before going to the bank door. He pauses in the safety of the bank door to look around just in case. Once outside, while he is still covered by town centre CCTV, he heads towards the motorcycle showroom but pauses to look in a shop window, using the reflection in the glass to see what is going on behind him, just to be sure!

So, having read how Sid and Colin withdrew their cash, are you closer to being Sid Stupid or Colin Clever? Change the scenario a little: if you were going to get just £40 out of the bank would that make a difference? Would you suddenly become Sid Stupid and not care?

That is the most important lesson I have to teach. To know or identify the circumstances in which you are vulnerable, and in everything you do to take simple and reasonable steps to make sure that you don't become the victim of a crime.

By being aware and careful, you are probably 95% less likely to become the victim of opportunist theft at a cash point! By reading through this security handbook you will identify vulnerabilities and implement effective counter-measures to greatly reduce your chances of becoming a victim of any crime. That is as hard as it gets!

Definitions

If we have a common understanding and definition of some basic terms, we will be able to make better progress.

Security

Security is the application of methods and procedures that are used to make our lifestyle secure against any vulnerability, threat or risk. By applying security appropriately, we will achieve safety!

Vulnerability

A 'vulnerability' is the avenue that a threat uses to reach you and cause you harm. For example, if you are in the habit of leaving your handbag in the bar when you go to the toilet, that is a 'vulnerability'.

An abandoned handbag would be easy to spot but the vulnerability isn't always so easy to see. For example, leaving a pair of low-heeled driving shoes visible in the car leaves you vulnerable in several ways. A criminal:

- knows that your car is owned/driven by a female
- knows that you are probably wearing heels (why else would you leave low-heeled driving shoes in the car?) so cannot run away from him/her
- guesses you are not under 15 or over 50
- guesses that you may be alone
- knows this is the night club area, so if he/she waits here in the bushes until the clubs close . . .

Threat

A threat is any occurrence that could cause you harm, loss or distress. Threats can be imposed on us by crimes such as theft, robbery, burglary and assault by drunks in the street. Though this book primarily concentrates on threats that can be imposed on us by criminal activity or accident, there are other threats such as illness or disease.

Introduction

Risk

Risk is the extent of our exposure to the threats to which we are vulnerable. Risk can be measured in two ways: the impact of the threat or the likelihood of falling victim to that threat.

The impact of a threat is a measure of the damage, injury or loss it could inflict if we fell victim to that threat. For example, the impact of somebody stealing my handbag is that I would lose some money and few personal items. However, on another day I might lose a lot more. All of my money, my cheque book, my driving licence, the car keys, my diary and my house keys! Now the thief has my driving licence and address, a set of house keys, plus credit and store cards and my identity pass to get into work. Thus the risk of losing a handbag can have radically different risks associated with it depending on the circumstances.

The likelihood of a threat is a measure of the frequency with which we are exposed to it and may become a victim of it. For example, you would agree that being targeted by an international gang of terrorists, who plan to kidnap somebody and demand ten million pounds as ransom, would be a significant threat. However the likelihood of that happening to me is so low that I won't be losing any sleep over it. I don't have ten million pounds and any international terrorist would know that. I am of no significance to them and they probably wouldn't be looking in the supermarket and the other places that I go for a worthwhile kidnap victim anyway. For that reason, though kidnapping and murder are decidedly serious and unwelcome, because I am not a senior politician, wealthy celebrity or national leader, I am pretty sure they won't be looking for me.

Countermeasures

A countermeasure is something that you can do to improve your safety and security. My aim is to teach you how to identify problems, then how to propose appropriate countermeasures to those problems. To do that I will discuss potential vulnerabilities, threats and risks then suggest a range of appropriate potential countermeasures. None of the lists I produce are exhaustive; they simply illustrate the problems and possible solutions. The lists will be a guide for you when considering your unique circumstances and lifestyle, you will need to spend some time identifying your vulnerabilities, threats and risks, then finding a countermeasure that is appropriate to your lifestyle and circumstances.

Generally when you identify a threat, there are four things that you can do about it:

- Ignore it and hope it goes away.
- Take action to reduce the risk.
- Take action to avoid the risk.
- Take action to remove it – without taking new and unnecessary risks.

For any given vulnerability, threat and risk some options might not be acceptable, because of the intrusive impact they will have on your lifestyle. To illustrate that I will use a simple example. Suppose the threat you have identified is the possibility of a pickpocket taking your money. Using the above strategy there are four options for dealing with it.

- **Ignore it** – keep your fingers crossed and hope it doesn't happen.
- **Reduce the risk** – put your money in an inside pocket, always do your coat up, and try to avoid crowds.
- **Avoid it** – never carry any money, and have your clothes specially made with no pockets so that nobody can ever pick your pockets.
- **Remove it** – carry money in a stainless steel money belt. Employ ten armed bodyguards to walk beside you to escort and protect you. They will be instructed never to let anyone get within six feet of you. You will only ever use your bullet-proof car and never ever travel on trains, tubes trains or buses.

Though all of the options would work, it is clear that some options are more acceptable and sensible. Some options are unrealistic or foolish. As with this example, for every threat and risk, only you know your circumstances sufficiently well to decide what course of action is best for you, or how you can adapt an approach to suit your circumstances. For me the bodyguard option is unachievable and unacceptable, but to an international pop superstar it may be a valid option!

In this example, for most people the second option 'reducing the risk' is the most effective and sensible solution. Knowing your lifestyle and circumstances you are free to adapt the approach to suit your circumstances.

Introduction

Throughout this book it will be your primary objective:

- To recognise the sort of threats that are out there and how they can affect you and your lifestyle.
- To look beyond the examples listed, to recognise additional or modified threats to which you are vulnerable due to your unusual or unique circumstances.
- To study those threats and to identify how you can remove or reduce the risks.
- To compile an action plan that sets out the actions you have to take in your lifestyle to implement countermeasures, reduce or remove the risks and vulnerabilities identified.
- To continually monitor your life, so that you can recognise change which will be a trigger to performing another personal security review, to ensure that your lifestyle remains as safe and secure as it can.

Though the security tutorial necessarily compartmentalises your life, in reality various segments of your life will almost certainly overlap. That doesn't pose any real problems for you, because when performing a security review you have an intimate understanding of all aspects of your life.

When you have reviewed your security, you may want to use your new skill and experience to review security for an elderly relative. If you are attempting to perform a review for somebody else, it should be clear that you will need constant access to and a close and detailed understanding of the person and lifestyle of the subject of the review. Without a fairly intimate knowledge of the lifestyle of the subject of a security review, you cannot hope to understand the impact of potential risks and countermeasures or how relevant they may be.

Safety

Safety is the status we all want to achieve. Safety can be defined as a circumstance in which vulnerabilities have been removed or reduced to insignificant levels, and threats and risks have been removed by the application of sensible, achievable and affordable countermeasures.

Non-security problems

While performing a security review people often identify 'problems' that are not security related. For example, while thinking about the possible theft of that handbag, you may realise that if somebody stole your handbag, you would lose the picture of your husband proposing at that big office party!

Not a huge loss, but it would affect you so obviously you should not ignore these non-security problems. They represent a potential threat so we have to take action. In this case, the countermeasure may be to go to the photographer to get a copy of that photograph. Until then perhaps you should keep the photograph at home where it will be safe!

Don't lose track of any problems that you identify: record them and take the opportunity to resolve them.

Review Method

The method I propose is easy to follow. The book is broken down into chapters and sections, where each one concentrates on a different aspect of your lifestyle security. A security review is completed in simple stages.

Stage 1: Review security

You will review an aspect of your security during which you will identify and record any vulnerabilities, threats and risks that you find.

Stage 2: Prioritise problems

When you have finished the review, you will need to prioritise the vulnerabilities, threats and risks that you have identified and recorded. When completed, you will have listed them in order of severity, putting those that present the greatest threat to you and your lifestyle at the top of the list, and those that present the least threat at the bottom of the list. This process allows you to concentrate on resolving the priority problems – those that will give you the greatest possible reward for your efforts making best use of your limited resources.

Introduction

Remember, addressing the highest priority problems as soon as possible will allow you to make the greatest improvements to your personal safety and security.

Stage 3: Define countermeasures

In stage 2 you prioritised the problems to allow you to concentrate on those that offer the greatest threat to your security. In this stage, you take each problem and attempt to identify and define sensible, achievable and affordable countermeasure(s) that will resolve the problem to your satisfaction. You may come up with only one possible countermeasure, or a list of three alternate countermeasures. When you have identified them, record them.

Stage 4: Adopt and prioritise countermeasures

For each 'problem' you should now consider the possible countermeasures that you identified and recorded. That is, look at the options and based on a range of considerations decide which countermeasure(s) you want to introduce. The decision will be based on a range of issues including:

- **Benefit** – try to decide by how much any proposed countermeasure will improve your safety and security. A countermeasure that delivers marginal benefits should possibly be shelved while you concentrate on a countermeasure that will deliver greater benefits

- **Cost** – try to identify the financial cost of introducing each countermeasure. The cost may be easy to identify. For example 'buy a new padlock for the garage door' will cost £15, plus £5 for extra keys to be cut. Sometimes there are hidden costs, which have to be identified and included. For example, suppose you had identified the countermeasure of 'replace the front door' to improve your security. The cost of the door is £325, but that is not the total cost. Fitting the door will cost an extra £125; new lock, letterbox, handles and house numbers will cost £75. The price of the door and fitting includes a new doorframe, which means the wall around the door will have to be plastered and painted at a cost of £55. So there is a hidden cost of an extra £255 to replace the front door!

- **Resources** – if you are paying somebody to introduce the countermeasure you will just ask for three independent quotes, and pick the quote that offers what you consider to be best value, which may not be the cheapest! As with any purchase, you should also consider reputation and recommendation, quality, availability and your feelings. When dealing with tradesmen and craftsmen, I always consider my 'gut feelings' about them. No matter how well he may be recommended, no matter how low he may bid, if I just don't trust him or I feel there is something not quite right, I won't use him.

- **Degree of risk** – you should also consider the level of risk you will be taking by not introducing a countermeasure. For example if you don't fix the lock on the front door, you may as well leave the front door open because the lock is useless. That would be a critical factor to be considered when prioritising your countermeasures.

Stage 5: Implement

When all of the decisions have been made, you have to implement the selected countermeasure(s) in the order you decided upon. The countermeasure may be simple, such as shutting the kitchen window instead of leaving it open for the cat to come in when it is cold or wet. It may be more involved, such as cutting back all of the hedges and shrubs around the back of the house then planting prickly bushes to stop intruders from hiding there. It could even be life changing, such as changing your job and moving to live in a safer area, while making the children change schools.

This is the most vital stage of the process, the time when you act to protect yourself against the vulnerabilities, threats and risks that you have identified during the lifestyle security review process.

Review Pace

The sooner you review your safety and security and implement countermeasures, the safer you will be, but don't rush the process. Take your time to read each section of this book carefully. Think about each problem that is discussed and consider how that problem or others like it could affect you. When you fully understand them, you will have a valuable insight into the way apparently inconsequential, innocent acts, omissions and decisions could put your safety and security at risk.

Introduction

When you have finished reading this book, using the examples and descriptions given and your intimate knowledge of your unique lifestyle, you will be able to identify and prioritise the specific problems that could turn you into a victim. More importantly, you will have learned and be practised at looking at everyday situations and be able to identify where new risks and threats lie, which will allow you to take steps to avoid them. Knowing that not only allows you to make changes to reduce or remove your exposure, it also allows you to continually review your life, identifying and avoiding new threats as they occur.

What You Will Need

To understand and be able to perform an effective security review, you need:

- This book and the methodology and explanations contained in it.
- Constant access to, and a close and detailed understanding of, the person and lifestyle of the subject of the review. Which means you can easily review your own lifestyle, you could review a close family member but almost certainly couldn't effectively review the lifestyle of a total stranger.
- Time to read the book, to consider the range and type of threats discussed and to take more time to think through and identify how any of the issues raised could affect your particular lifestyle.
- The ability to decide on the relevance and threat level to your lifestyle of the risks discussed, while taking a broader view to decide if you are subject to other more specific and unique threats and risks.
- A notepad and pencil or other means of recording vulnerabilities, threats and risks as you discover them as well as assigning appropriate and possible countermeasures.
- The skill, finances, time and resources to implement any countermeasure that you select.

Other than that there are no specialist skills or knowledge required to be able to perform a security review! But you must:

- Recognise and understand that there are threats and risks all around us.

- Accept that some of your activities will make you more vulnerable and hence at a greater risk of becoming a victim.
- Learn how to identify potential threats and risks in 'your world'.
- Learn how to identify acceptable and possible countermeasures that you can use to reduce or remove your exposure to those threats and risks.
- Remain alert to your surroundings, particularly in relation to some of your activities and actions.
- Become equally aware of the activities and behaviour of the people around you, and be prepared to take action to avoid developing or potential risks.

When To Do It

If you have never reviewed your security, review it as soon as you can. After that, you should perform a formal personal security review every 12 months.

However, during the year you should remember to maintain an awareness of your world and continually monitor your lifestyle, because a change in circumstances could invalidate previous reviews and countermeasures.

If you identify a significant change in your life, you should at least undertake a partial security review, but the more significant the change, the more reason there is to perform a new and complete security review! When you have a potentially life-changing experience, you should perform a new lifestyle security review. For example, if you:

- move house
- start a new job
- take a different mode of transport to work – e.g. train instead of driving
- have a child
- come into some money.

It's Your Decision!

Remember that this is general advice. Laws change, and people differ. You may have a totally different lifestyle to everyone else in the country. You may have strange allergies, a love for dangerous sports and a pet tiger! Because there is only one 'you', this has to be just general advice and you must treat it as such. *You* must decide if you want to act on any of this advice. *You* must select actions that are appropriate to you. *You* must check with relevant experts to make sure that you do the right thing for you.

2 Theft

Money is the target of most criminals. They may steal gold, diamonds, mobile phones, television sets, handbags and cameras, but their ultimate goal is to convert those stolen possessions into cash.

That being the case, it would be a lot easier and more lucrative if they could steal cash in the first place. Though a thief might steal a camera worth £300, he may only get £20 when he illegally sells it on. That means that he would much prefer to steal your wallet or purse and take the £85 you have in cash, giving a much higher reward and less effort.

Hard cash isn't the only way that money changes hands. Credit cards, debit cards, and store cards are also used to make purchases. Though they are used less frequently now, cheques are also used to make transactions. Alhough none of them are as good as cash, they are all valuable to a thief.

Credit Cards

Credit card fraud is a huge business globally and the UK is not immune. The figures involved are amazing. There are 65 million credit cards in use in the UK. Worldwide, billions of pounds are lost annually and the credit card companies are struggling to stop that loss. The total loss in the UK is estimated to be about £500,000,000. Cash card fraud has soared and is reported to be 85% higher than last year in the UK. The new Chip and Pin system is designed to reduce that level, but fraud using cards lost in the post rose 51% last year to a total of £61.2 million. Telephone fraud on credit cards reached £139 million. On top

Theft

of that one report claimed that a further £123 million was lost to counterfeit cards.

When the change to Chip and Pin is complete, it is expected that fraud levels will fall – at least they will fall until criminals discover a way of getting around the new security protocols. The biggest problem at the moment is careless credit card holders and users. Loss of cards, either on or after delivery, puts them in the hands of criminals and abuse of cards by dishonest shop retail staff adds a greater burden.

Lost credit/debit cards

A card can be stolen while in the post so it never reaches the owner of the account. A card can be stolen from a residence on delivery, or fraudulent applications can be made to get cards delivered to a false address. If you don't shred financial and personal documents, criminals can take them out of your dustbin and use them to commit crime against you, as well as committing crime in your name! Using your details and a gas bill, for example a criminal can get a bank account. With that he can apply for any number of debit, credit and store cards using your name and a phoney address.

Cards stolen from bags and wallets by pickpockets, muggers and sneak thieves in changing rooms and clubs find their way into criminal use. Cards are big business in every sense – there are reported to be an average of 75 cash withdrawals per second in the UK!

Lost cards – countermeasures

- ✓ Keep track of your cards and never ever leave them unattended.
- ✓ Never keep your cards with proof of identity or chequebooks. Don't let them steal one wallet, bag or case that contains all they need to actually prove identity and fleece your accounts.
- ✓ Make sure that when a new card is due, it arrives. If in doubt call the company to check. When it arrives sign it immediately and cut up the old card.
- ✓ If you suspect a new card has gone missing, report it immediately or at least query it with the issuer.

- ✓ If you receive any documentation, statements, new account letters or anything else through the post that you do not understand, query it with the company immediately. (It may relate to an account a criminal has set up in your name.)

- ✓ If your card is stolen or just goes missing, report it to the appropriate company immediately. Cancel it, and order a new one.

- ✓ Don't write pin numbers or passwords down and never ever write them down and keep them with the card!

- ✓ Think about what you are going to do and consider leaving your cards securely at home. For example, if you were going to help a neighbour clean out the ditches on his estate, would you really need to take your cards with you? If you do you stand a chance of losing your wallet, but you will also probably get hot and leave your jacket on a fence post while you are working! While your back is turned somebody may take your wallet. When else do you think it might be safer to leave your cards securely at home? Jogging, walking the dog, mowing the lawn, taking rubbish to the tip, taking paper to the recycling depot? Add a few activities relevant to you.

Dishonest retail staff

Because they handle them all day, dishonest retail employees are ideally placed to abuse credit and debit cards in a number of ways.

Clone. They have the technology to read the details off your card if you are not looking, so that they can create a clone – a duplicate of your card. They can then sell the duplicate card and the criminal who uses it can put his/her own signature on the card and use it. As your card has not been stolen, you don't know anything is wrong until you get your statement in a month or so and find a lot of purchases for luxury items that you know nothing about.

Theft/substitution. This is a riskier undertaking for the waiter or assistant in the shop, because to use this trick they have to return a similar but different card to you. For example if you are Mr Jones and you pay by credit or debit card, the waiter or shop assistant gives you back a card, but the card he gives you is in the name of, for example, Mrs Green!

If you spot the switch they will apologise, tell you it was a mistake and give you your card back. If you don't spot it, you put the card in your wallet or purse and leave, carrying a card which was originally issued to somebody else.

Theft

Meanwhile your card has been sold on and is already being used to buy electronics in the high street. You find out you've been carrying a card in the name of Mrs Green when you try to make your next purchase, when a sarcastic assistant asks Mr Jones if he has any proof he is Mrs Green!

If you don't use your card very often, you might not find out until you get your statement in a month or so. By that time your card has become too hot to use, so it has been 'recycled'. Another victim is now carrying your card and his/her card is being used by the criminal to make expensive purchases.

Double swipe. In this trick, the retailer swipes your card with the amount and gets a confirmation, but tells you it didn't work. They swipe the card again either for the same amount or any amount they care to key in. That sum is debited from your account and the retailer slides the 'profit' into his pocket.

Customer not present. With all card details, a retailer can sell goods to a customer who is not present. This system was introduced for the convenience of customers – you call the shop and order a laptop computer or something over the phone. The seller takes the details of the card and registers the purchase. Your card is debited with the value of the purchase without your card being swiped or you signing anything. If the criminal can arrange to intercept delivery of the goods, they are his. Perhaps he asks the store when the delivery will be made and then simply turns up and waits outside for the delivery. He walks out of your gate, says, 'I'm just on my way out, guys, give it to me,' then off he goes with the goods.

Internet abuse. Just to indicate the size of the problem, one million UK citizens reportedly fell victim to fraudulent online transactions last year. With card details it is relatively easy to make purchases. With a card name, account number, expiry date, address details and security code you can order almost anything over the Internet. By requesting that the goods are delivered to your 'work address', you collect the goods – not the card owner. Use that stunt 20 times in a day, set up in that temporary delivery address to collect the express next day deliveries, and then move on. You could even use an innocent address to receive goods that have been fraudulently obtained on a stolen or abused credit card. For example, by visiting an estate agent, viewing an empty property for sale, getting a key cut and then using that building for a while before moving on.

Dishonest staff – countermeasures

✓ Always keep an eye on your cards. Make sure that you know where they are at all times.

✓ If a shop assistant starts to do something under the counter with my card I politely ask them to stop and explain what they were doing. I explain that I am asking the question for security reasons. If they cause a problem I ask for the manager. (I have been known to report problems to their head office and to the credit card company), especially if the store manager is dismissive or obstructive.

✓ Always keep your cards with you. Never trust the staff, for example by leaving your card while you go to the toilet or to get your coat. Watch what is happening to your card at all times.

✓ When a transaction has been completed, before you put your card away check it carefully to make sure that it is yours and not a substitute. If given a substitute I would not say anything to the apologetic member of staff but report it to the credit card company and police immediately.

✓ If my card is double swiped or I am not sure what a member of retail staff is doing when they fiddle with my card, I ask them. Again, I will explain that I have security concerns and if necessary speak to the manager and call the credit card company to clarify what transactions the member of staff has processed.

✓ You should be very careful with any information, receipts, statements, old cards, new cards, letters, application forms – anything could be of use to a thief, who might be using your account.

✓ Be particularly vigilant if you are using a credit or debit card abroad. You won't know about it until you see your statement in a month's time, by which time you will be at home and in no position to go around to that car hire company in Brazil to ask why they charged the hire of ten cars to your card!

Cash Cards

Credit and debit card fraud will eventually lead to a cash reward for the criminals involved. For example, the goods they buy with a stolen credit card will usually be converted to cash, so that they can buy what they want.

They would much prefer to steal the cash in the first place. There are a number of tricks that they can use to get at your cash! UK crime figures show that criminals took £39,000,000 from UK cash point fraud and theft in one year alone.

Receipt left at cash point

When you withdraw money from a cash point, most machines give you the option of having a receipt, though some machines always issue one. That receipt contains personal information, information that can be valuable to a criminal. Just from a privacy point of view, would you be happy for a neighbour to follow you to a cash point, see you make a transaction then pick up your receipt to see how much you have in your account and how much you just drew out?

Receipts – countermeasures

✓ Always take your receipts and statements with you when you use a cash point.

✓ Shred all unwanted receipts. Never let the criminals get hold of them.

Bogus phone survey/check

Criminals sometimes call people pretending to be from 'the bank'. They make quite plausible claims and sound bored enough to really be bank employees. They say they are doing a security check due to criminal activity in your area. After getting your confidence, they tell you that for security reasons they need to confirm some information. You are asked for your account number, mother's maiden name, and postcode. After each answer they confirm you are correct. Then they apologise, but say it's for your own protection, and ask for the security code on the back of your card. They may also tap you for more information – your branch, and even PIN number.

If you answer all this they have enough detail to persuade your mother that they are you, let alone a bank or loan company. If anyone starts asking these sorts of questions over the telephone, be very, very wary, especially if *they* called *you*! Be safe – *don't* give details out over the phone.

Bogus survey – countermeasures

✓ No matter who it is, be very wary of giving any personal information out over the phone.

✓ If it is a genuine phone call, you don't have to give out irrelevant information anyway – most large companies only collect it so that they can build up marketing information. If I drive a car, the make, model and mileage are my concern and not the bank or credit card company's – if they want to sell me their car insurance they can find another way of doing it.

✓ If they have called you, assume that they are dishonest unless they can prove otherwise. For example, could they give you their head office phone number to confirm that they are doing their job and that they work for the bank. If they give you a number, check it in the phone book or with directory enquiries. If it is the real phone number for the bank you can consider calling back and discussing matters. Personally I won't give anything out over the phone. With the advent of automated call centres and centralised call handling on another continent, I do all of my transactions face to face in the branch or by letter!

✓ If you called them be ready to give them limited information. If they ask for more information than you think they need, ask them why they need to know that. Ask to speak to a supervisor if you have to and explain that the amount of information being requested over an open or mobile phone line is a security breach. (Always make a note of their names, any department, reference numbers and the head office number and address so that you can complain if you have to!)

✓ Never trust a mail shot; it may look official but you don't know. An official looking letter arrives through your front door, explains that everybody is switching to PIN number cards for security reasons and asks you to fill in and return the enclosed form to 'our processing centre'. So the form asks for the account number, expiry dates, security code details, mother's maiden name etc, and for you to return it in the conveniently post paid envelope to Mr C Riminal, Central Processing Centre, PO Box 1554, Crookstown. There goes some more of your money!

Cash point sleeve

Sometimes called the Lebanese Loop! Some criminals insert almost invisible sleeves into the card slot of cash machines. The victim slips their card into the cash point and tries to key in their number. It doesn't work because the plastic sleeve is stopping the machine from recognising the card. Sometimes the criminal, posing as a helpful customer, suggests that the card holder should try keying in their PIN number again. When they do the criminal takes a note of

Theft

that number. Of course it doesn't work, so the card owner assumes the machine has swallowed their card. If the bank is open they go in to complain; if the bank is closed they can only walk off and try to report it the following day. As soon as the card holder has walked off, the criminal removes the sleeve and the card. He has the PIN number so off he goes to get as much as he can from that account.

Shoulder surfing

A crude trick but it works. The criminal, and perhaps an accomplice or two, crowd you at the cash point while you are keying in your number. If there is only one person you can use your body to shield the keyboard when you key in your PIN number. If there are two or three of the criminals they position themselves so that it is almost impossible to shield the number as you key it in. If it works, the criminals have your PIN number. All they do then is to pick your pocket or snatch the bag containing the card and they have all they need to empty that account.

Sleeve surfing – countermeasures

- ✓ Before using a cash point, feel the card slot with the tip of your finger. If there is a problem, or something in the slot, do not use it but report it to the bank immediately. (When you detect a sleeve you will be able to see and feel what it is.) Don't make a fuss – the criminals are not far away!
- ✓ If the card slot is clear, insert your card and shield the keyboard with your body so that nobody can see you keying in the PIN number. If anybody is hanging around or seems to be taking too much interest in what you are doing, consider these options:
  - ➢ Going inside the bank to use a cash point there.
  - ➢ Reporting your suspicions to bank employees.
  - ➢ Reporting your suspicions to the police – don't forget to describe the suspects so that the police know who they are looking for. In most towns they can watch the suspects on CCTV without raising their suspicions so that they can gather evidence before they take action.
  - ➢ Use a different machine at another time.
  - ➢ It's not 'British' – but you could ask them to step back, or assume they are looking and hold a coat or bag up to shield the number you key in.
  - ➢ If you use a cash point and the machine seems to be ignoring your card, check closely for a sleeve. Look in the slot – you will see that your card has not been fully swallowed by the reader, and the edge

is still visible. Do not leave the machine – call the police if you can and inform bank staff. Do not touch the sleeve because police may be able to recover it and some get evidence they can use against the criminals. If you are with somebody, get them to report it while you protect the machine – warn people trying to use nearby cash points too.

Skimming

Skimming is a much more sophisticated version of the trick. Skimmers use false card readers to take and record the card details so that the criminals can make a copy or clone of the card.

For example, when entering a bank foyer at night you have to swipe your card through a reader at the door. That 'official' reader reads the card, recognises you as a bank customer and releases the door lock. Criminals have in the past mounted their own reader underneath the official reader, so that a customer swipes their card through both machines. The official machine lets the customer in, and the criminal's machine reads and records the card details internally.

In other cases similar devices have been fitted over the actual cash point card slot. They are extremely well made and designed to blend in with the machine. The customer feeds his card into the cash point through the false card slot. The criminal's device reads and records the card details as it feeds through into the real reader. The customer makes their transaction and then leaves, not knowing his card has been copied.

Unfortunately, there is also either a micro camera aimed at the keyboard of the cash point to see and record your PIN number, or the thieves are waiting posing as customers so that they can shoulder surf to see your PIN as you key it in.

With the PIN and the details to make a clone of your cash card, they can then go ahead and empty your account.

Skimmer – countermeasures

✓ Beware of badly-made, poorly-fitted, loose card readers. It may be a real reader but it is more likely to be a false one. If in doubt don't use it and consider reporting it to the police and or bank staff.

✓ Beware of multiple card readers – the bank won't fit more than one on a single door!

✓ Beware of any fittings that seem to be new or out of place. I saw one micro camera disguised as a box to hold leaflets, but the criminals had to stick the box inside the cash point recess to make the camera record the keyboard. If the cash point looks different, beware.

✓ False equipment is often held on with double-sided sticky tape. Beware of problems with loose or badly aligned covers, boxes, or other fittings.

✓ If possible use the cash points inside a bank during opening hours. It is highly unlikely that they have been tampered with.

✓ Often there will be several cash points at a bank. Skimmers can cost thousands of pounds so there is only likely to be a skimmer on one of the cash point machines. When approaching several machines check for differences. Does one have a new box holding leaflets? Does the card slot on one machine look different to the other two? Are there people who seem to be hanging around and taking undue interest in the cash machine on the left? Has somebody stuck out of order signs on the other cash points to force you to use the suspect cash point? If so, beware, don't use it and report your suspicions.

Micro camera

Beware of any unusual device or equipment at, near, or on a cash point machine. Criminals have been known to mount a micro camera at a cash point that will transmit all transactions to a nearby screen for them to watch. If they can see your card, they can get the account number and your PIN number. Within an hour there may be a clone on the streets spending your money or running up a bill on your account.

Micro camera – countermeasures

- ✓ Always check any cash point for unusual equipment or devices, especially if they look very temporary and/or unusual. The criminals are clever and have access to skilled engineers. The devices can look like part of the machine so beware.

- ✓ If you see something, don't use that machine. Draw the device to the attention of bank staff or call the police and report your suspicions.

Man in a box

Crude – but it worked. I heard of one case where criminals erected an official looking hoarding at a cash point on the Friday evening of a bank holiday weekend. They used yellow hard hats, yellow jackets, barriers and flashing lights. The hoarding had an official looking sign apologising for inconvenience during refurbishment and asked customers to use the temporary machine set into the hoarding. It had a screen, a slot and a keyboard, plus what looked like a cash drawer. A stream of people used the machine but it never worked. They all got frustrated and saved up their anger for the bank because they were left without cash on a long bank holiday. What they didn't know was that they were helping somebody to steal their money.

Inside the hoarding there was a man. When a customer put his card into the temporary cash point it fell into the criminal's lap. When the customer typed in their PIN number, there was a beep and the number appeared on a screen inside the hoarding. The criminal slid the card into the real cash point, typed in the PIN number the victim was still busily trying, then withdrew as much cash as he could. Then, to put the victim off, he pressed a button and the message 'systems error, please try later' appeared on the screen that the victim was watching. The criminal slid the card into the slot, pressed a button, and it whirred out for the victim to take. Nobody knew a thing until the following Tuesday when bank staff asked what the hoarding was for and dozens of customers started complaining that the cash point had been out of order all weekend.

Crude theft – countermeasures

✓ Be alert. Wouldn't that set-up have made you suspicious?

✓ If it doesn't look right don't use it, and consider reporting it to the bank or police.

Cash point robbery

Criminals are not stupid. They know that cash points hold cash and that people using cash points have access to it and are there to withdraw cash. Sometimes a muscular young thief or gang wait at a cash point for someone to withdraw money, at which point they threaten that person and take that money. Some victims have reported that they when they were walking towards the cash point they were concerned about the two big guys in hoods who were watching them, but they still withdrew and lost their money!

Cash point – countermeasures

✓ When going to use a cash point be aware of the surroundings. That includes lighting, dark corners, overgrown bushes, corners and alcoves where criminals could be hiding. If in doubt, don't use that machine, and report your security and safety objections and concerns to the bank. They can get the lights fixed and the bushes cut back.

✓ Look to see who is around you. If three louts are loitering nearby, decide if you really want to use the cash point at this time. If there is a rowdy group coming down the High Street towards you, wait for them to pass before you use the cash point.

✓ If you are in any doubt, don't even approach the cash point. Wait until they have gone before you go and take your cash cards out.

✓ If you are in any doubt, don't withdraw anything, if you *have* to take something out – for example because you are at a petrol station and you need money to pay for the petrol you just pumped into your car – only take out what you need. If there are suspicious people around but you need £15 to pay for your fuel, *don't take out £500 because you need some holiday money next week.*

✓ When you do draw money out, be discreet. Don't take it from the cash slot and then turn around so that everybody can see while you count out the £500 holiday spending money. Complete the transaction privately in the cash point alcove; don't give a sneak thief a chance of running up and snatching your cash while you try to count it. Don't show everybody in the street how much money you just took out; put it away safely and securely as soon as you can.

✓ Beware cash point beggars. Aggressive beggars sometimes position themselves by a cash point and then harass people withdrawing money. They know you have money because you just drew some out and if one in ten cash point users are intimidated enough to give them money, they are winning. If this is a problem at your bank, report it to the bank staff and to the local police. Get the authorities to move the beggars on.

✓ If you use a cash point in a bank or building society foyer, where you need to swipe your card to gain access to that part of the building after hours, be careful. Check through the window; are there any unsavoury characters waiting in there? If so, consider not using that machine and report the problem to bank staff as soon as possible.

✓ If you use an after hours foyer cash point beware of 'tailgating', that is somebody following you in without swiping their own card (if they have one) to get in. If anyone without an account at that bank wants to get in there, why do they want to do it? They may be homeless and want somewhere warm and dry to sleep for the night, or they may have criminal activities in mind. If somebody tries to follow you in, challenge them. If you are too small or too timid, or they are too big to challenge, simply wait until there is nobody else near enough to follow you through that door and make sure it shuts behind you before anyone else gets there.

Forced withdrawal

Quite rare, but criminals have been know to force a victim to go to a cash point and withdraw as much cash as they can. The criminals then take the cash and run. This is a hard one to overcome, because if violence has been used against you and you are in fear of your life or safety, any countermeasures you use could cause you to be harmed.

Forced withdrawal – countermeasures

✓ Avoid the problem and don't fall into the hands of the thugs. Be aware of your surroundings and make sure that you avoid anything that looks like trouble.

✓ If you haven't been able to avoid the trouble, you have two choices,
   ➤ **Do what they say** – if they are violent and or desperate there is no telling what they might do to force you to withdraw money.

> **Try to make the machine swallow your card** – key in the wrong PIN number, in which case after a couple of attempts the machine will swallow your card and they won't get any of your cash. You could claim to have made a mistake because you are nervous – but it is your choice. Personally I'd rather lose a few pounds than risk my life.

Pickpockets

The word 'pickpocket' conjures up images of Fagin and street urchins cleverly lifting pocket watches or a silk handkerchief from a gent in Ye Olde London.

Pickpockets still exist, and they are common especially in crowded tourist areas. Tourists are a rich source of income for pickpockets, because they are carrying cash, traveller's cheques, valuable documents like passports, cameras and video equipment. Some may even be wearing expensive watches and jewellery!

In any crowd, especially in a crowd of people who are a little lost and a little distracted, the pickpockets move in. They often work in groups, or even families, moving through the crowds and taking what they want. Age is no barrier, I have heard of families who go out working with children as young as six or seven. The adult criminals get their children to fight, run into people, knock over displays in stores, ask victims to reach things off high shelves and so on. When you are distracted their parents move in to steal your money or valuables.

In the UK there seems to be a trend away from dipping into pockets. The thieves more often target bags and rucksacks, stealing from pockets and pouches. Some use finesse to slide quick fingers into bags, others use cruder methods. Many rucksack wearers find that the pockets and pouches on the outside of their rucksacks have been slit open with a craft knife and the contents stolen.

Don't expect to be able to recognise a pickpocket. A pickpocket may be a smartly dressed business person, a confused-looking grandfather type, a family out seeing the sights, or a nice young woman. Remember they earn their money by blending in and looking like everyone else in the crowd.

The Personal Security Handbook

The operation is pretty standard. Some work alone and some work in a team. If they are working in teams, once something has been taken the thief who actually took the purse or wallet stays innocently where he or she is, but quickly passes the stolen goods on to a runner. You won't see the transfer. Even if you felt something and raise a fuss, the 'innocent' thief is quite happy to be searched because he or she knows that you won't find anything on them. Meanwhile the runner has dodged into a quiet corner, money is taken from the purse or wallet and everything else may be thrown away. They might keep credit cards and chequebooks, but that is risky because the names and details will link them to the theft. Sometimes they immediately pass on those identifiable valuables to another criminal, sometimes they stash them somewhere safe for collection later, it depends how much of a risk they want to take.

Pickpockets – countermeasures

- ✓ Accept that pickpockets exist. They are after your money and valuables if you give them the slightest chance to take them.

- ✓ Maintain an awareness of who and what is around you. If you can see problems or potential problems avoid them!

- ✓ Realise what you are doing and take steps to minimise the threat and vulnerability. For example, if withdrawing money from the cash point, or collecting your winnings from the bookmaker at the racecourse, be careful. Don't let anyone other than you and the bookmaker see how much money you are slipping into that inside pocket, then zip or button the pocket up so nimble fingers cannot easily slide into it.

- ✓ Realise that pickpockets are busiest at the busiest places, especially places where people are leaving or arriving:
    - ➤ bus stations
    - ➤ railway stations
    - ➤ airports
    - ➤ ports, docks and ferry terminals
    - ➤ hotel reception areas.

- ✓ Anywhere there is a big crowd that is surging or stopping and starting you are at risk. The crowd movement and jostling gives the thief an excuse to bump into you, push against you and take what he wants. For example:

Theft

- ➢ race meetings
- ➢ sporting events, especially finals and big matches
- ➢ passengers getting on and off over- and underground trains
- ➢ passengers getting on and off buses
- ➢ pop concerts
- ➢ sale time in busy shopping streets and especially inside the popular shops in that street.

✓ In many places you will hear announcements or see notices warning you to be on your guard against pickpockets. Pickpockets love these places. They stand around and watch for wealthy-looking people to come along. When those people hear the warning announcement or see the sign, they often feel their pocket or look to see if their wallet or purse is still where it should be. That tells the pickpocket exactly where to go for money! Make sure that your valuables are always secure so you don't have to check them!

✓ Pickpockets look for somebody worth stealing from. Don't stand out from the crowd! Try to blend in. That may mean dressing down, taking off the Rolex watch and leaving the heavy gold and diamond tiara at home with the expensive digital camera! Try to look like an average person.

✓ The same advice works with behaviour as well. If everyone on the street is busy going from A to B, and you stand still looking lost you will be noticed. Worse, if you pull a tourist map out of your pocket and stand looking at it, the pickpockets and thieves will be drawn to you like a magnet. Thieves will target somebody who is out of place. By looking confident and going about your business you will not attract so much attention. If you are lost, you can still do it. Confidently walk towards something that looks safe, such as a decent hotel or an office block. You may try approaching somebody in authority, such as a police officer or other uniformed civil employees. If all else fails, hail a taxi and get them to take you straight back home or to your hotel.

✓ When travelling be aware that transport centres such as airports and stations are a favourite target for thieves, so you should take extra care.

✓ Never put a wallet or purse in the hip/back pocket of jeans or trousers. That is what pickpockets call the 'sucker pocket'. If you put your valuables in a hip pocket in a crowd you may as well throw them into the first bin you come to, because the thieves will take them soon enough!

✓ If you have an inside pocket in a jacket or coat use it. Where possible make sure that that pocket also has a zipper or button fastening so that even if a pickpocket reaches in that far, they won't be able to slide your wallet out easily. If your inside pocket doesn't have a zip or button, you can get strips of Velcro that can easily be stitched on to fasten the pocket.

✓ You can try the old trick of wrapping a rubber band or two around your wallet or purse. A nice shiny leather wallet or purse slides easily and unnoticeably out of your pocket. If you wrap it with a rubber band or two, the rubber will catch on the material as it is being slid in or out of the pocket. That will stop it from falling out easily, and stop it being lifted out without your knowledge.

✓ Try not to put all your money and or valuables in one pocket. Consider putting your most valuable possessions in a hotel safe or leaving them at home. Put large sums of money in a money belt, and avoid putting everything else in just one pocket or zip-up section of your rucksack. Don't make it easy for the thieves.

✓ A money belt is the safest way to carry cash and valuables such as traveller's cheques and passports. It is a wide thick zip-up pouch that is designed to be worn unseen underneath clothes. A 'bum bag' or beach belt is NOT a money belt. They are usually brightly coloured, quite large and bulky and designed to be worn outside clothing as a big extra pocket on a belt. They are quite vulnerable to theft – in a crowd a thief can jostle you while cutting the belt with a razor sharp knife, and whisking the bum bag away. You won't even notice it is gone until you go to look for your sunglasses or cash to pay for something.

✓ Be wary of gathering crowds. Thieves sometimes create incidents to gather a crowd of people who stop to watch the argument, accident, fight or even passionate kiss. They pick areas where they know that a simple incident will stop people so they will quickly build a crowd. While the crowd watches, people apparently try to get through or get to the front to see what is happening. Actually, they jostle and push to take as many wallets and purses as they can. If you see an incident and or a crowd – avoid it.

✓ Never leave anything valuable unattended. It only takes a moment for a thief to sort through likely pockets and bags. It will take you days and a lot of your time and money to replace what was stolen.

Other Tricks and Methods

Thieves are quite inventive in their efforts to separate your from your money. A recent change is that international and transcontinental thieves are targeting people in the UK. They use a variety of methods and I have illustrated a few below, to show you what to look out for.

Chain Letters

An old trick that often attempts to intimidate people into keeping the chain going. You get a letter which tells you to send money to the person at the top of the list; add your own name to the bottom; and send it to ten new people. It doesn't work.

Chain letters – countermeasures

✓ Don't believe any scheme that seems to offer you something for nothing.

✓ If anything looks too good to be true, it probably is!

✓ Do you want what the letter is promising? If not, walk away – the best deal in the world is a waste of time and money if you don't want it, or don't need it in the first place.

✓ If you get anything that looks like a chain letter, throw it away.

✓ If you get something else that you don't understand, take it to the Citizens Advice Bureau and ask if they can explain it.

Phoney foreign fines

One of the latest tricks is fraudulent speeding fines. Criminals spot a UK driver on the continent, take the number and details of the car they are driving, then wait a couple of weeks.

The UK driver is surprised when the postman delivers a very official-looking speeding ticket, or parking infringement notice. Enclosed with the notice is a demand for the fine to be paid to a given address. More often than not there was no speeding or illegal parking – it is just a trick to part you from your money. It works because on the whole British drivers are quite law abiding. They don't remember the roads they went down or where they parked, so many drivers will assume they did it and pay up!

There are increasing numbers of these phoney fines coming through. If in doubt, don't pay immediately. Contact the embassy of the country where the fine is supposed to have been issued and check it with them. If you have been naughty – pay up. If not, submit a copy of the documents you received to the embassy and ask them to forward everything to the correct law enforcement organisation. Don't forget to include a request for them to tell you what has happened to the criminals.

Tricks and cons

There are any number of tricks and cons being tried by hundreds of different people and organisations. The common theme is that they usually play on your greed and all promise something for what seems to be nothing. The most common trick is the shady government funds transfer.

The victim gets a letter on what looks like official government stationery from someone in a developing country. The writer claims to be an official in the ministry of something or other and his letter goes on to explain that they want to transfer some money into the UK and need a UK citizen to help with the transfer. They want to transfer several million pounds to your account which will be there for a few days and then transferred to official accounts elsewhere. For allowing them to use your account you will be paid a fabulous reward, such as 1% of the funds moving through your account, or a flat fee of £250,000. The letter asks the victim to write back to an official looking address.

What happens even if they do make the transfer and you get paid for allowing it to go through your bank account? When the UK tax office finds out (banks automatically report large transfers), you will have a lot of explaining to do and a very complicated tax return to make. What about international terrorism funding? The FBI, MI5 and MI6 would start sniffing around if you were laundering millions of pounds in this situation. I think that the police organised crime units would take an interest in you as well, but that's just untrusting old me! Maybe you still think it sounds like a good idea?

So, if anyone is stupid enough to write back to them, these foreign criminals know they have a ripe fish on the hook. Somebody who has let their guard down, somebody who is vulnerable and a little greedy. Their next letter starts by asking for your bank details, which you should never give anyway. A few letters exchange telling you about the increasing sums of money that will be moving and how much you will be getting out of the deal. The letters promise further transactions when this one goes through without a problem. But you get a letter saying there is a problem.

The official writes to tell you that you have to have an account in their country through which the transfers will take place. By this time you have been swapping letters for a few weeks, maybe a few emails too, so you can almost smell all that cash.

Not wanting to lose the deal now you ask how you can open an account, and then the real sting starts. The official tells you that you need to send, say, £500 to open the account and make it look real. If you send that, he tells you he needs to make a few bribes to get officials to look the other way when the big transfer takes place, so you send some more money.

By now you have two or three thousands pounds, three months and 15 letters invested in this. Another £1,000 to bribe a few more officials seems to be such a small investment to guarantee the big pay off . . .

The trouble is there is no official, there is no huge payment, no funds transfer, nothing other than an elaborate trick to get you to send them some money. Bribes were probably paid to get some official headed paper. I even heard of one guy who, when he received the first letter, telephoned the government offices out there. When he asked to speak to the official by name and title he was put through somewhere to someone so he thought it was OK. He went ahead and sent out several thousand pounds. When he realised it was a scam, he called back on the same number but this time nobody knew of the official. Bribes can do a lot for you in some countries!

Tricks and cons – countermeasures

✓ Does it sound too good to be true? If so ignore it.

✓ Does it promise something for almost nothing? If so, ignore it.

✓ Does it sound reasonable? The official had three million pounds and wanted to transfer it to your bank account, but he had to ask you for a few hundred pounds to open a bank account and pay a few bribes. Doesn't sound sensible to me!

✓ Stay alert, and ignore these tricks. Throw the letter away.

'You've won a prize' letters

These letters are very common at the moment. You receive an official-looking letter. Stop there! What is an official-looking letter?

Headed paper? Printed neatly? It says it is official? It comes from an official organisation? It includes the name of a well-known bank, or has the logo of an international company, or claims to be supported by the UK government or some other group?

Some letters are genuine and most are junk mail at best, or outright attempts at crime at worst. That letter might look impressive, but you shouldn't believe a word it claims until and unless you can prove it.

Where were we? You receive a letter that attempts to look 'official'. It is worded very carefully, claiming that you have won a major prize. These letters are usually quite confusing, because they come with a number of leaflets, offers, prize draw stamps, reply slips and so on.

They usually claim that you have won a prize, but you have to phone a premium rate number to see what prize you have won. Or:

- you have to buy something from them to make your claim;
- you have to register to claim your prize;
- you have to send a fee to register with them to claim your prize.

Or, any other cheap confidence trick!

If you have entered a competition, you are informed if you have won a prize. If you haven't entered a competition, it is highly unlikely that you have won a prize anyway. If you have won a prize through any legitimate organisation, they will contact you and send you your prize. I doubt if they will ask you to send £50 to a foreign address, buy something, or spend any money in any other way to qualify to receive that prize.

'You've won a prize' letters – countermeasures

✓ If it seems too good to be true, it almost certainly is.

✓ If you don't remember entering a competition it is probably a con.

✓ No legitimate organisation is going to ask you to spend money to claim a real prize.

✓ If I get something like this, I shred anything with my personal details on it, and the rest goes straight into the bin.

Counterfeit money

At any large public gathering criminals are likely to attempt to pass counterfeit currency. There is so much counterfeit currency around that you will regularly see shop staff checking every note they are given. If there is enough around for companies to instruct staff to check every note, shouldn't you be checking notes given to you as well?

Counterfeit notes and coins have no value and it is a criminal offence to attempt to pass them on. Just to make sure you understand that – if you take a forged £50 note, then realise it is forged and try to pass it on to avoid the loss, *you* are now committing the criminal offence!

When discovered, all counterfeit money should be surrendered and the police notified. The person who has the note when it is discovered or identified as counterfeit unfortunately loses, because nobody has a responsibility to refund any money lost.

Counterfeit money – countermeasures

- ✓ Make sure that you know what the latest bank notes and coins look and feel like. Banks and post offices sometimes display notices explaining what to look for in new notes.

- ✓ When you accept cash from anyone, the higher the denomination the more careful you should be. Personally, I don't mind checking notes when a shop assistant hands them to me. They check the notes I give them, so they shouldn't feel too bad when I check notes they give to me!

- ✓ If you don't recognise it, if it is for example a Scottish ten pound note which you are not familiar with, or the notes handed to you don't feel right, ask for different notes.

- ✓ Counterfeit coins are rare, but they are around. You can usually tell by dropping them onto a table; they make a dull thud, not the sound you expect a genuine coin to make when dropped. Sometimes the edge markings are missing or the colour is wrong. If in doubt, refuse it. (Look out for foreign coins too; it may look like a tatty pound coin, but it could be something from abroad).

3 Everyone

Everybody is different, but generally people can be divided into broad groups – such as male and female. Some groups tend to be more vulnerable to certain threats and risks. This chapter discusses threats, vulnerabilities and risks to which everybody could be exposed. Later chapters concentrate on more specific groups.

Mobile Phones

Mobile phones are a useful tool and a highly desirable fashion accessory. There is always a new model coming out with ever more functions, and the mobile communications companies offer an increasing range of products and services from wireless ear-pieces to the latest ring tones. It seems that everybody over the age of about eight owns and frequently uses a mobile phone. The problem is that because they are so expensive, popular, small, portable and easy to conceal, they are also very popular with criminals.

Figures show that in 2001, at least 710,000 mobile phones were stolen. Some were stolen from desks or handbags but many were taken in muggings, (the police call this crime a street robbery).

Nationally about 40% of street robberies included the theft of a mobile phone, and very often the mobile phone was the only property taken! In London alone 1,200 mobile phones are stolen each month.

Everyone

In the UK, more than 2,000 mobile phones, palm top, laptop and other portable electronic devices are stolen *each day*. Many of these items are recovered by the police, but quite often the legitimate owner cannot be traced. When reporting the loss or theft of mobile phones and other electronic equipment, some owners find it difficult to remember the make and model, and details such as serial numbers and identifying marks are rarely available.

The mobile phone industry hit back against crime by agreeing and introducing a scheme where a stolen mobile phone handset can be rendered useless, as soon as it has been reported stolen, if the owner has the right details available.

IMEI Number

Every mobile phone has a fifteen digit IMEI (International Mobile Equipment Identity) number. You will need this number if your mobile phone is lost or stolen.

To find and record the IMEI number for your phone, key in star, followed by the hash sign, then zero then six, then another hash sign: *#06#

As soon as you press the final hash sign, your mobile phone will display your IMEI number. Write it down accurately and safely, with the phone number for that mobile phone, the make, model and identifying marks, so that you can report it should your phone be lost or stolen.

If your mobile is stolen

Report the theft to the police as soon as you can.

Report the theft to your mobile network operator, with the phone number and the IMEI number as soon as you can.

The network operator will then remotely immobilise it so that it won't work any more. The thief cannot run up a huge telephone bill making long distance calls to foreign countries. It will be a lot harder to sell as well.

The police and mobile network operators are hoping to stop thieves using or making money from the theft of mobile phones. If they can do that they could potentially stop thieves from stealing mobile phones at all. But, they need your co-operation to make it work.

Find and record the IMEI number for your mobile phone(s) now!

Mobile Equipment National Database

The Mobile Equipment National Database (MEND) is officially endorsed by the police and mobile phone networks. It was created to record the details of mobile phones and other electronic equipment, so that the police can track down the rightful owner if stolen property comes into their possession. MEND is free to use, and will allow you to record details of most portable electronic equipment such as

- mobile phones
- camcorders
- CD players
- desktop computers
- laptop computers
- computer games consoles
- hand held computers and personal organisers.

Visit www.menduk.org to register and record the details of your valuable electronic equipment for free. Then if any of your equipment is stolen, report it to the police and tell them that the details are recorded on the MEND database. Those details will then be recorded on the Stolen Equipment National Database (SEND).

Your Keys

Copying keys

Take a moment to consider this question. Sit and think about it for a while and then write your answer down. How many sets of keys there are to your house,

Everyone

and who holds them? Don't read any further until you have done that – then with your list finished read on!

So how many sets of keys do you think are in circulation? Now, how many sets of keys could really be in circulation?

When a house is sold, one or two sets of keys are surrendered and passed on to the new owner, but most families have more than two sets of keys. That means that anyone who used to own your house could still have keys that they kept for sentimental reasons. They may just be thrown in a box at the back of their garage with a nice brass tag showing the address they come from, but they exist somewhere!

Now widen the consideration. One or all of the previous owners may have given a set of keys to a relative for safe keeping, or to the lady who used to clean for them. They may have forgotten that they gave the plumber a key the time he had to replace the boiler when they were on holiday. That nice Mrs Biggins who used to live over the road had a key, because she used to pop in at lunchtime to let their dog out. And the man at number 73 used to service the car, so he had a garage key! Little Jason lost his keys at school three times so he had a new set each time! Then of course the six or seven estate agencies over the past 15 years they all had a set of keys when they were trying to sell the house and they may have taken copies.

So how many sets of keys did you write down on your list? Now that you have read the information above, how many more sets or individual keys do you think you could add to that list?

There is no point at all in improving your security when you are not certain who has a set of keys to the property. If you have no control over the keys, you have no control over the security and safety of you and your premises. If you haven't changed the locks since you moved in, any number of people you don't know and have never met may have keys to your house!

Looking after your keys

Even if you are careful when making duplicates and giving sets of keys to people, how careful are you with your keys? You may think that they are safe on a hook in the kitchen or in a little bowl in the hall, but they may not be. Window cleaners have snatched sets of keys, had copies cut and then returned the originals. That copied key with a list of the valuables the window cleaner has spotted in the house could be sold off to a burglar or used by him in his night job as a thief! Keys in the hallway could be taken by somebody coming in to deliver a parcel, read the electricity meter, or measure up for new carpets.

Even leaving keys in the hall can be a risk, because thieves have found that fishing through the letterbox with a cane with a hook on the end can be quite rewarding. While you are in bed, it's worth a criminal investing fifteen minutes of his time fishing through the letterbox, especially if the reward is that he gets the keys to your BMW or Porsche. All keys should be out of sight and out of reach of the door and any visitors who are passing through.

Keys – countermeasures

- ✓ Locks give you security, keys give you access. Remember that unless you are very careful with your keys, you might as well forget installing locks and locking things up in the first place.

- ✓ Never leave any keys unattended – for example in your car ignition while you go to open the garage or in your bag while you nip to the toilet. (Your bag will almost certainly also have something showing your address, so the thief will have your keys and your address.)

- ✓ Never leave keys inside windows, on desks at work, or in your car – anywhere that they may be taken or copied.

- ✓ Be wary of labelling keys. There is no point in telling a thief or any dishonest person who finds your lost keys where your house is or what the car number is.

- ✓ If you want to put a nametag on keys, make it your mobile phone number. If you lose your keys and somebody calls, don't give your address. Ask them to meet you at a convenient public place like the library or supermarket. Take the keys back, but on the basis of your opinion of the person who hands them back to you, consider changing all the locks anyway. He or she may be a criminal so trust your instinct.

- ✓ Always make sure you know how many keys you have cut for any given lock. Always record who has what key, then you know who has access, and know who to contact if you need a spare or have to replace the lock and issue new keys.

- ✓ Before issuing a key to anyone, decide whether they really need a key of their own. Is it just for their convenience? If so can they wait to be let in by somebody else? Do they really need unattended access of their own? Do you want them to have unattended access of their own?

- ✓ Make sure that when people leave, get transferred, get evicted, sacked or otherwise change, that you keep control of the keys. Get their keys back, and if they are leaving under any sort of cloud, or even if you just think it might be prudent, change the locks so that any duplicate keys they have had cut won't be of any use.

- ✓ How many keys do people carry? Most people have at least a few keys that they can't remember what they fit. When you change jobs or move, get rid of old keys. Spring clean your keyring today. Decide if you really need to carry the key to the lawn mower, or the key to your first motorbike that you have as a keepsake. Remove any keys if you don't need to carry them or don't know what they are. Discard any that you recognise but no longer need. Any you don't need to carry (like the lawnmower key) put somewhere safe like a kitchen drawer. Any keys you don't want, don't use and can't remember what they are, put in a sealed envelope in the back of a kitchen drawer marked 'unknown keys' with today's date. A year from now if you still don't remember what they are, and haven't needed them, discard them.

- ✓ Never allow strangers to have unattended access anywhere that keys are kept. It is too easy to take a key.

- ✓ Make sure that everyone keeps their keys safe, puts them on a chain, or on a clip inside a handbag or case. That way they shouldn't be forgotten.

- ✓ Avoid using key racks which are helpfully labelled BMW, garage, speedboat and so on – don't make it easy for a thief or burglar.

- ✓ If you find that a key doesn't fit any more, change the locks. It is not unknown for a criminal to simply switch keys, taking a door key and substituting one that looks the same. The key owner thinks they have the same number of keys they always carry including a back door key. Because they never use it, they have no idea that it has been replaced by a similar key. (A reminder that if you don't need to carry the key, don't carry it.) Meanwhile, the criminal is at large with a key to the back door of your house, or worse still the key to the back door to your shop! If you find a key doesn't fit the lock, assume it has been stolen and substituted – so consider changing appropriate locks.

- ✓ If you have lost a key, or have taken over a property and don't know what keys are in circulation, there is only one remedy and that is to change all the locks. With new locks, you have total control over who has a key to your house, garage, shop or shed. You will issue a new key to anyone you think *needs* access to the house.

- ✓ For extra security you can buy a security lock. Keys can only be cut at specialist security stores, not at any shoe repair shop or market stall.

- ✓ Seriously consider giving one key, not sets of keys. If you have children who may lose their key, only issue them with a single key to either the front or back door. (Given a choice, select the door with the lock that is easiest and cheapest to replace.) Then if the children lose their key, only that single door has been compromised, which means you only have to replace that single lock. If the child had lost a set of keys you would be regularly replacing every lock in the house!

- ✓ Are there any keys available to a criminal who sticks a cane with a hook on the end through the door? A lot of cars have been stolen with keys that have been 'fished out' through the letterbox or a broken window. Move keys away from letterboxes – fit a mail basket internal flap and brush draft excluder as well to prevent 'fishing'.

- ✓ Don't leave house keys in your car. If the car is broken into, the criminal has your house keys, could well have the full address from documents in the car, and from the state and quality of the car also has a fairly good idea of your wealth and possessions.

- ✓ If you have anything stolen, such as your car, coat, briefcase, and your keys were in it, change the locks.

- ✓ Never ever give, loan or leave house keys with a builder or other workmen.

- ✓ I would never, ever leave keys with estate agents or anyone else. The minute you hand a key over to an organisation rather than a person, you have totally and irrevocably breached your security.

Keys hidden outside

Most people have experienced the annoyance of being locked out of their own home for one reason or another. It is very easy to do – popping out to get something from the car and finding that the wind has blown the door shut. Alternatively you may have had the annoying doorstep conversation with your partner when you get home from shopping that has you both saying, 'But I thought you had the door keys.'

To avoid this problem, many people are tempted to hide a door key somewhere outside the house. Don't do it. Criminals know that many people do, especially where there are children in the family.

People used to leave a door key fastened inside the door on a length of string. All you had to do was fish through the letter box, pull the string out and use the key tied to the end to open the door. That 'clever' trick got to be as well known as leaving a key under the front doormat, so people stopped doing it. Hiding keys in or under a flowerpot, bricks and gnomes won't fool a criminal either. I have even seen adverts for 'secure' key hiding places made to look like cobblestones, gnomes or other garden items.

To my mind anyone who uses one of these plastic containers which are 'cleverly disguised' as something or other is foolish. Why spend a lot of time and money making your house safe and secure, then break your own security by leaving a key out for the criminals? No matter how clever your hiding place is, it will be discovered. If you were a criminal watching a target house for a few days and saw a child come home, move a brick near the garage door, open the front door then return to that brick, how long would it take you to guess where a hidden key might be? And criminals also see adverts for key stores in the shape of garden frogs, cobbles and logs, and will have made it their business to know what they look like, because finding a key makes it a lot easier for them to get into your house.

Hidden key – countermeasures

✓ **Don't hide keys outside.**

✓ If you have to have an emergency key, give one to two relatives or very close and trusted friends who live nearby. (Why two? One of them might be out when you need your emergency key!)

✓ Make sure that you trust your key holders and anyone who lives with them. Uncle Bob may be thoroughly trustworthy, and Mrs Biggins from number 42 may be a wonderful lady, but who else is coming and going in that house? Uncle Bob's daughter, or the new boyfriend of Mrs Biggins' lovely daughter may not be as trustworthy!

Defending Yourself

UK law currently allows you to use reasonable force to defend yourself, though the definition of 'reasonable' is a little vague. There is some pressure to change that law, but at the moment the bottom line is that if you do fight or otherwise use force, you might have to persuade a judge that what you did was 'reasonable' for the circumstances at the time.

For example, taking a shotgun and firing both barrels at a man you thought looked a lot like the guy who mugged you in London two years ago isn't reasonable!

On the other hand, if a robber runs up behind you and stabs you in the arm, punching him in the face to give you time to escape sounds very reasonable – *depending on the circumstances*.

It is impossible to say what is reasonable and what isn't because circumstances can be so different. In the above example, where somebody runs up behind you and stabs you in the arm, what if you are an unarmed combat instructor and an ex-member of the SAS? What if you are also the captain of the all county rugby team, and the robber is a nine-year-old boy who stabs you with a pencil? In those circumstances the courts might decide that punching him wasn't 'reasonable'!

Handling conflict

Drunks, drug addicts, criminals and louts are far too ready to resort to violence for no apparent reason. There are two ways you can handle conflict:

- Learn karate or some other form of self-defence and win any fight that they may start! Assuming that there aren't 10 or 20 of them and they are not carrying guns and knives. Assuming that you don't go too far in the heat of the moment and kill or seriously injure somebody by mistake!
- Avoid the conflict in the first place (my opinion).

The best way to win a fight is to not get into the fight in the first place! Fighting is and should be your very last resort. This book is all about preparation, awareness, planning, prevention and avoidance. Using the same techniques, most of the time you can see a fight coming and 99 times out of 100 you should be able to avoid it quite easily.

Assault

Anyone can be the victim of an assault or an attack although luckily these are quite rare. The legal definition of assault is quite wide. For example if somebody bumps into you in a crowd, technically that physical contact could be an assault, but most people recognise it as an accidental bump (or was it a pickpocket?).

If somebody stands ten feet away and shouts and screams telling you they are going to come and punch you, and if you genuinely think they will, and they are capable of doing so at the time, then that constitutes an assault as well!

Conflict Management

We live, work and socialise in close proximity to other people, which unfortunately leaves us open to disputes and conflict. Ordinary disputes and disagreements within the office and family are easily resolved. For example, if there is a disagreement about who uses the office coffee machine or photocopier first, or which television channel to watch at home, common sense allows you to resolve those issues quite easily. Unfortunately, when a conflict is initiated and fuelled by alcohol or drugs, it has the potential to become life threatening.

Most people rarely come into contact with pure aggression, rage and violence. This irrational behaviour is not encountered every day, which means that people are not skilled and experienced in dealing with it. This section is designed to help you to identify the signs that somebody may be working themselves up towards an explosive act of violence, so that you can walk away before that violence becomes reality.

Approaches to violence

The army approach may be to go in first, go in hard, outnumber the opponents, use superior fire power and overwhelm them before they know what's hit them.

The police approach may be to decide if an offence has been committed. Decide if it is a criminal or civil matter. Decide if police intervention is called for. Observe the situation. Close the road off. Call up appropriate resources and be prepared to wait until the situation can be handled peacefully.

Two fairly different approaches, but totally irrelevant to us. The job of the army and the police is to face aggressors and to end conflicts, but yours isn't. Your job is to keep you and your family safe. You should avoid conflict just as you would avoid a burning building.

Your approach should be:

- to maintain an **underlying awareness** of your surroundings at all times.
- to maintain an awareness of the **actions and behaviour of those around you**.
- to be able to **identify signs** that people around you are losing their temper.
- to recognise important **impact factors**.
- to be able to recognise the impending escalation from harsh words or threats to actual violence.
- on recognising that a conflict is building, to have **already identified a means of escape** to allow you to extract yourself and your family from that situation safely.
- as a **conscientious citizen** to be aware that on leaving the scene, you might need to call the police to report the disturbance, so that they can attend to restore peace.

Quite a simple approach, but some explanations are in order.

Underlying awareness

I am not proposing that you treat every moment outside your home as a potentially fatal patrol behind enemy lines. I don't suggest that you should study everyone who comes within ten metres of you to decide if you would win a fight with them if necessary, if you can't keep them more than ten metres away from you.

I am suggesting that you simply maintain an underlying awareness of your surroundings. Imagine I was in radio contact with you all day. Then at some stage I surprised you by calling up and saying, 'Shut your eyes now, and tell me what's going on around you.'

If your reply was **vague**, e.g. 'I'm not sure, I think there might be some bloke behind me. I'm cold and ten minutes late for my train. Um, there was a hole in the path – or was that yesterday? Oh yes, there is some noise over the road', I would say that you are not sufficiently aware of what is going on around you.

If your reply was more **specific**, e.g. 'It's quite busy, a dozen or so people ahead of me, most walking away. One man coming towards me – a businessman type. There are two or three adults behind me, one woman with a small girl – I saw them coming when I came out of the car park. I just walked past a road works, there is a hole in the path where they are repairing a water leak outside a house that has been painted white. The road is quite busy with commuter traffic. There are five kids on skateboards over the road on the pedestrian precinct and one of them just made a loud noise when he crashed and fell off', I would say that you were very aware of your surroundings.

Your attention will wander. You may be straining to see if the bus is coming, worrying about an exam the following day, or trying to figure out how you can impress the love of your life on your big date tonight. That's OK, but you can still do that while maintaining a level of awareness!

I know that you have an ability to automatically monitor your surroundings. For example, you walked along the path, not in the road where traffic is passing at 40 miles per hour! You didn't trip over the rubbish bag on the footpath, and you ducked when you walked under a low branch. It's automatic. It's something you do naturally without really thinking about it, even if you were trying to remember what you have to buy from the shops on the way home.

All I am proposing is that you should extend that awareness. Practise and learn to include recognition of place, conditions and people. With that information coming in by sight, sound and smell, you are in a position to decide whether there is an actual or potential threat to you in time to take steps to avoid that threat.

Actions and behaviour

When walking with your family toward a cash point, intending to draw out a large sum of money, being aware that there are four people around you helps. But who they are and what they are doing is very important to maintaining your safety and security. For example:

- Person one is Mrs Biggins who is sitting at the bus stop waiting for a number 42. She is a known quantity. You know Mrs Biggins, you know where she lives, and you can see that she is waiting to catch the number 42 bus that will take her home.

- Person two is unknown. He is wearing a hooded top and has a scarf wrapped around his face. He is behaving nervously, looking up and down the road. There is a motorcycle parked at the kerb and he has left the engine running. Your sense of self-preservation should start raising alarm bells. Why is he so nervous? Why has he left the engine running? If it is his bike why isn't he wearing a crash helmet? Why has he covered his face with that scarf? He is standing outside a jewellery store and you can now see that he is holding a large brick and looking at the window and then nervously looking up and down the street. Adding two and two and based on circumstantial evidence you think he is about to smash the window and escape with a few trays of gems. If that was the case, I wouldn't want to get too closely involved; he may be armed or may have accomplices inside the shop. I would move away from him and the shop, make a mental note of the motorcycle registration number, his description, the name of the shop and call the police to explain my concern!

- Persons three and four are loitering at and around the cash point. You can see that they are young males. They are also hooded, but they are taking a great interest in the people coming and going at the cash point. They are whispering and looking closely at wealthy-looking people. They seem to be taking more interest in elderly people than in fit young men. Could they be thinking of stealing some money from a careless cash point user? I would call the police anyway to explain my concerns about the jewellery shop and the motorcycle-riding suspect, so I would also tell them about the youths at the cash point. The police will probably request that town centre CCTV cameras are directed on the area to record the suspects for future reference, while sending a police officer to take a look. Meanwhile, I would have withdrawn to safety with my family, retracing my steps and telling Mrs Biggins to come with me to take her to safety as well!

Thus, knowing that there were four people around me was of little value. Taking just a little more interest and recognising clues has helped. By looking more closely I have seen that of those four people, three present an actual or possible threat to Mrs Biggins, to me and to my family. Being aware of my surroundings has allowed me to take simple steps to avoid and reduce that threat!

Identify the signs

Human communication is complicated, and comprises three different elements:

- **Words**. Talking accounts for a surprisingly low proportion of our ability to communicate. In fact, experts say that less than 15% of our everyday communication is conveyed using words!
- **Body Language**. Most people have heard of body language. It includes gestures, movement and stance. If somebody is relaxed, leaning back against the wall and smiling at you, you can read from their body language that they are no threat to you. On the other hand, if they are standing tall, rigid, leaning in towards you and scowling, you can just as easily see that they aren't a happy bunny! Up to 55% of human communication is achieved through body language.
- **Paralanguage**. The remaining 30% of our communication is delivered by paralanguage, or the *way* we speak. By speaking softly, quickly, enthusiastically or sounding bored, the listener quickly tunes in and understands more than the words we may be saying.

Apart from the communication elements described above, we also betray our feelings in certain involuntary actions. These signs are usually classified as **warning signs**, and they show that a person is becoming angry or agitated. When somebody takes the next step towards violence they may display **danger signs**, which show that they have reached the point where they could become violent.

In a one-to-one situation, by being able to recognise these signs you should be able to 'read' the state of mind of the person you are facing and thus be able to withdraw before violence erupts.

Warning Signs – the person could display warning signs that include, but are not limited, to the following:

- Fixed eye contact – they won't look away or blink. They see you as a threat, so keep their eyes firmly on you.

- Breathing rate changes: they breathe faster and deeper. Subconsciously they are preparing for action, sucking in more air to boost their oxygen levels ready for a fight.
- Standing tall – stretching to look as big and frightening as they can.
- Blushing – adrenaline and high heart rate make blood flow around the body. That includes the skin which changes colour when blood runs through it, making it look like blushing.
- Quick behavioural changes – they can be on edge, unsettled and unable to concentrate on what they are trying or pretending to do. Sometimes they might stop doing one thing and move to something else – for example they could abandon looking through a magazine, toss it down and start rearranging the ornaments on the shelf.
- Misdirected aggression – for example if the subject is eating a sandwich, they may throw it at the door, punch the sliced loaf on the table or kick a rubbish bin.

Even though you have just met this person for the first time, you could be unlucky and be the innocent victim of an eruption of violence over something which is nothing to do with you but has been bubbling and brewing for days. You could meet somebody in the supermarket who clearly displays these warning and danger signs. You could just be unlucky and be in the wrong place at the wrong time and at risk of suffering from the pent-up tension and anger that this person is displaying. When you see these signs or anything that resembles them you should withdraw. They clearly show that the person displaying them is rapidly approaching a state where they will resort to violence.

After the warning signs come

Danger signs – the person may display the signs which include, but are not limited, to the following:

- Fist clenching – they might clench their hands into fists, then hold them as fists or release them and clench them again.
- White face – when preparing to make an attack, the body automatically draws blood in from the extremities to protect vital organs. This means blood may drain from the face making the person look white-faced.

- Boxer's stance – another involuntary action where the subject drops their shoulders and stoops. Their arms are in and held at, or above, waist level, making the fists ready to use, and feet spread for balance.
- Target acquisition – this occurs immediately before an attack. The person suddenly narrows his focus and concentrates on you, looking for weak points and choosing the best place to attack. For example, you might notice that he seems to be taking a great deal of interest in your chin, because he is very close to punching your chin.
- Pounce crouch – if you are close to the person you will not see this as it occurs when you are some distance away. They have to leap towards you to make the attack, and to do that they will have to crouch down ready to make that leap. If you see the pounce crouch you may be too late – you should have backed off a long time ago. Wait one second then step back and towards your exit.

I don't expect you will ever see any of these danger signs, because you will have left when you recognised the warning signs. If you see anything that looks like a danger sign, get out and get away immediately.

Impact factors

In any confrontation you should be considering a range of variables that are or could be important to the outcome. In some circumstances, even the biggest and strongest martial arts expert could find that he is at a disadvantage when faced with a violent teenage boy!

For example, if our martial arts expert happened to be carrying a baby at the time he was confronted by the violent teenager, he would be at a distinct disadvantage. Having the baby in his arms is an impact factor that he has to consider because the presence of the baby would have an impact on his ability to use his skill and strength to defend himself. Other impact factors include:

- **sex** – the sex of an attacker and their proposed victim.
- **age** – the relative ages of the people involved.
- **physical fitness** – the relative fitness and health of the people involved.

- **use of weapons** – where one person is armed with a knife or other weapon.
- **location** – if one person is on the edge of a cliff or railway platform.
- **drugs and alcohol** – where one person is drugged or drunk
- **mental disability** – where one or both people have a mental illness.
- **numbers** – where one person is outnumbered by attackers.

The above examples are not exhaustive but they illustrate how, in a confrontation, a person could be disadvantaged by any number of factors. In all cases, the effect of the impact factors means that the result of a conflict is unknown. You should never get into a fight, and you should never, ever get into a fight that you don't absolutely know that you will win.

Recognise escalation

If you work in a shop for example, you know what a normal customer looks and sounds like. Take that up a notch and think what an angry customer would sound like if you told him that his order still hasn't arrived three weeks after you promised it would.

Now take it up another notch again. This customer is reaching over the counter to grab you – he wants to do something more than complain to express his displeasure. You can see that there is a clear escalation in his behaviour.

In life that escalation in behaviour should be clear to you as well. Common sense tells you when somebody is not happy, but the addition of the warning and danger signs listed above should show you where that person is on the scale of displeasure to violence. Your job is to withdraw and defuse the situation that is causing that escalation before any violence actually takes place, while staying safe yourself.

Remember that in a work environment, when you identify the warning and or danger signs, you should also be warning colleagues, customers and anyone else around to withdraw, so that nobody is in danger.

Identify escape routes

You should always be aware of your escape routes. It should be an automatic, subconscious part of your life. In some professions and circumstances it should also be part of official company policy, procedures, staff training and awareness!

In simple terms, don't get trapped! In any circumstances keep the exit or exits in mind. For example, if I enter an office building for a meeting I make a subconscious note of the signs directing me to fire exits. When I reach the conference room I know that the nearest fire exit is to the left outside the conference room door. Everybody should maintain that awareness, but I suggest that some professions should make that a priority. For example, female estate agents should be sufficiently aware of entrances and exits, so that if they were showing a client around a house, they could always retreat to an exit easily if the client's behaviour gave cause for concern.

Personal space

Most people have a fairly rigid perception of personal space: an area that surrounds them and 'belongs' to them. Get too close and step into their space and they will immediately feel uncomfortable, threatened and under pressure due to your presence.

As a rule that personal space is about arm's length, though in some circumstances we mutually waive our right to personal space. For example, if you walk up to a stranger in London and stand within inches of his shoulder he will step back, probably with a comment such as, 'What's your game, mate?' On the other hand, on a crowded tube train you can stand with your head in the armpit of that same man and he will studiously ignore your presence while you consider introducing him to the concept of under-arm deodorant!

If asked to deal with an angry customer, maintain personal space, remembering that as a person becomes more upset and agitated, his personal space expands. Ten feet may be too close when he is angry – even being in the same building as somebody may be viewed as a threat!

That being the case, in any circumstance, especially where there is scope for conflict, remember to maintain your escape routes.

Conscientious citizen

As I have indicated above, a conscientious citizen will also think of other people. Protect yourself yes, but remember that if you are aware of a threat you should be taking steps to warn other people of that threat and if possible protecting them as well.

Warn them, tell a member of staff, stop people going towards the danger, call the police, do anything you have to, to prevent people being hurt in a conflict or dangerous situation.

Internet Security

A great many people use the Internet, and as time passes and technologies converge Internet access may be almost inescapable. You send emails at work and at home, research your family tree or edit your club web site, and that has it's own security issues, but they are nothing compared to the problems you could be facing.

If you buy goods over the Internet or access your bank account via the Internet you could be susceptible to fraud. You might find that your Internet connection has been tampered with and is costing you a fortune, or that your computer has been hijacked and is being used by parties unknown to store suspicious files.

If you use the Internet you are vulnerable. Criminals are using ever more sophisticated methods to commit cyber crime. The greater your use of the Internet, the greater your risk of being targeted by criminals. Internet security is a huge and complex subject, so I will attempt to summarise some key points for you to consider.

The criminals

Most people think that computers are complicated and that you need to be very smart to hack into a computer system (illegally break into a computer). To an extent that used to be true, but today there are so many hacking tools available that almost anyone can commit a crime.

Everyone

There are even hacking sites that will describe a range of vulnerabilities for different software, and even give step-by-step instructions in how to break into different systems or write viruses.

Your equipment

When you install your computer equipment, there are some steps you can take to make it as secure as you can.

Your equipment – countermeasures

- ✓ Buy from a reputable dealer (you don't know what you are getting through a small ad in the local paper).

- ✓ Ask your dealer to include and configure the security of the computer before they deliver it. This should include a firewall and anti virus software etc and possibly power surge protectors. (Many computer users believe that their computer is protected because they have a firewall. Unfortunately because that firewall is not correctly installed or configured it may at best be partially effective).

- ✓ Ask to be shown how to check log files and exception reports as well as keeping all of the security software up to date.

- ✓ Assuming your computer will be used for more than playing games, make sure that it includes a method of taking backups (safe copies) of important files in case of a problem.

- ✓ Ask your dealer about a maintenance contract, which will keep you informed of and include the application of software patches and software upgrades.

Software updates and patches

Computer software is very complicated to write, which is why they make mistakes. When those mistakes are discovered, the software company issues a 'patch' to correct a minor problem, or a new release of the software to deliver an upgrade that fixes a lot of small problems and delivers better functionality.

If you don't identify and apply those patches and upgrades to your computer software, you will be running a computer with increasing numbers of faults in the software. The criminals look for those faults and write viruses and other illegal programs to take advantage of those loopholes in your computer software and security.

Some software, such as anti-virus software relies on a regular update to identify the latest viruses that are in circulation. If you don't update the definitions, your anti-virus software won't recognise the latest viruses and so cannot stop them from infecting and damaging your computer.

The longer you leave it, the more likely you are to suffer a hacking attack on your computer.

Software upgrades and patches – countermeasures

- ✓ By some means make sure that patches and upgrades are applied to your computer when they become available.

Passwords

Passwords are critical to the security of most computer systems, which means that you probably have at least a dozen PIN numbers and passwords to remember. That means that you probably write them down – which means that you have breached your password and PIN security.

Passwords – countermeasures

- ✓ Some systems come with a default password – the criminals know them so change it as soon as you can.

- ✓ Don't make your password too easy to guess. 'Password', 'Secret', 'Sales', or your name or the company name are often used and are far too easy to guess.

- ✓ Make your password at least 8 characters, of mixed letters and numbers, and try not to use recognised words. 'Passw0rd' replacing the letter o with a zero is better than nothing, but still too simple.

- ✓ To remember your password, make it memorable. Use a string of letters and numbers that means something to you. If your kids in age order are Sarah, Brian, Kate and Chris. If your mum's house number is 12. If your old school was Surbiton Comprehensive. Your password could be 'SBKC12SC'. Nobody will guess that, but you can remember it because the clue is 'kids, mums place and school'.

- ✓ If your password is compromised – you think somebody was looking when you typed it in – change it. You should change it every few months anyway.

Illegal software

There is a whole raft of illegal software out there, but it might be illegal for different reasons.

Malicious – They may be called viruses, trojans or worms, but they are not wanted and could cause you harm. They may have effects that are annoying or disastrous, from simply spreading themselves to infect other computers, to deleting important files on your computer. They might find and transmit your bank details to a criminal, or change your dialler to use a premium rate number costing you a fortune in phone calls. Whatever they are – you don't want them.

Illegal Copy – They may be simply illegal copies of commercially available software. Rather than spend money buying a legal copy, some people borrow a software CD and take an illegal copy of the software for free. Software manufacturers will take legal action if they find somebody making illegal copies of their software.

Sharing – Software is available to locate and share computer files, for example music or videos. Generally this sharing is illegal, and music and film companies have taken legal action against people who illegally copy and share these files.

Virus – countermeasures

- ✓ Buy and make sure that any anti virus software is properly installed and configured.
- ✓ Make sure that the anti virus software is regularly updated with the latest virus definitions.

- ✓ Make sure that your anti virus software is automatically loaded and running in the background when your computer is turned on.

- ✓ Check your dial up numbers regularly, or better still become familiar with the warbling of your modem when it connects to the Internet. If that warbling noise changes from the familiar Brrrr – De – Dahhhhh – De – De etc, it means that you are dialling a different number. Disconnect immediately even if you have to unplug the modem, and check the dial up number.

Spam

Spam is the name given to unwanted emails, the electronic equivalent of junk mail. Most email systems have a facility to 'filter' incoming emails, to remove the mass mailings of Spam. You should also have your anti-virus software running in the background, because at least 80% of computer viruses are spread by email.

Spam – countermeasures

- ✓ Check with your Internet Service Provider, computer supplier, email system and anti-virus system to make sure that they are configured to protect you from Spam and viruses.

- ✓ Never open an unknown and unexpected email attachment – that is where viruses are usually hidden and opening them will infect your computer.

At work

Know and obey your company policy relating to computer use. Your employer may take a dim view of you spending half of the day sending and receiving private emails, or looking at Internet holiday offers for a last minute break.

It could be worse, you could be dismissed or even charged with a criminal offence under the Computer Misuse Act for some things.

Work – countermeasures

- ✓ Know what your employer expects from you.
- ✓ Don't share passwords or access computers and data you are not supposed to access.
- ✓ Don't email suspect material from work and don't access suspect web sites and material at work.
- ✓ Use your common sense, work is for work!

Computer privacy

To prevent computer theft, personal stalking and abuse or the unwanted interest of paedophiles, the whole family must think Privacy.

Computer privacy – countermeasures

- ✓ Never give out or disclose usernames or passwords in any form.
- ✓ Never reply to emails asking for bank or other personal details.
- ✓ Remember to make your password secure and change it frequently, especially if you think it may have been disclosed.
- ✓ If you have Broadband (where your computer is permanently connected to the Internet), make sure you have a firewall properly installed and configured.
- ✓ If you use a free email provider, try to make sure that your email name and address does not give away your real name, sex, or location. Being BracknellSue24@freemail.com tells people too much.

Shopping and on line theft

There are several ways in which shopping on line can make you vulnerable to theft. From disclosing bank details to bidding for non-existent items on auction sites, criminals can part you from your money.

Shopping and on line theft – countermeasures

✓ Be sensible and take all precautions you can.

✓ If it looks too good to be true – it probably is, so don't fall for it.

✓ Be wary of spending more than you realise, you don't know how it adds up until the bills come in at the end of the month.

✓ Look for the little padlock or key at the bottom of the web page and the https:// in the address that indicates that a web site is secure.

✓ Use the sites of known companies, but be wary of those you have never heard of or who are based abroad.

✓ If in any doubt – don't buy!

✓ Gambling on line is increasingly popular, don't get carried away! Consider blocking gambling sites if you have children.

✓ When buying on line DON'T answer irrelevant marketing questions and always tick the box that indicates that you don't want offers and other junk email sent to you.

Ergonomics and health

When you buy your computer ask about ergonomics and health. Make sure you know how to site the computer, have a decent chair, good lighting etc. Computers can seriously damage your health!

Ergonomics and health – countermeasures

✓ Have a comfortable, adjustable chair and footrest.

✓ Buy and use wrist rests.

✓ Consider having a 'tracker ball' instead of a mouse. Ask to see them in the shop. (The mouse has to be moved around the desk but the tracker ball does not move, giving you more desk space for your use).

✓ Site the desk where you won't get light reflecting on the screen from windows or strip lights etc.

Everyone

- ✓ Have a keyboard that can be tilted to your comfort.

- ✓ If your screen flickers, get it repaired or replaced and adjust the colour, brightness and contrast to comfortable levels.

- ✓ If possible position the computer so that you do not face a blank wall. By facing an open room you will allow your eyes to focus to different distances as you glance up – reducing eyestrain.

- ✓ Take a regular break. Children should take a break every 20 minutes, I like to take a break at least every 30 minutes.

- ✓ Get up and take some exercise.

- ✓ Computers run on electricity, take great care with cables and plugs, and never remove the cover from a computer – especially when it is plugged in. Get your computer store to make any repairs or upgrades.

- ✓ Don't overload any power points with computers, scanners, printers, modems and other gadgets.

- ✓ Look out for trip hazards caused by trailing cables.

General security

Don't concentrate on the computer and lose track of your personal information outside the computer.

General security – countermeasures

- ✓ Don't position the computer in a conservatory or near an open window where it can be seen by and tempt a passing thief.

- ✓ Take regular backups of important information in case you lose the computer to theft or mechanical failure.

- ✓ Remember to keep track of information that is coming out of the computer! Print outs of invoices or personal information should be retained or shredded so that they don't fall into the hands of criminals.

- ✓ Decide what you will do with floppy disks or CD's that contain personal information, you don't want to throw them away where they could be picked up and read.

- ✓ Decide what you will do if there is a hardware failure. If the repair centre tells you that you need a new hard disk (that is OK because you have copies of important information and files), but what happens to the old disk? It should be destroyed safely so that nobody can access or retrieve any information left on it.

- ✓ Decide what you will do with the computer when you eventually dispose of it, can you be sure that all confidential information has been deleted from the hard disk? Take advice, and don't give information away with your computer!

Identity Theft

Identity theft is sometimes called information theft or identity fraud. Basically, criminals look through the rubbish you throw out to find documents and information that they can use to commit crime. That crime can be as simple as using your credit card details to order something, or at the other extreme using information you have thrown away, in order to pretend to be you and establish a false identity.

Most people have been in situations where they are asked to produce proof of identity, where household bills or perhaps a bank statement are accepted as proof that you are you. That means that anyone else with a copy of your bank statement could pretend to be you.

A recent test by a local authority gave some alarming results. When they looked through the dustbins of 100 houses, 70% of them contained enough information for a criminal to be able to engage in identity theft fraud using the identity of somebody in that house. The information that people throw away includes:

- bank statements
- pay statements/pay slips
- CVs and job applications with full personal details on applicants
- income tax documents
- receipts for purchases containing bank information
- cash withdrawal receipts

- insurance documents
- personal letters
- personal loan information
- court papers
- mortgage statements and details
- utility bills
- credit card statements and receipts showing numbers and expiry dates
- council tax statements
- notes showing cash card and other card personal PIN numbers
- discarded and out of date credit cards, membership cards etc.

Are you happy that strangers could have collected that sort of personal information about you and your family so easily? Are you happy that businesses are so careless with your details that they throw similar information into a bin to which anyone has access? Do you care that strangers know what you get paid, what your regular monthly payments are, or what your bank balance is?

Other than this being an intrusion into your private affairs, criminals could use all of this information to run up huge bills using your name. Credit card numbers are quite handy. Some unscrupulous employees working for companies which carelessly overlook criminal transactions can earn thousands from your credit card. You may discard enough information to give them on line access to your bank account, or deal in stolen cars in your name!

Taking your identity

The criminals could abuse your identity in more extreme ways. With the information from your dustbin they could quite easily get a duplicate of your birth certificate by pretending to be you. With that they could begin to create a parallel identity, perhaps renting accommodation and setting up bank accounts, then taking out huge mortgages or perhaps importing drugs. During 2003 identity theft increased by 54% over the previous year when identity fraud had cost us a total of £1.3 billion. It is widely reported that identity fraud is a growth criminal industry and that figure will continue to grow each year.

Information is all the criminals need and it is possible that you are happily tossing that information into the bin for them to take their pick. Criminals are happy to pay the homeless and others to search bags and bins, which coincides with a surge in reports of interference with rubbish bags all over the country. While searching for information they slit bags open and toss through the rubbish looking for likely information. When they get it, they can either use it or sell it on. Apparently the going rate for personal details is surprisingly low. About £5 to £30 buys you a name and address with credit card details with expiry dates etc. A top rate of about £50 will be paid for a full range of personal information that can be used to establish an identity.

With your information being misused you could lose money from your accounts and you could find that your credit rating has fallen to a point where you can no longer get loans. People have been refused a mortgage or loan because of debts that they knew nothing about, or even had the police asking them questions about fraudulent transactions completed in their name. Don't get caught out.

Phishing

Criminals want to find out all about your bank account details, and what better way is there of doing that than by asking you what those details are?

Of course you wouldn't give them those details, would you? Well actually you might just be gullible enough to do just that. Thousands of people have been tricked into giving out their details. Phishing is an appropriate name for this con because the criminals are fishing for details. The way they do it is to telephone or email hundreds or thousands of people.

The caller or the email is quite business-like and explains that 'the bank' is updating records, or that there have been some suspect transactions on your card, or any other plausible-sounding excuse. Whatever the story, they need you to confirm your account details over the phone or in a reply email. If you give them, they will empty your account before the banks close.

Everyone

Information theft/phishing – countermeasures

✓ The answer is to destroy any personal documents, and you can do that in a number of ways. Anything that contains personal information, for example, bank account details, National Insurance numbers, pay slips etc should be destroyed, not thrown away! Though you could destroy everything, you don't need to. For example, credit card statements and bank statements often come with pages of information about interest rates and special offers tempting you to buy various products. You don't have to destroy them if they don't contain personal information, just throw them away if you don't want them. You don't need to destroy the parts of a credit card statement that invite you to apply for a loan if they don't contain account and other personal information. If you are certain that something has no personal information on it, just throw it away! You can destroy documents containing personal information in a number of ways.

> **Scissors**. You could sit and snip everything into tiny unreadable pieces, but this is a slow process.

> **Fire**. You could keep all of your personal documents and then have a monthly bonfire to totally destroy any trace of personal information. You have to have the space to do it safely. You have to make sure that everything has been completely destroyed and that the fire is completely out before you leave it. You also have to clean up the ashes or leave them blowing around the garden and put up with the mess!

> **Office Shredder**. People have access to an office shredder, and many employers do not object to their staff bringing in and shredding the occasional document, but before you try, it would be best to check with your employer. If they allow you to do so, don't abuse it. Once word gets around in the family you could end up with all the personal documents for your mother, father, aunt, grandmother and your cousin Bob. Your employer would not be pleased if you were spending two hours per day destroying family documents.

> **Home Shredder**. You can buy shredders for home use. They range from hand-cranked plastic boxes to almost office specification machines which start at about £60. Most shredders are graded by how fine the strips are. The more strips you cut a page into the harder it is to reassemble them and gather the information. A cross-cut shredder is even more secure, because it not only shreds a page, it cuts each little strip into sections cutting across the strip – hence the name. That makes re-assembly of a cross cut shredded page even more difficult. You can manage with a hand-cranked machine, but they are quite slow. An electric shredder is quicker and more convenient. (Caution – remember that if abused a shredder can be dangerous and that shredded paper could be a significant fire hazard!)

✓ Don't give out personal information over the telephone unless you are absolutely and totally sure of the identity of the person calling. You should never give personal details over the telephone to anyone who calls you, no matter what their reason or excuse.

- ✓ If you need to give personal details only do so if you telephone them, so that you are sure of their identity. But only call them if you are sure of the real telephone number. Only ever call them on a telephone number that you can confirm, e.g. it is on your bank statement, or is taken from a telephone directory etc.

- ✓ If somebody calls and asks for personal or financial details, *never* call them back on the number they give you. You could be phoning a criminal. If they require details tell them to write to you, or tell them to give you a name and address so that you can look up their legitimate number in the telephone directory.

- ✓ Remember that the Internet is just another telephone call. Some criminals are now trying to collect personal information via emails. The email looks official. The email seems to come from an official source, for example fraudoffice@mybank.com but they are quite easy to create. To all intents and purposes anyway, the Internet and emails are not secure. Never give personal, financial or any private information out over the Internet. When buying over the Internet, only do so if you are totally and absolutely sure that the web site is secure and legitimate.

- ✓ False web sites are quite easy to create as well. If I were a criminal I could create a web site called www.ukbanksecurity.com. I could set that up to look like it was an official site run by your bank. I could entice you to log on and register for reduced rates, free gifts or a chance to enter our million pound draw. Of course when you register you have to prove you are a real customer of the bank by keying in your account number, credit card number, security code, mother's maiden name and the last purchase you made over £100 on that card. With all of those details, they are spending your money before you log off! Never give personal, financial, medical or any details over the Internet in any survey, quiz, competition or other transaction.

- ✓ Emails are just as bad – banks and building societies will never ask for personal or bank details in an email. Never disclose those details in an email, and be very careful about filling in official looking on line forms with any of those details. If in doubt go to the bank and ask.

- ✓ When you fill in any form, think before you fill it in. A lot of organisations issue forms for such things as extended warranty, or asking for a quote for a new kitchen, or anything. (I never buy an extended warranty because they are not worthwhile. Unless of course they are telling me that their product is so unreliable that I need to insure it against breakdown, in which case I won't buy the product anyway!). Have you ever wondered why they were asking some of the questions?
    - ➢ Do you own your own home?
    - ➢ Do you have a mortgage? How much?
    - ➢ Which banks do you use?
    - ➢ What is your annual income?

- ✓ They are collecting information on *you*. Nothing to do with what they are selling. They are collecting marketing information that they use or sell to other people to use. When you fill that form in, marketing men are sitting around rubbing their hands in glee. For example they now know that you are a young married couple with no children, you own your own house and have a high income, so suddenly all sorts of marvellous offers start coming through your letterbox. Do you want to buy a luxury timeshare in Costaripoff? Do you want to buy exclusive designer handbags, or maybe a top-of-the-range set of golf clubs? When I am presented with a form, I fill in what is pertinent and cross out the 'information gathering' questions that have no bearing on the purchase or enquiry.

Junk Mail Avalanche

Apart from the nuisance value of an avalanche of junk mail, your letterbox and front step are important to maintaining your security, especially when you are going on holiday.

Do everything you can to stop the flow of unwanted deliveries that could be a problem. Free newspapers, circulars, flyers and pizza advertisements all flow through the letterbox or more often are just dumped on the doorstep. I haven't asked for any of them, I have no interest in them and they all go straight into the rubbish bin. Unfortunately, these are the deliveries that can cause you problems.

If not collected and disposed of, within a few days they could overflow your letterbox and doorstep, cascading out to blow around the garden for all to see. A clear indication that you are not at home and, by the time the doorstep is stacked up with this rubbish, you clearly haven't been there for some days. That will attract the attention of local criminals.

In my area free 'newspapers' are tossed onto the doorstep, usually several days after the publication should have been circulated. The indifference as to the timing of their delivery shows the value the publishers put on their publication. If you don't want it, phone them and tell them to stop delivering it!

Junk mail and circulars – countermeasures

✓ If you would like to try to stop **junk mail** being sent to you by direct marketing organisations, you could try contacting the Mail Preference Service. Please see www.mpsonline.org.uk or call 0845 703 4599 for details and to register your desire to be excluded from junk mail postings. It doesn't stop all junk mail but it considerably reduces it. You will need a valid email address to complete the online process and they warn that it can take up to four months to have full effect.

✓ A similar organisation which deals with **telephone marketing** is the Telephone Preference Service; visit the site www.tpsonline.org.uk or call 0845 070 0707. All you have to do is register your phone numbers and you should soon be excluded from most UK telephone marketing.

✓ **Fax marketing** is dealt with by the Fax Preference Service; visit the site www.fpsonline.org.uk or call 0845 070 0702. All you have to do is register your fax number(s) and you should soon be excluded from most UK fax marketing.

✓ As for the paper and glossy cards that are delivered, try posting a sign on your door reading 'No circulars or advertising leaflets'. That probably won't work for everything, so try to make sure that your mail is cleared each day while you are away.

✓ I did see a house that had a special delivery slot for circulars and free newspapers. Actually it was a large box with a lid and a wide access slot, near the front door. The owner told me that inside the box was a plastic crate. A couple of times a week he would take the crate out and throw each item into his recycling bin. He only checked it in case some genuine post had been put into the circulars mailbox in error.

4 Vehicle Security Review

Your house is probably the most expensive purchase you will ever make, with your car coming in as the second most expensive and valuable possession you own!

Your car is important to you not only because of the money you have invested in it but also because it is your safe little kingdom when you are away from home. A protected mobile environment where you feel safe and secure. It is a shelter from the weather and the world. Your car must therefore live up to your expectations of reliability, security, safety and protection.

In one survey 24% of people asked assumed that during the next year they would become a victim of car crime by theft of, theft from or damage to their car. They could be right: 2004 statistics show a 40% increase in car crime, with over £1 billion worth of property stolen. Most people seem to think that car crime is inevitable and that there is nothing they can do about it. They are wrong.

Theft of and From Cars

To implement and maintain security, you should undertake a security review of your car. While doing the review, try to look at your car and its contents the way that a criminal would look at it. All he wants is to make some money, and cars are the easiest and biggest source of crime-derived income in the country. Perhaps a few UK car crime statistics will show you how serious the problem is and how easily you could be affected.

The Personal Security Handbook

- 22% of all car crime takes place in car parks.
- Vehicle crime costs the UK at least £3.5 billion a year.
- Each year 2,500,000 car owners suffer loss due to car crime.
- 400,000 vehicles were stolen in 2004.
- There were 1,800,000 cases of theft from vehicles in 2004.
- On average one in every 28 vehicles is broken into each year.
- About 55% of cars that are stolen are never recovered.
- The UK has the highest car crime rate in Europe, and accounts for 30% of all European car crime.

Buying a car

What can you do about car crime? Stealing a car is quite easy if you know how! Though most manufacturers will charge thousands of pounds for a new car, they only spend a few pounds on the security features that they build into each vehicle. Vehicle security is slowly improving, but it could still be a lot better.

When buying a vehicle, you should ask about the security levels. Let the salesman and manufacturers know that you care about quality, price, specification, safety, miles per gallon and *security*. With that message feeding back to the small group of super manufacturing groups who own and run most vehicle makes in the UK, they should get the message and move quickly to meet that demand. If they don't respond to your demands, shop elsewhere. Buy a foreign vehicle – the cost is often lower, security, basic specification and build quality is higher as well!

Your car told me!

Realise and remember that the make and model of your car – the colour, state and visible contents can often say quite a lot about you, the owner. For example do you think that the following list matches vehicles and owners quite accurately?

- A late model German sports saloon = successful businessman
- Quirky pink little saloon of modest age = single young female

- Hot hatchback with racing body kits = single boy racer aged 23
- People carrier = mum with kids
- Battered old mini = impoverished student.

Yes, a very rich student might be driving a German sports saloon, but generally the profile of cars and owners is quite accurate. By looking at the make and model of the car a criminal can decide which one of them may be a worthy target for him in more ways than one. Which car or owner he picks depends on what his objective is.

If the criminal's drunk and wants an easy car to steal for a ride home, he will probably try for the student's battered mini. If our criminal is stealing to order, he will go for a BMW, Range Rover, or other top of the range vehicle and will probably have already stolen the keys so that it can be taken quickly and easily.

Additional Security

Although manufacturers build a basic level of security into their vehicles, the owner can increase security levels by purchasing, fitting and using additional car security devices and systems. Remember that your objective is twofold:

- to make the car more secure so a criminal cannot steal it
- to deter the criminals in as many ways as you can, making other cars in the street more appealing to them. If they are they will walk past your car and leave it untouched.

There are a number of ways of doing this.

Steering wheel locks

Steering wheel locks come in a wide range of styles, designs and sizes, which are made by a variety of manufacturers.

The basic concept is to lock or clamp a device to the steering wheel, which will prevent a car thief from turning it. As the vehicle cannot be driven away, it is of no use to them, so they will not attempt to break into or steal that car. (Of course if the driver has been foolish enough to leave valuables on view in the car, the device won't prevent a thief breaking in to steal those valuables.)

Other devices available allow the car owner to lock various controls, for example, the clutch pedal to the steering wheel, or the gear lever to the handbrake, with the car in reverse gear and the hand brake locked on. All of them prevent a thief from operating the controls of the car so they cannot drive away.

Immobilisation

Most of these devices have to be wired into the ignition circuit or other critical system in the car. When the owner leaves his vehicle, he arms the immobilisation device, usually with a remote control. When activated, no matter what they try, the criminal will not be able to start the car. If they cannot start it they cannot steal it – unless they are really bold. (I attended the report of a stolen luxury car, and found that dozens of people had not only witnessed it but were glad when the car was taken away! The thieves had reversed up with a breakdown truck and tampered with the vehicle. When the alarm sounded they declared it an 'electrical fault' which was why they were recovering the vehicle. Local people watched and were glad when the thieves managed to get into the engine bay to silence the alarm. They then used a winch to drag the car onto their breakdown vehicle and drove off with it. The best description I could get was 'two nice men who stopped that noisy car alarm'.)

Key codes

These are an extension of the immobilisation device, because they introduce a numeric keypad, or transmitter/receiver that prevent the engine running unless the code is keyed into the pad, or the key ring transmitter is present in the car. If the person trying to start the car is the owner he will be able to start it. If it is a criminal, he won't have the code or transmitter so will not be able to start the car. Newer and more exotic versions of this system even use the driver's fingerprints as an authorisation to start via an on-board computer and fingerprint reader.

Alarms

Third party manufacturer's alarms are widely available, from a simple system that honks the horn if the vehicle is tampered with, through to sophisticated systems that flash lights and play voice tapes that loudly proclaim something like 'This car is being stolen – call the police.' Some systems will send an emergency signal to a base station operator who will call the owner and ask what is happening to the car before they call the police to report a theft in progress.

Unfortunately, standard alarms are sometimes too sensitive. A cat jumping onto the bonnet of the car, or the draught from a passing van, can set them off. This causes them to activate too easily, sounding thousands of false alarms, which have over time had an adverse effect. When a car alarm sounds, most people assume it is another false alarm and grumble about it; very few bother to look out of the window, let alone investigate or call the police to report it.

Beware of 'grabbers'. Many vehicle alarms and door locks are operated by remote control. Criminals have some quite sophisticated electronic equipment that they can use to 'grab' your remote signal. They set their monitoring device near an expensive car to listen for the signal. When the owner arrives and presses his remote control, they intercept the signal and record it. Later when they want to they can use that signal by simply playing it back through their grabber device to open the car, turn the alarm off and steal the car!

Stickers

Some schemes have attempted to cut down on car thefts by persuading owners to place various stickers in their car windows. For example, if a commuter usually drives to the station and then always travels to work by train, his car will, or at least should usually be, in the railway car park from about 08:30 each morning to say 17:00 at night every weekday.

If he joins one of these schemes he places an 'I'm at work' sticker in the back window of his car. The police will be aware of those stickers and will be free to stop any vehicle with such a sticker in the window at any place at any time between 9 am and 4 pm from Monday to Friday each week.

If they see a car with such a sticker being driven around town at say 1.15 on a Tuesday afternoon they can stop it. It might be that the car owner explains that he has been to the dentist, and proves his identity. On the other hand it may be that the person driving the car stole it from the station car park!

The car owner then accepts that by joining the scheme he may be stopped when driving around on a weekday when he is not at work. That annoyance is offset by the fact that he hopes that by doing so the police will be able to stop a thief stealing his car while he is at work.

Etching

Glass fittings for cars are expensive. A full set of windows, headlamps, mirrors and even plastic light clusters is very expensive. If you have the vehicle registration number etched onto them at a cost of a few pounds (or for free because some insurance companies will pay for it to be done at a windscreen replacement centre – check with your insurance company) the car will be protected. A car thief will not want to change all of the windows, mirrors, headlamps and front and rear light clusters to hide the real identity from the police or a buyer because it will be too expensive. Anyway, walking in to a dealer and asking for the full set of windows, lights and lenses for a luxury car will raise a few eyebrows, if not suspicions, anyway. Etching is simple, easy, fast, and very, very cost effective.

Radio transmitters

These transmitters are installed in a vehicle and wired into the power system. They are hidden in any one of dozens of different places where they can be fitted in each model of each car, so the criminal never knows where to look for one. Each transmitter has a unique code. If the car is stolen the owner phones a control room and reports that his car has been stolen, and then the control room triggers his transmitter so that it starts broadcasting its unique signal. Police and other services can then track that signal to where the thief has either hidden the vehicle or where he is still driving it around. These transmitters are very effective. They are quite expensive to buy and install, after which there is often a subscription to pay, but the cost of ensuring the safe return of your car is a lot less than buying a new one. Some owners with these radio transmitters fitted do not display any marks to show they have them; others display radio transmitter warning signs, clearly hoping that criminals will realise they cannot get away with it and will leave their car alone. Insurance companies usually offer a discount if you fit and use an approved security device.

Mapping transmitters

An extension of the above system, where the radio transmitter fitted to the vehicle is always transmitting. The benefit of this system is that the control room staff and the vehicle owner can log in to a live mapping system that actually shows where that vehicle is at any time of the day or night. Some people use it as an advanced anti-theft device. Some employers use it to watch their fleet drivers, to see where they are and if they are where they should be.

Stealing a Car with the Car key

Because security measures are improving, especially on top-of-the-range cars, criminals have started stealing car keys to make stealing the car a lot easier. Rather than attempting to bypass the sophisticated security equipment being built into the more expensive vehicles, they break into a house, take the key and simply drive off in the car.

House breaking

In some cases the thief steals to order, and may even be sent out with a shopping list to find specific vehicles. For example they may be sent out to find a brand new top-of-the-range blue Range Rover, with a manual gearbox. He spots one and trails the owner to see where the car is being kept. The next step is to relieve the owner of his keys, because with the keys and the usual remote locking device, he can drive off in seconds.

Another way of getting the keys is that a thief may raid a house and by chance find a nice set of car keys with a new BMW key fob. It is easy for him to go out into the street and press the key fob transmitter to see which BMW in the street outside flashes its lights in a welcoming way, as it pops the door locks open. In either case, the thief is away down the road in your car.

The stolen car may be destined for a shipping container to be exported and re-sold in a foreign country, or it might just be a free ride home for the criminal. In the worst cases, it will be damaged in high speed and reckless driving, then burned out to prevent the police collecting fingerprints and other evidence.

Sometimes louts steal cars just to use them to race around, often careless about damaging other vehicles and sometimes deliberately ramming them. Sometimes they drive to a quiet spot and steal the wheels and the radio/CD before leaving the vehicle at the low water mark by a tidal river, relying on the river to wash away any evidence.

The UK trend of breaking into houses with only the intention of stealing the car keys is increasing. In the Home Counties alone, in one year top-of-the-range cars collectively worth over £40 million had been stolen by thieves who had obtained the keys during household burglaries. You could try taking your keys, mobile phones, handbags and wallets into your bedroom each night; it is unlikely that even a sneak thief will be able to get in and take them without waking you.

Leaving the keys in the ignition

You should always remember to take your keys with you when you leave the vehicle, even if you have left your husband, wife, granny or children in the car. A thief is likely to steal the car and may even take it if family members are still sitting in it. The family members will be terrified and dumped down the road somewhere, while the thief helps himself to your car and anything you left in it elsewhere.

Selling your car

Criminals have been known to steal cars when taking or arranging a test drive of a car that is for sale. Some car owners are happy to stand at their front door and let a stranger drive off for a test drive, trusting them to come back with the car.

Some thieves take the owner with them on a test drive, then when they get to a remote location they get the owner out of the car and drive off. There are at least two ways to get the owner out of the car: threaten them, or trick them. Threats are easy to understand, but how could a stranger trick you into getting out of the car? Thieves are quite clever and manipulative. What if a stranger is taking a test drive and tells you he can hear a rattle from the back? What if he mentions it once or twice then tells you he thinks the exhaust is loose? What if he pulls over a few miles up the road, gets out and asks you to dab the accelerator while he listens to the exhaust, then comes back and says, 'Yes, it's rattling against the back axle; you go and listen and I'll dab the accelerator.'? You go to listen to the invented noise, and very soon wave goodbye to your car as he jumps in and drives off leaving you miles from nowhere and minus your car!

Car theft with the key – countermeasures

- ✓ Don't leave your car keys where people will expect to find them, such as in a bowl inside your front door, on a hook in the kitchen or even on your desk at work.

- ✓ Consider removing the manufacturer's tag from your car key ring so that even if they do steal the keys, they don't know what make or model they are looking for. (This won't work where manufacturers have helpfully stamped the make into the key itself.)

- ✓ If you want to be really clever, put a Ford key fob on your luxury car key ring to confuse them. In the boasting stakes you lose a few points with a Ford instead of your treasured Aston Martin or Rolls Royce key fob, but making life hard for a thief who manages to walk off with your car keys may make it worthwhile.

- ✓ Although most people are tired of hearing it, they still do it! Never, ever leave your keys in the ignition. It takes just a moment for somebody to jump in and drive off. Some insurance companies are refusing to pay out if owners are careless and allow their car to be stolen with the ignition keys. Leaving the keys in an unlocked car on the garage forecourt while you go in to pay is a tempting invitation to a criminal. Don't do it. Even when you reverse out of the garage, turn the engine off and take the keys with you to shut and lock the garage door.

- ✓ Make it a strict rule – whatever the reason, if you get out of your car always turn the engine off and take the keys with you. If you walk away from the car you should shut the doors, windows, tailgate or boot, sunroof and lock the doors. Be safe not sorry.

- ✓ If somebody is going to collect your car, for example a mechanic who will take it for repairs or service, never leave the car unlocked with the keys in the ignition. Never leave the car unlocked and the keys hidden in it, for example under the driver's seat, behind the driver's sun visor or in the driver's door pocket. Never lock the car and leave a hidden key balanced on the top of one of the tyres or in the end of the exhaust pipe. Never leave a key hidden in a magnetic key box. These are sold for people who lock themselves out of their car; you put a key in it and attach it to the bodywork somewhere. Expect criminals to look for them – and anyway they can fall off!

- ✓ When using a car park, if you see any damaged cars or broken windows report it to the car park attendant, or the local police. If criminals are active in the area the police may catch them, but at least the police investigation will deter the criminals from attacking more vehicles. If cars have been damaged in that car park it is vulnerable – don't use it!

- ✓ When looking for a place to park, look for a car park that is staffed, is regularly patrolled, has automatic barrier access, closed circuit television and good bright lighting. If it is a busy car park (which it almost certainly will be with all those defences against crime), the constant flow of cars and people will help to deter criminals as well.

- ✓ Whenever you park your car, at work, in a car park, while shopping or even when parking at home in your own garage, always use steering wheel locks and other secondary security devices. The more barriers you erect, the more problems you present to the criminal, the less likely he is to try to break into your car or home. Your aim should always be to make your property such an unappealing target that the criminals will walk past to look for an easier and more lucrative target elsewhere.

- ✓ Test drive – When selling your car, never let a prospective buyer take the car out alone. You should also avoid being taken to remote places in case the prospective purchaser is a thief and intends to threaten you to steal the car. If you have to get out of the car while on a test drive (to fill up with petrol or check the allegedly rattling exhaust) make sure that you turn the engine off and take the keys with you. Tell the prospective buyer that you will check the exhaust when you get home again!

Car Jacking

Car jacking is a violent crime that has come from the USA. Car jacking is the common name for robbery, where a criminal steals a vehicle being driven by, or in the possession of, the victim.

More criminals are resorting to car jacking partly because of improvements in anti-theft technology used in higher-priced vehicles. The immobilisation equipment, remote locking and alarm systems in use on newer cars make it almost impossible for the average thief to easily steal a locked top-of-the-range car. Car thieves soon discovered that it was a lot easier to steal a car that already had the keys in it, even if they had to pull the driver out and assault him or her to get possession of the car.

As far as some thieves are concerned, violence is an acceptable part of car theft now. To steal a modern car you have to silence an alarm, hot-wire a protected ignition, bypass a sophisticated immobilisation device and then probably find and disconnect a satellite tracking system. Car jacking simply requires the thief

Vehicle Security Review

to spot a top-of-the-range vehicle, take the driver by surprise, and steal the car using as much violence as they need to.

They deal with any satellite-tracking device that may be installed by stealing the car and then leaving it somewhere. If it is still there a week or so later, they assume there is no device so they take the car and probably export it. If they come back and find the car gone or the police present, they know it was fitted with a tracking device so they go out and steal another car and repeat the process.

How do criminals get you to stop so that they can attack you to take your car?

Accident

The criminals will approach your car from behind and gently nudge into the back of it (they don't want to damage it because they want your car, so it will be a very gentle nudge). You stop and get out to check the damage and exchange insurance details. The driver behind talks to you then gets back into his vehicle and pretends to look for his insurance details. Suddenly an accomplice appears, jumps into your car and drives off, followed by the motorist who shunted you.

Something wrong

A slightly different version of the car jacking trick, but it has the same result. When you pull up at a junction or traffic lights, a helpful passer by points to the rear of your car and tells you that you have a flat tyre, or broken light, or damage to the rear of your car or leaking petrol! You get out to take a look and the criminal or his accomplice jumps in and drives away in your car – sorry – 'his car' now!

Assault/attack

The aggressive version of this method is used when the criminals cannot be bothered to, and don't need to, do it any other way. They often pick on female or elderly drivers who are more likely to let them take what they want. When the driver of a good quality car is trapped in traffic so cannot drive forward or backwards, they simply gang up around the car, pull the door open, pull the driver out and then one of them jumps in and steals the car by driving it away. The level of violence used in these cases can be horrific, with fists, knives, coshes and even guns being used.

Car jacking – countermeasures

- Firstly, accept that the chances of any individual becoming the target of a car jack are extremely low; being prepared may actually save you and your car.

- The most important lesson to take away is that if it does happen, it is just a car! It isn't worth fighting to the death over a car; don't risk serious injury by fighting violent criminals. If confronted with violence let them have the car, but make sure that you remember all the details you can so that you can pass them on to the police.

- Be safe when you approach and get into the car. Look around to see who is nearby, especially if you are a woman. If you don't like the look of somebody hanging around near your car, don't go to the car. For example go back into the office or shopping centre, report your concerns and ask a security guard or member of staff to escort you to the car.

- If it is dark, or there is nobody around when you go back to your car, you didn't park in the right place to start with. Learn a lesson from that and be more careful when you select your parking place in future. Consider getting somebody from your office or the shop to escort you to your car – better to be safe than sorry.

- When you reach your car, before you open it, look inside just in case somebody has broken in and is waiting inside to surprise you. For example there may be someone lying on the back seat or in the back of a van or estate car. If there is somebody in the car, pretend you didn't see and that it isn't really your car. Don't tip them off that they have been seen or that you suspect anything – you don't want to give them an excuse to jump out and chase you. Walk past and take the most direct route to bright lights and assistance then call the police. If somebody is in your car, it could just be a drunk sheltering from the cold – but you never know.

- When nearing your car, look in the surrounding vehicles. Somebody could be parked up near your car waiting for you to return. Just scan the cars; you should be able to see if there is anyone near enough to attack you. Be particularly careful of vans parked beside your car. A criminal could hide in the back of a van then when you get near enough slide the side door open, drag you in, slam the door and attack you.

- When you are at the car and you can see it is empty, with the key ready in your hand open up, get in and quickly and safely drive off. Don't delay by searching your handbag for a mint, or folding your coat up neatly and putting it on the rear seat out of the way. Leave the car park as soon as you can.

- Be aware of the tricks used by car-jacking gangs. Be cautious if a gang of youths in a car 'nudge' the back of your car with no apparent reason or excuse. You are legally required to exchange details if there is an accident, but if you are worried don't get out of your car. Keep the doors

Vehicle Security Review

locked and talk to them through the closed window. Consider driving to a police station or at least onto a garage forecourt where the video surveillance cameras will capture anything the gang may do.

✓ If somebody tells you that you have a flat tyre, or oil leak, or anything else, consider driving to a garage forecourt (or other well lit and busy place) to take a look, just in case that 'friendly passer by' had motives other than helping you.

✓ If, when you are driving, you think you have a flat tyre but don't feel safe stopping in the area you happen to be in, think safety. If it is safe, carry on driving slowly. Do not obstruct other traffic, but make your way to a safer area with better lighting or at least in a more public place. Get off the main road, and if possible stop on a garage forecourt; they are ideal locations. They have CCTV coverage, staff with a phone available so they can call the police if something happens, as well as a lot of people coming and going. With so many potential witnesses and people who may come to your assistance, any criminals should stay away while you change the wheel. (Remember all the aspects of basic safety when changing a wheel.)

✓ If someone approaches you when you are getting into your car and demands the keys, it is probably safer to hand them over. You could foil them by disposing of the car keys, which is the one thing they really need to steal the car. If rather than hand them over you throw the keys into a river, over a wall, into the bushes in fact anywhere out of reach, the criminal will probably run off. They won't want to stay around to look for the keys, especially if you have chosen somewhere safe to park – and where CCTV, patrol staff or other members of the public are coming and going. Unfortunately throwing the keys into the river or otherwise out of reach could provoke a drugged or drunk criminal to offer violence as a revenge for your depriving them of the car. It is your car and your choice. If in doubt it is better to be safe than sorry.

✓ When in traffic always leave 'rubber and road' showing over the bonnet of your car. That is, when stopped in a queue of traffic you should be able to see the back tyres of the car in front and a stretch of tarmac between the back of their car and the front of the bonnet of your car. Stopping far enough back to see rubber and road will ensure that the gap between your car and the car in front is enough for you to drive out and around it if it is broken down. That means that if a car jacking gang try to take your car while you are stopped in traffic, you have the chance if not the opportunity to pull out of the queue of stationary traffic to get away. ONLY IF IT IS SAFE for you and other road users.

✓ **Lock Yourself In.** If you are in any doubt I suggest that you should drive with your windows and sunroof shut, and the car doors locked. If you are alone at night, in an area with which you are unfamiliar, worried about a car that is following you, or suspicious of a group of youths loitering at the traffic lights ahead, lock yourself into the car and head for somewhere there are lights and people!

- ✓ With a brick someone can break the window, but if they do you can reverse or drive off to escape them. Perhaps they aren't hard-core criminals, just some louts who have drunk more lager than they have the brain capacity to cope with. They might try to snatch your mobile phone in this sort of incident because it seems a good idea at the time. A locked car and a mobile phone that is out of sight and out of reach might just be enough to put them off their plan of stealing something from the next car that stops at the lights.

- ✓ **Risk of being in a locked car.** Locking yourself into the car could pose a slight risk to you and any passengers you may have. The circumstances would be quite unusual, but it is possible that you could be involved in a traffic accident and be knocked unconscious, or be immobilised by injury. If there was a fire, or a high risk that other vehicles might run into you, rescuers might want to pull you from the wreckage to save you. If the doors were locked, they could not easily do that. Taking a minute to find something to break the glass and pop the doors open could, no matter how unlikely it is, leave you open to suffering more serious injury. For that reason, I have a general rule. When on motorways or other high-speed roads, my doors are not locked. Nor are they locked when in my home area or at low speeds. When in an area I do not know, or when I think there may be a threat to people or property in the car, I will lock the car.

- ✓ In a car jacking, never let the criminal take you as well as the car. Basically, the car jacking goes wrong if somebody is in the car when it is taken. On the other hand you have to consider the fact that it may not be a car jacking gone wrong, it might be a kidnap or terrorist attack. If you find yourself in the car with the carjacker/kidnapper, you might try a few things. The objective is to get out of the car and get away. That may be impossible if, for example, a mother has her child strapped into a child seat in the back of the car. If you can, try to jump out when the car stops at the next junction. If the only way to stop the car is to grab the steering wheel and force the driver to have a minor accident at slow speed – run the car into a wall! If he is too strong or you are in the back seat, consider getting behind him and attack his eyes to cause a low speed accident that won't harm other people. If you are in the boot of the car, consider using a mobile phone to call for help – you can give your last known location, car make, colour and registration number, as well as last-known direction of travel. You could kick out a plastic rear light cover and wave your hand out through the gap – other motorists will see it and report that to the police. If I saw a car with somebody waving from the boot, I would also follow the car and give a running commentary to police as to where it was going.

- ✓ It is your judgement call; you have to decide what is best for you. If a kidnapper is driving you towards a remote road, as long as you don't injure innocent people, running the car into a bus stop or wall may be the only way to stop the kidnapper getting you where they want to take you.

Stealing Valuables From a Car

The theft of cars is a huge problem, but more cars are broken into to steal the contents or parts of the car, than are broken into to actually steal the car. No matter how many warnings are issued, people still leave valuables on show in their car and are surprised when they return to find that their car has been broken into and that the valuables have gone.

As a basis for some quick sums, let's assume that we know a drug addict who has a £200-a-day habit. That is, to buy sufficient drugs to meet his cravings, he has to find £200 each and every day to buy those drugs! He isn't independently wealthy so he has to find the money somewhere else. Because of the effects of the drugs he isn't capable of holding a job, and in his state no employer would take him on anyway. To raise the money required he could beg on street corners, but I am told that at best that would raise £150 at a good spot on a very good day after at least eight hours of begging, so begging won't feed his drug habit.

Bank robbery would work, but he isn't good enough, co-ordinated enough or clever enough to do that. Street robbery might raise that sort of money, but he probably couldn't cope with a victim if they fought back, so he either has to find and use a weapon or find another way to feed that habit. Theft works. Shoplifting, burglary or breaking into cars to steal things will allow him to steal cash, valuables, credit cards, anything that will bring him the money he needs.

Now consider this! Suppose our addict decides to raid cars to earn his drug money. He smashes the car window (cost to you, or your insurance company, at least £200). The breaking glass damages the metallic paint on the door (cost of repair can easily be £150). He takes your new mobile phone, which was priced at £175, but you got it on contract during an offer and you only paid £25. Unfortunately you didn't take insurance on that so you have to buy a replacement phone (cost to you £175). The incidental cost to you of all of this including insurance excess, replacement phone costs, car insurance loss, time off work and higher insurance premiums next year at least £1,000. Our drug addict took your £175 phone, and he sells it on to somebody else but all he gets for it is £20 if he is lucky.

In round terms that means our drug addict will have to break into at least 10 cars, to steal at least 10 top-of-the-range mobile phones at a total cost of £10,000 to society, just to get the drugs he needs for one day.

In one year, if he lives that long, our one addict will have broken into 3,650 cars (a lot more if they didn't conveniently contain top-of-the-range mobile phones). All of that activity for one addict will cost society (and remember that society is us – you and me) at least £3,650,000 – and that is just the cost of the cars he broke into and was lucky enough to find a phone. If he has to break into an average of five cars to get one phone the figures are astronomical – based on these figures you can see that this one addict can easily be costing us all at least £10,000,000 a year!

Consider how many drug addicts there are in the country. Accept that those top-of-the-range phones are not always conveniently left in cars for all of those addicts and you begin to see how absolutely huge the problem is that we face. Use your common sense and read, understand and follow the countermeasures below to keep your property safe.

Stealing from cars – countermeasures

- ✓ Lock your car whenever you are not in it.
- ✓ If you have a trailer, a caravan or a luggage box on the roof, lock that too.
- ✓ Buy and use a trailer hitch tow lock and, or wheel clamp to secure caravans and trailers when you leave them at home. Any device that prevents the trailer being taken will help to deter a thief.
- ✓ Never ever leave your car keys in the car, even if you have left a passenger in there too! Make it a habit that when you get out of the car, the car keys go in your pocket. That has a double benefit in that it stops the car being stolen and also avoids the embarrassing problem of being locked out of the car, with the keys still in the ignition.
- ✓ When you lock your car, use secondary security devices too; apply a steering lock or gear lever and handbrake lock.
- ✓ Make sure that you don't leave valuables on display in the car. See 'What they will take' below!
- ✓ Anything you do to make your car a less appealing target is a good thing. The idea is to make the criminal walk past your car to look for a more tempting and more vulnerable target further down the road, or in the next car park.

✓ Make a note of the make, model and serial numbers of your car radio, CD player, DVD player or any other in-car entertainment systems. At least if they are stolen you will be able to report them, so there is more chance of them being found!

What They Will Take

They will take anything! If the car is in the wrong place at the wrong time, they will literally take anything and everything. If there is something visible in the car, it will attract their attention.

- Bags – You might know that the Tesco carrier bag on the back seat only contains a bar of soap and some toothpaste, but they don't know that. You might think that nobody could possibly be interested in the tatty old coat you wear when you wash the car every Saturday afternoon, so you leave it on the back seat of the car.

You have to learn an important lesson. You have to realise that you know what these things are, you know that they have no value, but the passing car thief doesn't know that. Where possible, you must see things through their eyes! All they can see is a Tesco carrier bag, as far as they know it could contain an expensive new digital camera!

- Coats – They can only see a coat on the back seat, they don't know it is your tatty car-washing coat. As far as they know it could be your favourite coat, the one you wear every day, so it has to be worth looking through the pockets. If you were careless enough to leave that bag and that coat in the car, you might just be careless enough to have left your house keys and a wallet in that coat. You may have left a chequebook and £75 cash in the pockets so it is worth the criminal breaking into the car to see. The only way to avoid this problem is not to leave anything on show in the car. If they can't see anything they won't try to steal it.

- Laptops and briefcases – Certainly don't leave real identifiable valuables like a laptop computer, briefcase or digital camera visible in the car. If you do leave your handbag, mobile phone, personal CD player, digital music player or anything visible, you may as well walk up to the nearest criminal, hand him the goods and ask him to damage your car if he has time. Don't invite crime!

When you next go to your car take a fresh look at it. Walk around it and look it over as though you were looking for something to steal. That expensive-looking golf umbrella and the quality sunglasses are just sitting there, waiting to be taken.

You might think that nobody would break into a car for a golf umbrella and some sunglasses, but they will! You know they are only worth a few pounds but the criminal doesn't. Remember the criminal only has to invest a large stone and two seconds of his time to smash your car window to see what he can find in the car. It costs the criminal nothing – so don't tempt them!

- Car park change – Do you think the additional temptation of what looks like about £10 or £15 in change in a little tray on the dashboard will tempt a criminal? You keep the change there because it is convenient for you to pay car park fees or feed a parking meter. Any money is valuable to a thief, because with a £200-a-day-habit, any contributions are gratefully accepted.

- Keys – Keys are a major problem in cars. Many people keep or leave a set of house keys in the car. Most people have a house key on the same keyring as their car keys. If your car is stolen, the criminals will have a car full of evidence pointing to your address (letters etc.), employment (work documents, business cards) and habits (railway station car park season ticket which means you go to work by train so the house may be empty all day). If someone gets the car and all of that evidence and you leave a house key for him too, he will almost certainly come back for more! The only other thing you can do to make life easier for the thief is to pack your valuables and leave them just inside the front door so it is that little bit easier for the thieves when they come to steal them.

- Documents – Some people also leave their vehicle registration documents in the car. Don't leave anything for them.

What they will take – countermeasures

✓ Don't leave anything visible in the car. Never, ever, leave anything with any value on show in the car even for 'just a minute'.

✓ Don't even leave things you know are not valuable where they can be seen. Carrier bags, shopping bag, coats, boxes or parcels will be too tempting. A criminal will smash the window and take them just to see what is inside.

✓ Don't leave loose change visible. It may be convenient for car parks and parking meters but a criminal will think £7.48 in change makes it worth smashing the window. After all, if the car owner helpfully leaves some money visible in the car for the criminal, you never know what else there may be in the glove compartment.

✓ Never leave house or office keys in the car. Avoid leaving any documents with your home or office address on them. If you give them the keys you don't want to give them the address so they can go round tomorrow to take everything valuable out of your home or office.

✓ Don't leave vehicle documents in the car. Some people leave the registration document, which is a mistake. Most people assume that somebody with a vehicle, the keys, and the registration document is the owner of the vehicle, so they can sell it or trade it in. Our criminal could easily steal the car, and if the registration document is in the glove compartment it makes it a little easier for him to convert that car to cash by selling it to some unsuspecting victim.

Where They Will Steal It

So, thieves are likely to take just about anything at all from your car. But, where are thieves likely to break into your car? There are hot spots, just as there are places that are more likely to suffer from vandalism, or assaults. I have attempted to list some considerations below, but the real answer is that if you leave your car insecure, or leave something valuable on show, it can and will eventually be taken wherever you are.

Car parks

Public car parks are favourite places to raid cars. The obvious reason is that there are hundreds of cars to choose from and many of them have valuables or potential valuables visible inside the car.

After the morning rush the car park is full of cars, but very few people are moving around until the lunchtime and evening rush. If we call those people moving around 'witnesses', we have identified times when there are few, if any witnesses in the car park – that sounds quite a good time for a thief to work, doesn't it?

Most car parks have multiple entrances and exits for vehicles and pedestrians, giving the thief a number of entry and escape routes to use if he is disturbed. A major benefit to car thieves is that car park tickets are usually designed to clearly show the expiry time, and the local authority insists that you display that ticket in your car so that council staff can fine drivers for staying too long.

The time printed on that ticket could be in the format of a bar code that council staff could read using hand held scanners, but local authorities are not really interested in the safety of your car and the contents. They just want to make money off the poor oppressed motorist! They insist on printing the departure time in large print, but unfortunately the time on that ticket also clearly tells a car thief when a driver is likely to return to their car.

If the ticket is paid up to 6 pm, the owner is highly unlikely to come back to the car before five. Nobody pays more than they have to, so the pay and display tickets tell the criminal which cars to target! They even tell when the owners of surrounding cars are likely to come back to disturb him.

If it is 10 am and the ticket is paid until 6 pm, our car thief knows it will be six or seven hours before the owner discovers that his car has been stolen or broken into.

In most public car parks, if a member of the public sees a car with a broken window they will just rush to make sure their car is OK. It is very unlikely that they will bother to stop at a kiosk and report the damage, which is just as well, because most car parks are unmanned. The pay and display machine is the only council representative in the car park.

Car parks – countermeasures

✓ Don't leave anything on view in your car.

✓ Given a choice, park somewhere that people can see your car. If there is a manned kiosk park opposite it. If the car park is unmanned park close to one of the exits or entrances where passing traffic or people walking by will make it less likely that a criminal will target your car.

- ✓ If there is CCTV coverage of the car park, park in front of one of the cameras. Criminals don't want to be on film doing their nasty deeds, so they are less likely to target a car being filmed on CCTV. You won't have left anything on show in your car so they won't be interested in your car anyway.

- ✓ If you see anything suspicious in a car park, or if you see a car with a broken window, report it to the car park staff, or to the police if the car park is unmanned.

- ✓ Remember security. When you park in the car park, don't leave the car keys in the ignition while you wander off to find one of those pay and display ticket machines. The car will be gone when you get back! Lock it and take the keys with you, and don't leave your case or handbag in the car while you go to get a ticket. It only takes a moment to steal that bag.

- ✓ If you have a steering lock or other secondary security device, use it whenever you park and leave your car.

- ✓ If you have a car alarm, always use it. When you hear a car alarm always respond immediately.

Home – on-street parking

When they get home, most people are in for the night. That means that from, say, six in the evening until about eight the following morning their car is on its own. If you use on-street parking your car is vulnerable, but because it is in a residential zone, where most houses are occupied, theft is less likely during the evening. Later, in the early hours, it has been know for gangs to tour an area to spot good targets then swoop back in and break into 20 cars in as many minutes and vanish.

Home – on-street parking – countermeasures

- ✓ Be aware of any noise outside. I don't expect you to sit at the window all night with binoculars scanning the road for gangs of criminals. If you hear what may be breaking glass, or shouting in the street outside, take a careful look. Go upstairs if you can – you get a better view from upstairs. Don't turn the lights on – you will draw attention to yourself and warn the louts outside. Peek out through the curtains. If the noise is Mrs Biggins from number 42 dropping a bag of shopping that's OK. If it is a group of youths clustering around your car, or any car, call the police. Keep watching and stay in touch with the police to pass on new details. If you stay on the line you can even say to the police operator, 'Your car is coming down the street now. Tell them the two lads by the phone box are two of the gang and three more are hiding behind the white lorry.' Anything that helps the police to find the suspects will be appreciated!

Home – off-street parking

Off-street parking is a little safer. The car or van is hopefully parked closer to the house, so the resident is likely to hear noises outside and will investigate, disturbing and preventing any criminal activity. Unfortunately some town planners organise off street parking that is positioned away from homes, in little clusters which are often 'tastefully' landscaped with shrubs. That is very unfortunate because the town planners have isolated the vehicles from their owners and given the criminals some nice bushes that provide a screen to hide the criminal's activities and mask any sound that they may make.

Home – off-street parking – countermeasures

As above, plus:

✓ Where off-street parking is provided, if possible select a parking space that is in full view of the road, houses and any passing pedestrians and which is as close as possible to your house.

✓ Check out any bushes surrounding the parking area. If they are overgrown ask the council to cut them back. If there has been any criminal activity in the area, use that and ask the council to make cutting those bushes back a priority.

Home – garage parking

Garaged parking at home is the safest option. Garages are often built either next to or attached to the house, so the car and garage are near enough to be protected by the fence, gravel path, security light, family dog and so on.

The garage itself will protect the car for several reasons:

- The criminal doesn't know if the garage contains a car, or just a wheelbarrow.

- The criminal doesn't know if any car in the garage contains any valuables or if the car in the garage is worth more than scrap value.

- The criminal would have to take a greater risk by gaining access to the property, then break into the garage, which might be empty anyway.

Most criminals don't want to get caught. If presented with the option of risking discovery to break into a garage that may be empty anyway, or walking past and looking for an easier target, they will walk on by. Remember that the surrounding roads and car parks are full of easier targets than a car in a garage.

Where planners have designed and built blocks of garages away from the houses, take extra care. Very often these 'garage ghettos' are heavily vandalised, frequently broken into and subject to a wide range of anti-social and criminal activity.

Home – garage parking – countermeasures

As above, plus:

✓ If you have a garage don't clutter it up with cardboard boxes, broken televisions and all of the other rubbish people seem to like filling a garage with. Use the garage to keep the car safe.

✓ Always keep the garage door shut. You don't want criminals to see what interesting things you keep there, like a ladder, a ride-on mower, three brand new mountain bikes and so on. You don't really want them to know if the car is in the garage or not; that way they don't know if you are at home or not, which gives you a higher level of home security! If they don't know if you are in or out, they will probably walk on by.

Cars at petrol stations

Most people feel that a garage forecourt is a safe place. There are a lot of other cars around, there is often a CCTV system in place. If the garage is open there will always be members of staff on duty. Unfortunately, a garage is an ideal place for criminals to operate.

- It is a public place, where anyone, including criminals, have a right to be.

- There are a lot of people coming and going so they can merge into the crowd.
- There is a never-ending supply of cars and their valuable contents and naive drivers flowing on and off the forecourt.
- The criminal can wait and take his time selecting a worthy target.
- With luck the driver will leave his keys in the car and the criminal can take the whole car, drive off and search it at his leisure in some quiet back road. If he does that he may get alloy wheels, new tyres, engine parts, tools from the boot of the car, top-of-the-range car entertainment system, golf clubs etc; quite a star prize to an opportunist thief.

Always treat a garage forecourt as though everyone else there is a criminal. They aren't, but that will put you in a security frame of mind and prevent you suffering loss.

Petrol stations – countermeasures

As above, plus:

✓ Think security.

✓ Put any valuables discreetly out of sight. For example put your mobile phone in your pocket after you turn it off, close your briefcase and leave it in the boot, or at least slide it down into the passenger footwell. Your objective is to leave nothing tempting on show, nothing that a criminal would think they could steal in two seconds.

✓ When you get out take the keys with you. Get into the habit that if you turn the engine off, you lock the car then the keys always go into your pocket or handbag.

✓ When you have filled up with fuel lock the car before going to the kiosk to pay.

✓ When entering the kiosk, fiddling with your purse or wallet or stack of £20 notes, be aware that a criminal could snatch them and run off.

Main road service areas

Main road service areas are a cross between a car park and a garage forecourt.

- They are designed to hold a large number of vehicles.
- They offer various services, fuel, food, toilets etc.
- They are usually established on motorways or busy main roads.
- Because they are on busy main roads they attract a lot of visitors.
- A range of different vehicles use the motorway service areas, including trucks with expensive loads, coaches, cars, caravans, delivery vans and motorbikes.
- Members of the public have free access to the service areas via a network of inter-linked fast roads and motorways!

All of the above points make them an ideal target for vehicle crime. From hijacking lorries and vans with valuable loads, to breaking into a tourist coach while everyone is using the toilets (and making off with an arm full of cameras and other valuables). Service areas can be a crime hotspot.

Main road – countermeasures

✓ Be particularly careful when parking at service areas.

✓ Make sure that whatever vehicle you are in, you secure any valuables out of sight, lock all doors and windows and use any secondary security measures.

✓ Park as near to the main building as you can; criminals are unlikely to be bold enough to attack a vehicle in clear view of passing drivers and shoppers.

✓ Park under a light and in view of a CCTV camera if you can.

✓ Make a point of carefully locking and securing the vehicle. The criminals are usually already there and are watching drivers as they come in. By showing how careful you are you may just put them off trying because they now know you are aware of crime and actively combating it.

✓ If you are in a large group in something like a minibus or coach, and carrying anything of particular value that cannot easily be hidden (suitcases, rucksacks and bags etc), arrange for one or two of you to stay with the vehicle at all times.

✓ If you are using a service area and see anything suspicious, report it immediately.

Badly-managed leisure centre and hotel car parks

Hotel car parks are a favoured target for criminals. People using a hotel:

- are away from home;
- affluent enough to be able to afford to use a hotel;
- are likely to be travelling on business;
- may be carrying valuable laptops, samples, mobile phones;
- may be distracted enough to have left wallets, credit cards and cheque books in their car;
- unlikely to come out to the car until after seven in the morning.

That is a tempting target for a criminal, especially when many hotel and leisure centre car parks are vast, and designed, landscaped and built to look pretty, rather than to be secure and safe. I was once called to a hotel car park where 17 expensive cars had been raided in a single night. Remember the risks associated with these car parks.

Leisure centre and hotel car parks – countermeasures

- ✓ Even though it is inconvenient when using a hotel, take all of your valuables to your room each evening. The hotel porter should be available to help you if you have two cases of valuable samples, a laptop computer a briefcase and your suitcase.

- ✓ If using a leisure centre, don't take unnecessary valuables with you. You won't need them while swimming or playing squash so leave them locked away safely at home or in the office.

- ✓ Remember to park where the car can be seen, where it is well lit, where it is in view of a CCTV camera.

- ✓ If you find that a hotel or leisure centre car park is unsafe, badly designed and subject to crime, ask to see the manager, and tell them you will no longer be using their facilities because the car park is unsafe. If they lose enough customers, they will soon improve security in the car park. Follow up any complaint with a letter to their head office and marketing people. The more people that know, the more questions will be asked and the more likely they are to do something about it.

Garage workshops

Most mechanics are honest (though when asked to pay labour charges of £95 an hour some drivers would dispute that). Unfortunately no matter how many honest mechanics there are, there are some dishonest ones. To maintain security we have to treat all garages and all mechanics as though they are, or at least could be, dishonest.

You can still be polite when dealing with them, but before leaving the car with them you should take some steps to maintain your security. Remember your car is a private little home from home. Even though it is a small metal box with windows all around, most people treat their car as though it was an extension of their living room, oblivious to the world around them.

The security problem is what you leave in your car or hand over to the mechanic when you put it in for service and repair.

Garage workshop – countermeasures

- ✓ Don't leave valuables in the car! I have a friend who owns a garage and he tells me that he regularly finds chequebooks, credit cards, purses, wallets, handbags, and other undoubtedly valuable possessions in cars. To avoid that, when the owner signs the car in for work, he quickly checks the vehicle and points out these things so that the owner can take them away.

- ✓ Don't leave private documents in the car! It is surprising how many people leave bank statements, receipts, confidential papers from work or private letters in a car. When the car is due to go into the garage for service or repair, take the opportunity to give it a spring clean, check to see what is in the boot, under the seats, in door pockets and the glove compartment! Remove anything that shouldn't or doesn't have to be there.

- ✓ Check the car keys! You have to leave the ignition key, locking wheel nut key etc, for the mechanics to move the car and make repairs, but you don't have to leave any other keys. When they drop off their car, most people hand over the car and a bunch of keys that they refer to and recognise as their car keys. The trouble is that most sets of car keys have a lot more than the car keys on them. So you greet this mechanic you have never met and don't know at all. You hand over the car, make sure he has details of your exact name and address, then you tell him that you will be away in London until at least 5.30. Your car keys might hold:
    - ➢ the car ignition key
    - ➢ your garage key

- electronic fob for free access to the company car park
- a key to the steering wheel lock you usually use
- a spare key to your husband/wife's car
- the key to turn the burglar alarm on and off
- a key to the front door of the office
- a front door key to your parents' house.

✓ Be aware of the possible security implications of handing over the set of car keys described above. Check the vehicle, and spend a minute to remove the actual car keys from your bunch of keys, and only give these to the mechanic!

Getting into a car

When they get back to their vehicle, drivers can and often do make themselves a potential and tempting target for thieves. They are not aware of what is going on around them, because they are usually off guard concentrating on searching for the car keys or wondering what the traffic is like on the main road. Perhaps they are putting a briefcase or valuable laptop computer down to free a hand to dig in a pocket or handbag for the car key, or carefully balancing their purchases on the car roof while they do so.

A thief on a mountain bike can have swooped down and taken the laptop or briefcase and be gone before you can turn around to see what the noise was. That thief could be half a mile away before the driver even realises that he has become the victim of a theft!

Remember, snatch thieves could just as easily swoop down and take a handbag or shopping from a passenger who is waiting to get into the car, while the driver keeps them waiting as he searches for the elusive keys.

Women should take particular care. Handbags and shopping can be taken at this time and a violent criminal may also demand that she hand over watches and jewellery too.

Another risk at this time is that a thief will threaten or assault you, take the keys and drive off in the car. This is more likely if your car is an expensive sports car, or luxury limousine but don't relax just because your car is a cheap and rusty runabout; in the past thieves have stolen the cheapest car, just for a ride home!

Getting into the car – countermeasures

- ✓ You know when you have decided to go back to the car, so have your keys ready. Get the keys ready before you leave the shop or office. Avoid stopping when you get to the car to concentrate on looking for the keys.

- ✓ As you approach the car keep an eye out for suspicious activity. Stay aware of what is going on around you. Is that youth on a mountain bike just slow, or is he waiting for something?

- ✓ When you get to the car, take care when putting cases, bags and packages down to free a hand to let you get into the car. Have the key ready and available so that you don't have to put valuables down. If you have to put something down, make sure that you protect it by putting it down between you and the car where it will be harder to snatch. Consider opening the car boot and putting the valuables, shopping, laptop, or briefcase straight into the boot before you get into the car.

- ✓ If a stranger offers to take the key and open the car for you, or take the packages while you open the car, be suspicious. Are they helping you or intending to help themselves?

- ✓ If there is somebody or a group of people you don't like the look of hanging around at or near your car, don't go to the car! Wait until somebody else walks that way. Ask a shopping centre security guard to walk you to the car, or go back into your office and ask a member of staff to escort you to your car. If all else fails and you are really suspicious call the police and ask if somebody can come over while you get to your car. No matter what the group of youths may be doing, if they have the resources available the police should be interested in asking them why they are waiting around in the car park with no apparent reason.

Stopped at the lights

When a car pulls up at traffic lights, or a junction at a main road anywhere, it is trapped in the queue of traffic, which is a time when thieves often target cars. They simply run up, smash a window, lean in and snatch anything they can see. Women's handbags, men's jackets containing wallets and other valuables, briefcases, mobile phones and anything else that can be snatched goes in the blink of an eye.

These snatches can escalate into violence or the loss of the car. If the victim tries to fight back the criminals may assault them and weapons are sometimes on hand as a method of last resort to the thieves who will do anything to get away. Sometimes they work in pairs; one thief will loiter at a junction to look into cars. He then uses his mobile phone to call his partner who is waiting at the next junction – the spotter tells the grabber to go for the 'briefcase on the rear passenger seat of the blue Jaguar'.

If the driver jumps out of the car to chase a thief, another thief may jump in and drive the car away. Sometimes this is an orchestrated plan, where the first thief with the mobile phone or jacket makes a slow getaway, tempting the driver to think he can retrieve his belongings. The driver jumps out, not realising that he is leaving his £25,000 car vulnerable as he chases a thief, trying vainly to retrieve a £30 mobile phone or £50 jacket! Remember if they get the car, they may also have the handbag, jacket, wallet, briefcase, house keys, addresses, cheque books, credit cards etc as well.

Stopped at the lights – countermeasures

You have to stop at the lights and some major road junctions, but you can take a few measures to reduce the likelihood of your being targeted.

- ✓ Realise that this sort of smash and grab from occupied stationary cars does happen.

- ✓ Make sure that tempting valuables are not on display. When you get into the car, put your case, jacket and maybe your handbag into the boot out of sight and lock the boot.

- ✓ You don't need the mobile phone on the seat beside you or on the dashboard, so hide it away in a pocket. You cannot use the mobile while driving so you may as well put it in the boot with your briefcase or in the glove compartment, anywhere out of sight.

- ✓ Remember, if you have passengers, they can tempt thieves as well, so get them to hide their valuables so that thieves are not tempted to try smashing a window or two.

- ✓ When stopping in a queue of traffic, don't wedge yourself in. Always leave 'rubber and road'. That is, when stopped in a queue of traffic and looking over the bonnet of your car you should be able to see the back tyres of the car in front and some road surface between you. If you do that, you will have a little space to manoeuvre and if safe and necessary you would even have enough room to pull out of the queue of traffic and drive off if you had to.

Vehicle Security Review

- ✓ When stopping, especially in an area you don't know and if there are suspicious looking people hanging around – lock the doors and close windows and the sunshine roof. The more you can do to protect yourself, protect your property and to deter the thief the better.

- ✓ If somebody does break your window, don't try to detain them or try to fight them off. Don't try to chase them. Stay in the car, it is the safest place to be, and when it is safe, drive to the nearest police station or other place where there are a lot of people. A garage forecourt, with CCTV, plenty of light and a lot of people around is a good place to stop and call the police. You could also stop on a railway station forecourt, a supermarket car park, the front car park of a pub, in fact anywhere, that is well lit and has a lot of people around.

- ✓ If your car is attacked, try to make a note of any vehicles and car numbers etc that are involved. Otherwise try to make a note of the car numbers of drivers who have witnessed the attack. Most people won't want to get involved so they will drive off, and with their car numbers you can at least tell the police what vehicles were around at the time.

- ✓ If you can see a crowd of youths waiting at or near the next set of lights, try pacing your approach. That is, if it is safe, slow down so that you reach the junction or lights when they are on green, which means you don't have to stop. If they are criminals they will not have a chance to attack your car if you don't come to a stop at the lights. BE CAREFUL, remember traffic is moving around you. When you slow right down and leave a large gap in the flow of traffic, other drivers may try to overtake and cut past you, or cut into the gap you leave, so when you accelerate to drive through with the lights on green be extra careful. Don't get into an accident by ignoring other traffic. For example the driver of a car in a side road may think you are slowing to let them out, then when you accelerate to catch the green light you could drive straight into the side of his car as he pulls out onto the road. Try to pace yourself IF IT IS SAFE.

'Lapping'

Lapping is a speciality of the stationary traffic smash and grab thief. Criminals target business areas, where office staff will be going home and will be trapped in rush hour traffic jams. The criminals pick an area where there are a lot of offices, and where the badge of management tends to be an expensive laptop computer. A computer that is probably worth at least £800 (without the value of software and confidential corporate information) is more often than not casually tossed on the front or rear passenger seat. Our dim-manager stops his car at the traffic lights and is stunned when a brick comes through the side window, followed by a hand that snatches the laptop computer! He then sits trying to regain his composure as he watches his laptop in the hands of a young thief sprinting off down the road and vanishing in a labyrinth of alleys and underpasses.

Lapping – countermeasures

- ✓ If possible, disguise something like a laptop. If you cannot or do not want to put it in the boot of the car, at least don't advertise it.

- ✓ Never leave a laptop on the seat of a car, even if you are in the car.

- ✓ If possible try to avoid using those nice stylish padded laptop cases. You shouldn't be surprised to know that thieves know that posh and expensive laptop bags usually contain posh and expensive laptop computers. Consider putting your laptop into a sports bag, even put an old (dry) towel on top of it as camouflage. Very few self-respecting thieves will attack a car at the lights to steal what looks like some smelly sports kit and a potentially soggy towel.

- ✓ Even better, don't carry your laptop if you don't need to. It will be safer locked up in the office or at home than being carried around the streets or left in parked cars when you don't really need it.

- ✓ Remember that there is now a device that thieves can place on a car window to see if there is a computer in the car. The device apparently picks up electric signals, which invariably come from a laptop computer, even if it is turned off! That means they can tell if you have a laptop in the boot of the car even though they can't see it. Knowing there is an £800 laptop in the boot means that it is worth them taking the risk and going to the effort of breaking into the boot of the car!

'Spotting' in car parks

Everyone knows that if they have to carry them, they should lock valuables in the boot of their car. A few people even follow that advice, but at Christmas and sale times they fall foul of 'the spotter'.

Breaking into a car is easy when you know how. Criminals practice on different makes and swap methods so that they know how to quickly get into all of the common makes and models of car and van.

Getting into the boot is quite simple as well if you know how, but before they break in they ask themselves a question. Is there anything in the boot that will reward their efforts and make it worth taking the risk of being caught breaking into that car?

That is where 'spotting' comes in. A criminal will hang around a car park entrance at Christmas or when the sales are on. When somebody comes back to the car park loaded down with loads of interesting looking purchases, they will discreetly follow them all the way back to their car.

Who is targeted

A shopper with two economy size packs of toilet rolls will not be of any real interest! On the other hand, a shopper with bags marked with the name of a camera store, or a shopper carrying a brand new boxed DVD writer/player, iPod or similar expensive electronic goods will be of great interest. They will watch to see what car that shopper goes to, and what they do when they get there. They obviously intend trying to steal those goods, but if the shopper loads the shopping into the car, gets in and drives off it doesn't matter, because there will be another shopper along in a minute.

Eventually they will be rewarded. A driver will return loaded down with shopping and lock it all in the boot of the car before going back to the high street to finish their shopping expedition. They may have been security conscious and put the valuables in the boot of their car out of sight, but that doesn't matter to the spotter. He now knows that there is something worth taking in the boot of the car because he just watched the driver put it in there!

He breaks into that car, then two minutes later he emerges from the car park with the crowd, looking like a normal everyday shopper. Just a guy walking through the car park loaded down with purchases – only in his case they were your purchases until he popped your car boot open and took them!

Another opportunity for spotters is at remote car parks. At country parks, churches, etc, where the local authority has helpfully erected signs asking motorists to lock valuables out of sight in the boot of their car. Our criminal watches the dim motorist drive up, park and look at the sign. With security in mind, that dim motorist then locks his CD player, a handbag, and some expensive-looking shopping in the boot of the car before he goes shuffling off for an hour or so. Guess what our criminal spotter does as soon as Mr or Mrs

Dim-driver wanders off? He opens that car boot and removes the valuables, and he is miles away before any crime can be discovered let alone reported.

Spotter – countermeasures

- ✓ If you are going to go for a walk in the park, or go to church or otherwise leave the car for a long time, don't take unnecessary valuables with you.

- ✓ If you have valuables go home and put them somewhere safe before you go and leave the car at the local park, church or other unattended car park.

- ✓ If you cannot leave valuables somewhere safe, make them as secure as you can. Stop somewhere (before you reach your destination car park), to hide the valuables away in the boot of the car. There shouldn't be a spotter around where you stop and if there is, it doesn't matter because you are going to drive off straight away anyway. By doing it before you reach the church (or whatever) car park you will foil any spotter working there.

- ✓ If you carry valuables, disguise them. Try not to walk out of the electronics shop with your purchase in one of their distinctive carrier bags. You don't have to be too bright to figure out that an electronic shop carrier bag probably contains some valuable electronic items. I try to carry a supermarket cool bag around with me. They fold up quite well so they are easy to carry. They are strong and large enough to hold most things. Best of all, to a spotter I look like I am putting frozen food in the car, not a new digital music iPod.

- ✓ If you are doing a big shop, consider getting your first armful of shopping, putting it in the boot of the car then driving home with it. Better to be safe than sorry – go back to the shops later if you still have things to buy.

General safety – countermeasures

- ✓ Keeping your car tidy will usually prevent you from carelessly leaving things in it. In a clean car something left on the seat stands out, in a messy car something valuable left on the seat is just another part of the clutter so you may not notice it. A clean, tidy and empty car is less likely to attract the attention of a thief.

- ✓ There is another important benefit to be gained from securely storing the things we all carry in our vehicles. That is the safety of you and your passengers! Would it hurt if I threw a tin of baked beans at the back of your head? What if I was to pick up your whole week's shopping and then throw it at your head and shoulders as hard as I could? What about your toolbox, car jack, spare

Vehicle Security Review

wheel, tyre lever and various windscreen sprays, scrapers and oily rags too? You risk the equivalent of just that if you have an accident in an untidy car. Even if the accident isn't your fault, if you are sitting quietly minding your own business in a marked parking bay, and you are hit head on by a drunk doing 50 miles an hour. Your seatbelt might protect you from the worst of the impact, but all those loose things lying around in your car would hurtle towards your windscreen and your head!

- ✓ What is in your car? Does it need to be there? Now that you can see that the clutter could kill you and the friend you give a lift to work that morning, is there anything that should be taken out of your car, van, estate or MPV? Those metal fence posts are now potential weapons that could kill your two daughters on the way to school tomorrow. The week's shopping you put on the back seat because the car boot is full could kill you at the next junction where people always seem to be going too fast. Check the car. Remove anything that doesn't have to be in there. Weed out the toolbox, only carry what you really have to carry. When you have arrived at the bare minimum store and secure it properly. Put as much as possible in the boot of the car where it will be out of sight and won't hurt you in an accident.

- ✓ If you drive an estate car or van, remember that anything and everything you carry really wants to jump up and hit you in the back of the head. Install a bulkhead if you can, but always tie everything down as well as you can to stop it moving around, and take it out of the vehicle as soon as you can. Consider using a cargo net or tie down bags to stop things flying around in an accident.

- ✓ If a business person really has to have their briefcase on the front passenger seat, the front passenger seat belt can be looped through the handle to stop it flying around in the car if there is an accident.

- ✓ Handbags can be secured with a seat belt, but the bag would be more secure if it was pushed out of sight under the passenger seat. (Don't hide things under the driver's seat, because in hard braking any objects can slide out from under the driver's seat and interfere with the accelerator or brake pedals.)

- ✓ By spring cleaning your car, you will not only make it safer, you will reduce the weight and so reduce wear and tear on the car as well as improving your miles per gallon. If you aren't pulling around half a ton of bikes, unwanted tools, fence posts and other junk, your engine won't be working so hard so you simply won't use so much petrol.

- ✓ Be aware of your surroundings and act on gut feelings. If it doesn't feel right it probably isn't right! If you don't like the look of the louts hanging around the car park, find another car park, and report the louts.

- ✓ Don't leave driving documents and personal letters in the car. They have a different but nevertheless worthwhile value to criminals.

- ✓ If your car entertainment system is removable, or has a removable faceplate, take it with you when you leave the car. If the entertainment system or front control panel aren't in the car there is one thing less to attract a thief so they should walk on past. Make sure that you have recorded the make, model and serial numbers of any in-car entertainment equipment.

Criminal Damage

For some reason unknown to science there is a subspecies of human being which has the scientific name of *the brainless doofus*. This subspecies has a genetic need to mindlessly damage things. They are mainly nocturnal in habit and usually travel in small packs, but are timid, usually presenting no signs of brain activity or courage especially if they are alone.

This subspecies is genetically predisposed to seek out and unnecessarily damage the property of people it does not know and has never met. Though they can attack the property of somebody they think has transgressed against them, that is rarely the case.

Signs of their passing are scratches on car paint work, slashing of car tyres, pouring of corrosive fluid on car paint, smashing of mirrors and bending of car aerials and in extreme cases the taking and burning of cars.

As there seems to be no known pattern to their behaviour, countermeasures are restricted. It is likely that the countermeasures you take to protect your car and house from theft and intrusion will be quite effective to control and prevent this behaviour.

Unfortunately, the courts only appear to consider criminal damage to be of 'nuisance' value. If caught offenders are likely to just be told not to do it again. Not much punishment for the mindless damage they have caused.

Criminal damage etc – countermeasures

Some of the countermeasures have already been discussed, but the golden rules of avoiding criminal damage are:

✓ Always lock your car and garage.

✓ Don't leave tools and equipment around that these morons can use to damage your car.

✓ Don't park in an area where there are bricks, chunks of broken concrete, lengths of wood or bottles etc. that a passing lout could see and decide to use those objects to damage your car.

✓ Always be aware of your surroundings. When looking for somewhere to park, don't just look for a space that is big enough. Think about what you want to do, where you are, what time you will come back to the car. If you can see broken car window glass all along the road, that indicates that criminals are active in the area. If you can see a good quality car minus its alloy wheels and sitting on bricks, do you really want to park there?

✓ Is this a quiet side street now? If so, when you come back to your car from a theatre or cinema show that ends at midnight, what will the street look like then? If you can't see any streetlights, that means that the area will be in total darkness after sunset. Pick your parking area sensibly.

✓ Do you really want to park next to those overgrown bushes? How many robbers could be lurking in them when you come back after a late meeting? Be sensible and take time to really look at the area. What evidence can you already see, and what problem can you foresee this area giving you when it is late and dark?

✓ If you made a mistake or are later than you expected and find you have to get into your car in a lonely, dark and remote place be ready and do it quickly. With the key ready, check nobody is inside, open the door, get in, lock the doors and drive off as soon as you are ready. Don't take time to put your briefcase in the boot and don't delay by tuning the radio to your favourite channel. The sooner you have left that place the sooner you stop being vulnerable. When you get to the main road you can pull into a garage forecourt or supermarket car park to tune the radio, and take your coat off if you really need to.

✓ If you have an aerial, retract it. It takes a second to put it down, but it can prevent the criminal or vandal leaving you with an expensive repair.

5 Mostly Men

This will be a short chapter, but probably not for the reason you think! It is abundantly clear that becoming a victim of crime is not a measure of masculinity, intelligence, strength or any other supposedly male attribute. An adult male can make himself vulnerable to crime by being stupid, careless and forgetful just as much as a woman or a child.

There is a slight difference, as men probably assume that they can take care of themselves in most threatening situations, so their motivation to read and follow the advice in this book is probably quite low. No matter what your thoughts are, I strongly suggest that you read the whole book.

Don't skip any pages, and certainly don't assume that any of the chapters don't apply to you just because of the chapter titles I may have given. All of the advice is relevant to everyone – or rather you can learn from all of the advice given in this book.

Allow me to illustrate that point. There is a section in chapter 6 that describes the threats, risks and vulnerabilities that women face when shopping. As a man you may have decided to skip over that entire chapter. If you do you will miss some valuable lessons and advice. The advice to women about handbags could also be relevant you, if you look at the lessons and countermeasures and use your skill and intelligence to apply them to your circumstances. For example, the advice might inspire you into adopting some similar countermeasures to protect your wallet, rucksack or toolbox. Similarly, the advice on shopping may be relevant. Men shop! The real lesson is that no matter what we have in those carrier bags, we are just as vulnerable to having our shopping stolen as the ladies.

You may be able to make use of specific advice in a different way. If you read and learn from the advice to women about avoiding potentially dangerous situations, you might be able to help and advise your girlfriend, wife, daughter or mother to ensure their safety. At the same time you should become more aware of how a fun night out with the guys could be intimidating or frightening to women, as well as realising that that woman could be your sister, daughter, mother or even future wife!

While everyone needs advice, statistics show that it is usually younger men who often become the victims of violent crime. Whatever the reason, the result is that younger men are more at risk.

Why Young Men?

On average, young men between the ages of about 17 and 19 are 25 times more likely to be the victim of an assault, robbery or other violent crime than anyone else. There is a sliding scale that extends beyond 19 years of age, and only really begins to reach a normal/average level of risk when men get to the age of about 34. If you aren't a young man aged between 17 and 19, don't skip this chapter though. The common sense and advice may be helpful to you.

Why young men in particular? I am not medically trained but I will attempt to paraphrase what I have been told! In summary, there are physiological and psychological reasons why young men are more likely to be involved in disputes, crime and violence.

Young men want to establish their own independence, to take their own path, to compete with other males to earn a rank and status in the 'pack' – no different to wolves or other animals really! When they approach adult status, their physiology changes and hormones start to flow and any 'young buck' wants to pose and make a name for himself. He wants to establish status and display his strength.

Psychologically, they want to prove themselves, show their parents that they have achieved adulthood, as well as the important need to be seen to be strong so that they can attract a mate. Anything that allows them to prove their strength and, in their eyes their masculinity, is a good thing. The smallest apparent slight, insult or challenge has to be met with verbal and physical resistance. They want to prove to themselves and the world that they are men! Given that, there is one other important factor that is a major cause of trouble.

Excess alcohol

Unfortunately, it is just these activities that lead to young men becoming involved in criminal acts. Assaults, gang fights, public order offences, drunken stupidity and anything else you can think of. They may be perpetrators or victims, but if it is a crime where some violence is involved, statistically they will be young men and in a majority of cases somebody involved will be under the influence of alcohol. In the UK the statistics are quite clear.

- The vast majority of robbery victims are young males, and more often than not the property stolen is a mobile phone.
- As many as 45% of violent crimes are committed by young men who are drunk.
- Young men who have had too much to drink, were responsible for nearly 80% of assaults in one survey . . .
- . . . and drunken young men committed nearly 90% of criminal damage offences.
- Based on the latest figures it is estimated that there were approximately 1.6 million incidents of alcohol-related violence in 2004.
- It is widely accepted that alcohol is a crime multiplier. That is, the use of alcohol greatly increases the number and seriousness of crimes committed by young men.
- One government reports shows that alcohol abuse is costing the country nearly £16 billion a year in crime, injuries, health-care costs and lost productivity.
- Nearly 11% of young people taken to hospital for treatment following a binge-drinking session are under the legal age to be drinking alcohol.
- One casualty unit reported treating nearly 900 young drunks in one year, who were treated for a variety of injuries from assaults, including punches, kicks and stabbing with bottle and knives.

- It is reported that children under the age of 16 drink twice as much alcohol as they did just 10 years ago.
- Statistics show that drunks are responsible for 40% of cases requiring emergency treatment at hospitals.
- In some city centres, as many as 30% of arrests involve people who are under the influence of alcohol.
- In nearly a quarter of all cases, those apprehended for street robberies are under the influence of drink or drugs.
- In over 50% of cases, victims of assault report that their attackers appeared to be under the influence of alcohol.
- From disputing neighbours, to prostitution and from aggressive begging to vandalism, excessive consumption of alcohol is a significant factor.

There is no simple explanation as to why there is so much trouble, or why alcohol seems to be such a significant contributory factor. There are some factors which appear to have a bearing on the problem.

- Young men are more affluent than ever before so they can afford to indulge themselves and have plenty of leisure time available to them.
- Alcohol is available in many different forms almost 24 hours a day.
- Clubs, pubs and bars try to attract customers by offering free drinks, happy hours, two for the price of one and other offers.

Whatever the reasons, it is clear that with young males as many as 40% of all of their drinking sessions can be classified as binge drinking. (Binge drinking is defined as drinking the equivalent of four pints of beer or eight glasses of wine in a single session.)

Binge drinking

Most binge drinkers come within the age range of 18 to 24, but there are older and younger binge drinkers. A recent survey showed that nearly 30% of young people admitted to participating in binge drinking, and many of them also admitted experimenting with illegal drugs.

A few more sobering statistics (pun intended).

- When the perpetrator is drunk, over 30% of acts of violence are committed against innocent strangers.
- Nearly 25% of violent crime in one city occurred in and around the area frequented by young binge drinkers.
- When drunk, a young person is nearly five times more likely to commit criminal offences.
- When drunk, young men are just as likely to attack an acquaintance as they are to attack a stranger.
- The most worrying statistic I have seen is that it is estimated that 75% of drunken assaults are never reported.

Effects of alcohol

Given the statistics listed in the last few pages, I defy anyone to refute that there is an increasing alcohol-related crime problem in the UK. If the appalling crime statistics are not enough to make you monitor your alcohol intake, perhaps the following information on the effects of alcohol may make you reconsider.

- **Male/Female** – because they have a higher proportion of body fat than men, the same amount of alcohol will have a greater effect on a woman than it will on a man. (Though evidence suggests that men will lose control more quickly than women.)
- **Full stomach/eating** – drinking on an empty stomach will make you drunk more quickly than if you eat a meal while drinking. A full stomach slows the rate at which alcohol is absorbed into the system.
- **Your height/weight** – the bigger you are the more alcohol it takes to make you drunk, though that may be affected by . . .
- **Your drinking patterns** – The body adjusts and builds a tolerance to alcohol, thus reducing the effects. Therefore a habitual heavy drinker will need to consume greater quantities of alcohol to become drunk.
- **Current state** – your current state in terms of physical health and fitness and emotional status will change the effects of alcohol. For example a person who

is under stress or recovering from an illness may get drunk on a smaller quantity of alcohol.

- **Drinking speed** – the speed with which you drink has an effect. A large quantity of alcohol flooding the system in a short time has a greater effect than the same quantity of alcohol consumed over an extended period. So, knocking back five drinks quickly will quickly make you drunk.

- **Mixing drinks and drugs** – mixing drinks, prescribed and illegal drugs will have an unknown effect on the person consuming them. The effects can vary wildly, from slumping asleep to dropping dead, from getting amorous to making violent attacks for no apparent reason.

- **Reactions** – after consuming even a modest quantity of alcohol, your brain becomes less efficient, and the effects are cumulative. Under the influence of alcohol you will take longer to see what is happening around you. When you do, your brain will take many times longer to decide what to do about it, and then your muscles will be slow in attempting to deliver the action your brain is requesting.

- **Multitasking** – alcohol can slow your reactions by up to 30%, while severely limiting your ability to multi-task. That is, as you consume more alcohol, your ability to do more than one thing at a time is sharply reduced. The effects on drivers are well known; for example, a drunk driver may find that he cannot drive and talk to a passenger at the same time.

- **Reduced vision** – using alcohol reduces your ability to see and focus on different objects, and can reduce the effectiveness of your night vision by as much as 30% while reducing peripheral vision too.

- **Stimulant** – alcohol can be a powerful stimulant to the nervous system, creating a false sense of security and confidence, allowing a drunk to take risks that they would ordinarily recognise and reject as foolhardy.

Why it happens

The consumption of alcohol is often regarded as a relaxing and convivial activity, in many cases enjoyed with little or no ill effect. However, for some people, drinking can cause many problems. This section looks at the extent of problem drinking, the factors leading to it, and the types and proportion of crimes committed by intoxicated offenders.

As the effects of alcohol are variable based on a range of parameters, users should take great care when consuming it. A drunk who says he will know when he has had enough is deluding himself, because alcohol is known to affect your judgement. A drunk almost never has the mental capacity to realise that he has had enough, though there can be early warnings.

Alcohol always takes effect on muscular co-ordination first, then affects the brain by removing inhibitions and ruins the judgement of the drinker. If you feel you are losing co-ordination and getting clumsy, that is a warning that you have consumed too much alcohol. The lack of co-ordination in a driver first represents itself in an inability to steer in a straight line. If you notice you are having problems steering a vehicle and you are weaving along the road, stop the car and take a bus home. If you are a passenger in a vehicle where the driver is weaving, stop the car and do them a favour; seize the keys and take the bus home! Better still, realise that they have been drinking and order a taxi for you all, so they never get into the car

Remember that a small amount of alcohol will first make the driver feel overconfident, and they often lose control on roundabouts and at junctions, or misjudge distances between cars, having small accidents and near misses.

The bottom line has to be that alcohol is a dangerous drug if it is not used sensibly.

Excess alcohol – countermeasures

It may be hard to do, but all you have to do is behave reasonably and sensibly. Aim to be as mature as you claim to be. You should be able to see and identify a pattern in the actions and behaviour listed here. If your drinking behaviour leaves you recognising any of these problems in yourself, I suggest that you should seriously consider restricting your alcohol intake. If you have tried and can't cut back, seek expert help.

- ✓ For at least two weeks, keep a note of the amount of alcohol that you consume – and be honest!
    - ➢ Record how many times you go to the pub or bar.
    - ➢ Make a note of the amount of time you spend there.
    - ➢ Record what drinks you have had and how many.
    - ➢ Make a note of how you feel, especially if it is alcohol related, e.g. throwing up, hangover, skinned

Mostly Men

knuckles (unknown origin), lost time – for example too drunk to remember where you were after midnight last night.

✓ When you come to review the record, I suggest that you are drinking too much if:
  ➢ you have consumed alcohol every day of the week.
  ➢ you get drunk at any occasion other than Christmas, weddings and birthday parties etc.
  ➢ your friends tell you that you are aggressive when drunk.
  ➢ you forget or lose track of the record of how much you are drinking.
  ➢ you go out, but next day cannot remember the details of what you did.
  ➢ you are spending more than £30 a week on alcohol in any form.
  ➢ you are spending money on alcohol rather than food, rent, lecture fees etc.
  ➢ you commit any crime during or after drinking.
  ➢ while you were out, you got into a dispute or fight for any reason.
  ➢ you are asked to leave any premises because of your behaviour.
  ➢ your family or loved ones are worried about your drinking habits.
  ➢ drinking or recovering from drinking has an adverse affect on your studies or work.

✓ Cutting back is hard, but possible. Try to make it harder to drink at home.
  ➢ Don't buy and keep supplies of alcohol at home. If it isn't easily available you won't be tempted to drink it.
  ➢ If you do buy alcohol for home consumption, limit the amount you buy, avoid buying the strongest brands, and aim to drink it only when you have company.
  ➢ Avoid drinking alone.

✓ If you begin to feel that it is time you had a drink, divert your attention.
  ➢ Go out for a run, take the dog for a walk, or go and visit relatives.
  ➢ Go out and wash the car or motorbike by hand. Don't just drive to the nearest garage – they have too much tempting alcohol on display. Spend an hour or two in the fresh air with the hose, sponge and car wax.
  ➢ Go and tidy the garden. Cut the grass, rake up the leaves, pull up some weeds and do anything else that needs doing.
  ➢ Watch something you like on television, or rent a video/DVD. Consider taking time to scan what is on each week and tape some good programmes or films to watch when you want to avoid drinking.
  ➢ Spring clean the garage or workshop, tidy your tools or sort out your car magazine collection etc.

- Avoid situations where you are almost expected to drink. If everyone knows that when you aren't at work you are in the pub, you have a problem. Avoiding pubs will allow you to avoid alcohol.
- From the log of your drinking above, see how many days of the week you go to the pub.
- From the log see how many hours a week you spend in the pub.
- Aim to reduce your visits to pubs and the time you spend in pubs by at least 33%.
- Aim to reduce your alcohol intake while in the pub. Talk more and drink less. Play darts or dominoes. Sit out in the pub garden if you can – the fresh air is better for you and you are a little further away from the next pint.
- Drink half pints instead of pints. Psychologically a nine-pints-a-day man feels as though he has had his nine drinks, even if they were only half pints – alcohol intake reduced by 50% at a stroke.
- Consider drinking something other than alcohol. Pubs serve orange juice, fizzy lemonade and even tea and coffee.

✓ Peer pressure is quite strong among drinkers, especially young men. For example, the lads may want to know why you are having a girl's drink if you order orange, or question your manhood if you only order a half.
  - If you have the courage tell them the truth: you have decided you are drinking too much and you are doing something about it.
  - Tell them how much strength and willpower it is taking to achieve that.
  - If they challenge you, challenge them to do the same. Bet that they don't have the willpower to cut their alcohol intake by 50%. Of course you will have to help them draw up a log and probably surprise them with how much they drink now!
  - Set yourself a target, for example tell them that you have entered for the London Marathon and that reducing your alcohol intake is part of the regime. Maybe go so far as setting yourself a goal and actually entering and training for the marathon – or a local race!
  - If the marathon is beyond you, try lying! Use the marathon as an excuse for cutting back on alcohol, and then make an excuse later in the year 'my doctor advised against it, because of an old knee injury I got playing school rugby' is quite a good excuse).

✓ If you do try to cut down, you must keep up a diary of alcohol consumption. As before, make a note of the visits, time spent, type and quantity of drinks taken and how you felt.

✓ Try to keep up your alcohol avoidance activities for four weeks, then compare your diary entries for the first week you recorded against your last week. Look at and list the differences, for example:
  - no headaches/hangover for more than a month.

- haven't been sick for over a month.
- have spent £175 less this month, only because I don't buy alcohol.
- haven't taken any sick days off work this month.
- feeling fitter and healthier, more alive than I ever remember being.
- can actually taste my food now.
- my boss told me I am working well and in line for promotion if I keep it up.

✓ Make a list of the other hidden benefits, for example:
- The garage is tidy and I know where all of my tools are.
- I have started doing a home study course, which will boost my promotion prospects at work.
- I have started watching documentaries on television; I am amazed at how much I have learned and how much it has broadened my outlook, or how much more interesting it has made my conversations.
- I have started rebuilding a motorcycle I got from my uncle.

✓ And maybe one day 'Finished the London Marathon in 4 hours 38 minutes in 11,328th position'!

✓ You may wish to visit www.drinkaware.com for more information on alcohol consumption.

6 Mostly Women

Though most of the content of this book is of use to almost everyone, some might be a little more appropriate to a specific group of people. Why do I call this chapter 'Mostly Women'? I had to divide the contents into chapters, and this seemed a reasonable way to do it, but if you are a man, you should still read this chapter even if the advice is aimed at women more than men.

The bigger argument about rights and freedom doesn't concern me here. Should women have to take extra safety precautions just to live their life? No! Should women be scared to leave home after dark? No, of course not, but I shouldn't have to lock my car, or not draw cash out of a cash point because I think there are louts nearby either. I know that the results of a woman being attacked and me having my car window broken can't really be compared. It's the world that we live in, and until the government resolves the problems, we are stuck with it though we can do a lot to make ourselves safe!

Some research claims that victims pick themselves. There is the argument that by being somewhere you should not really have been you are accepting the risk of an attack. One report I saw went further; it stated that by 'appearing' to be lost, vulnerable and confused, a person could actually attract an attacker. If that theory has any truth, remember to never look lost, try not to look vulnerable or confused. Exude confidence at all times, even if you *are* lost walk confidently to the nearest bright lights and crowds of people.

General

The world can be a dangerous place to live but your chances of being the victim of a violent crime are statistically very, very low. If you aren't a drug addict, alcoholic, addicted to attending back street clubs, always going to those football matches where violence is guaranteed, or a member of a street gang, the chances of you being the victim of violent crime in a public place are very low. On the other hand, some reports show that as many as one in four women will at some stage in their life be the victim of domestic violence.

If you have read this book and have taken the advice I have given, the chances of you becoming a victim should be minute. So don't worry unduly, just take sensible precautions and don't let your guard down.

On average a woman is physically smaller, not as strong as a man, not as used to fighting, as well as possibly restricted in what she can do by her clothing or shoes. Add all of that up and you realise that a woman is probably more vulnerable to an attack than a man. Women must therefore protect themselves. Though self-defence skills are useful (and 'all women' self-defence classes are generally available), I suggest that you can better defend yourself with preparation, knowledge, intelligence and awareness.

It is clear that women probably make up a significant majority in some professions, so advice relating to dangers relating to work has been included in this chapter as well. However, the advice is usually also appropriate to men in the same circumstances.

Read the information below, but remember that just reading it isn't much use to you. You have to understand and use it to protect and defend yourself. The two words you have to avoid in your life at all costs are *if only*. If only I had checked the car, if only I hadn't taken that shortcut and if only I had taken an official taxi! Be aware and use a little intelligence in everything you do. The following general countermeasures should indicate the way you should be thinking. Make it a way of life so that you naturally think of risks and threats before you do anything.

Don't think of it as an intolerable and unacceptable burden on women, think of it as just an extension of something you already do. Before you cross the road you consider the risks and threats to avoid being run over. Before you take a bite of pizza you consider the risks and threats of burning your tongue if it's too hot or of getting a mouthful of those nasty little anchovy things! When gardening, before you pull up a weed you consider the threats and risks associated with that; is it a stinging nettle or does it have thorns? All I am suggesting is that you extend that a little to cover other circumstances.

General – countermeasures

- ✓ Especially when you are alone, when you are going to use a lift wait for the doors to open and look to see who is inside before you get in. If you don't like the look of them don't get in! If they hold the door, say something like, 'That's OK thanks, don't wait, I'm waiting for my 6'5" husband. He used to be a sergeant in the SAS but he got thrown out for killing three muggers! He and his six big friends will be here any minute.' Well OK, you don't have to be that obvious but you get the idea. Make an excuse and take the next lift.

- ✓ If you are in a lift alone and somebody, or a group, that you don't like the look of gets in, you should consider stepping out. If you can see a group of men and women on the floor where he/they got into the lift it is probably safer to get out than to stay in the lift. If the floor is deserted, it may be safer to ride down – especially if you are casually standing and balancing by keeping one hand on the control panel. It's obviously coincidental that you have your finger near the emergency alarm button! If you do feel the need to step out of the lift, if necessary make an excuse such as a more realistic, 'Oh sorry, this is our floor.' You are out of the lift, away from the person or people you did not like. Saying 'our' instead of 'my' indicates that you are not alone and that your partner or party is nearby. Take the next lift down.

- ✓ When in the lift, always try to stand next to the buttons. When you get in, make sure you look at the buttons, know which one is the alarm button, which one closes the doors and which one sends the lift to the reception area. In that way you are more in control. You can close the doors if that nasty-looking man is coming, you can hit the alarm if you have to, or push the ground floor button to get you to reception where there are usually at least a few people around who could help if you needed it.

- ✓ At night, if at all possible travel with somebody else. Consider asking a member of staff to escort you to your room or out to the car, or to call a taxi etc.

- ✓ If you have a home telephone, make sure that your entry in the published telephone directory lists only your surname and initial. 'Miss', 'Mrs' or 'Susie Biggins' clearly shows that you are female and that might attract uninvited attention. S Biggins is enough for people to track you down if they know you. See also section on nuisance telephone calls, page 123.

- ✓ When you answer your telephone, just say hello. Don't give information away to strangers. Whoever they are, they are strangers until you find out who is at the other end. Never answer, 'Susie Biggins 2667546.' By saying that the stranger knows your full name and your phone number, and he can then use the telephone directory to get the address. Knowing your first name he could approach you and put you off guard by making you think you know him. For example, if he walked up to you at a bus stop in town and said 'Susie? It is Susie isn't it? Haven't seen you for God knows how long. How are you? Tell you what, have you got time for a drink?' Does he know you? Do you know him? Would it be safe to go with him? Never be too embarrassed to answer such a question with 'Sorry, do I know you?' and leave it to him to prove he does. If he turns out to be cousin Boris from Brighton then it's OK, if not, make your excuses and stay somewhere safe or get to somewhere safe as soon as you can.

- ✓ If you receive a telephone call and it is a wrong number, the caller often says something like; 'What number is that?' Don't tell them ask what number they wanted. When they tell you, you can say no, sorry, wrong number. If they persist and keep asking for your number, just say 'Sorry, not the one you wanted,' and hang up.

- ✓ When using the phone, never reveal any information about yourself to a stranger and never ever say you are alone in the house.

- ✓ If you have a flat and a mail box or door nameplate, use the same trick as you used for the telephone directory. Your mailbox or doorbell nameplate should read 'S Biggins' never 'Susie Biggins'. Don't let a nameplate make you appear to be a potential victim.

- ✓ When you get home, if there is any sign of tampering or a break in, do not go in. For example, jemmy marks and splintered doorframe, broken glass, an open window or lights that shouldn't be on. Go to a neighbour or other safe place and use a mobile or fixed line telephone to call the police. Don't go into the premises until they have been checked.

- ✓ If you think that someone is following you, turn around and look to make sure. Looking at a person, especially if you make eye contact, gives you important information about his appearance and intent. It also sends him the message that you are alert and therefore will not be an easy target. Head for the nearest place of safety, given a choice a place with bright lights, lots of people, telephones and CCTV if possible. If he really is following you contact the police and explain your concerns.

The Personal Security Handbook

At Home

You may wish to read *The Home Security Handbook* for advice on home security. This section of the book aims to address or reinforce some issues that are more specific to the security of a woman and her house, or the house she is in, though once again men may learn things of interest to them.

You should be able to feel secure in your house, without spending a lot of money on fancy locks and alarms. Remember that no security measure will work if you don't use them. The best alarms are useless if they are not turned on and the most expensive locks won't work if you leave the door or window open, or give keys to everyone!

At home – countermeasures

- ✓ If you are going to be out after dark get an attack alarm and carry it in your hand ready for use. It will not do you any good if it is in the bottom of a handbag, in the glove compartment of the car or in the back of a kitchen drawer at home.

- ✓ Though it sometimes isn't possible in rented property, because the landlord refuses to meet the cost or refuses to let you 'damage' his property, try to fit good locks, and aim to have a two-point locking system on all external doors. (A two point locking system refers to two locks on the door. It is generally advised that one lock is fitted approximately two fifths of the way down from the top of the door and another just under half way up from the bottom. At least one lock should be a properly installed mortice lock.)

- ✓ Self-locking window locks are best, especially on the ground floor and anywhere else that a window can be reached easily – for example from a flat roof. Self-locking window locks don't rely on you remembering to lock them; when the window is shut the lock operates and needs some sort of key to release it. With a window lock in place the criminal will not be able to cut or smash the glass then reach through to open the window and climb in. With window locks in place he *could* break out all of the glass but that is a very noisy and time-consuming process. He *could* crawl in through the frame, but that would be dangerous to him with all of the shards of glass still in the frame so it is highly unlikely

- ✓ Some people advise that a venetian blind is a good deterrent. By lowering it and then fixing it to the bottom of the widow frame you prevent easy access, even if the window is open. If you are wondering why a venetian blind is such a good security device, try bending the louvers of a venetian blind and reaching through to open or close a window and see how much noise that makes. Now imagine the problems and noise associated with climbing through the window *and* the venetian blind and you will realise why it could help to make a burglar or intruder decide to walk on by!

✓ All external doors should be of good quality. Solid timber or possibly UPVC with steel core or reinforcement offer good protection, as long as the door, door furniture and door frame are of equal quality and properly fitted.

✓ If you work and leave or come home in the dark, external lights triggered by a sensor help you to see what you are doing and show you if anyone is hiding near your house. If it is your house, don't plant hedges and bushes around the building that an intruder could hide behind! If you have shrubs and hedges, consider cutting them down or removing them.

✓ When you come home, have your door key ready in your hand. You don't want to have to stand in the dark, hunting through your handbag and pockets looking for your door key. The sooner you open the door and get inside, the sooner your potential exposure and vulnerability is removed.

Bogus Callers

Bogus callers may be men, women, children, or even a nice young couple. Their business is to look innocent and sound plausible so that they can talk their way into your house. Once there they can have a range of motives but all of them are criminal, with theft high on their list of objectives. Always stay alert and aware of the dangers so that you stay in control.

Bogus callers – countermeasures

✓ Display a notice on the door saying that you do not buy from door-to-door salesmen, do not want a discussion on religion, do not hire tradesmen on the doorstep and already give to charitable collections. These notices are often available from your local police or council crime prevention offices, and should deter most callers.

✓ Even if you are expecting a visitor, use a door viewer, a window, an intercom in a flat, or call out to see who is there. If you don't like the sound or sight of them, tell them you don't wish to see them and ask them to go away. If they don't, tell them you will call the police, and call the police to report them. They may be innocent, but they may not be and if they are criminals they may find a more vulnerable and less aware victim up the road. If the police have resources available to respond to your call and come and check them out, you are protecting other possibly more vulnerable people in the neighbourhood.

✓ If you are going to open the door, use a well-fitted good-quality security door chain that will prevent the visitor from pushing the door open. Make them wait until you are ready to open the door. If you don't have a security chain fitted, get one!

✓ If the visitor comes after dark and you have an outside light fitted on the porch, turn it on so that you can clearly see who it is and what or who they may have with them. If you don't have an outside light fitted, consider having one installed.

✓ If they claim to be an official from the gas board or other official agency, ask them for identification. If they are genuine they will not mind you asking and will not mind waiting if you decide to check it. Even if your door chain is on, tell them you are going to check their credentials and shut the door politely. Always examine their identification closely. Keep hold of it and if in any doubt call the gas board or other agency to ask if they have a Mr Paul Bloggs checking for gas leaks in Bogford High Street today. You can even ask them to describe Mr Paul Bloggs to you, to see if he matches the man on your doorstep. If you still are not happy for some reason ask them to call back later, when you will have that nice Mr Biggins round from next door to sit with you while the alleged gas man does what he has to do. If you are really suspicious about the caller, consider calling the police to explain your concerns.

✓ If there is any doubt, abuse or problem, or if the 'official' gets angry and demands his identification back call the police. Give them the identification, even if the man is still there. If he is a bogus caller, it will be evidence to the police and could hold his photo and fingerprints on it. A fake gas board ID will be useful if the case goes to court. Remember – though I keep saying he, the bogus caller may just as easily be a female claiming to be a gas board official, district nurse or school truant officer!

✓ If the meter reader has said he will be coming on Tuesday morning and you don't want to be alone in the house with him, plan ahead. Invite people round for a coffee morning so that you have company when he comes – then when he does, keep an eye on him – don't give him any opportunity to take anything.

✓ If you are trying to sell your house, never allow prospective buyers (who in other circumstances you might call 'strangers' or even 'suspicious people'), to come around when you are alone. Make an appointment and make sure that the estate agent you are dealing with personally comes with them, or that you have company when they do come around to view the property. If more than one person comes to view make sure that one doesn't distract you by asking about the central heating while the other slips into the bedroom and helps herself to your jewellery!

- ✓ When selling your house, remember those keys! A lock and solid door are no good if 'everyone' has a key. Don't give keys to an estate agent unless you absolutely have to (and in my view, you NEVER have to). You never know who might have access to use your key or take a copy of it for suspect reasons. A genuine buyer will be willing to wait for a mutually convenient time and date to view the property so they don't need a key.

- ✓ The golden rule is to look after yourself. Don't weaken because good manners tempt you to. Never let them in because it is raining hard, or because it would be rude to make them wait outside. Keep them outside, until you are totally happy to open that door.

Nuisance Telephone Calls

Many abusive calls are made at random. The abusive caller probably hasn't got your number, they just dial a random number or get what they think is a 'lucky' wrong number. Nuisance calls may be threatening, offensive, coarse, rude or just silly and persistent. The objective of the caller is to get you to react. They then feel as though they are in control, which makes the 'game' much more enjoyable to them because they imagine they have some power over you.

Nuisance calls – countermeasures

- ✓ If you receive a single random nuisance call, remember not to react. Don't play his game. The callers are very often male – though some women do make these calls. Don't react and give him what he wants, because he will think the call was worthwhile. You will then have reinforced his desire to make the calls. If he enjoyed the encounter he will want to make more calls – probably to you!

- ✓ When you realise what sort of call it is, don't say anything. Just put the receiver down beside the telephone and leave him to talk to himself for a while. Leave the phone off the hook for half an hour if you can and cover it with a pillow or thick towel. Check to see if he has got bored and hung up after half an hour or so. If he has, replace your receiver. The chances are that it was a random call so he won't be able to call straight back. Even if he has last number redial, if you waited long enough he will have got fed up and tried a new random number so your number won't be in the memory of his phone. Remember, if you do leave the phone off the hook, be careful what you say. If you or a visitor are talking, he may be able to hear you, so don't mention any personal details, addresses, names, phone numbers etc.

The Personal Security Handbook

- ✓ If nuisance calls persist, make a note of the calls, the times, dates, duration and what is said. Try to use any 'caller number' facility to get their phone number. If you do, make a note of it with the time, date and call details. Don't listen to the call, don't respond or let them know you are listening but try to hear what the caller is talking about, and make notes, e.g. male, London accent, asking what I am wearing and suggesting. Do the same after each call. By the time you are sure it wasn't a random call, you will have evidence to take to the police. Call the police and report the problem, tell them what evidence you have. If you suspect somebody, for example an old boyfriend or that creepy bloke in the warehouse at work, tell the police. Then follow their advice.

- ✓ If the calls are coming in on a landline (not mobile), when you hang up immediately pick up your phone and dial 1471, and listen to the reply. 1471 automatically triggers the system to tell you what the number of your last caller was. (It sometimes doesn't work if the call came from an extension on a large switchboard – for example from an office number – or the caller has barred caller number).

- ✓ If the calls are coming in on a landline (not mobile) try calling 150 and explaining to the British Telecom operator what the problem is. They should be able to help you.

- ✓ If the calls are coming on a mobile telephone, call your service provider and explain the problems to them.

- ✓ Try blocking calls where the caller number is withheld – some service providers allow you to do that.

- ✓ Get an answering machine and try screening calls before you answer them. Your friends will understand if they are really friends!

- ✓ You have ultimate control of your phone. Hang up and unplug it.

- ✓ Remember not to give your name or telephone number to anyone, even if they do claim to be doing a survey for something that sounds official. Never give out any personal information over the phone. You do not know who they are or why they want that information.

    - ➢ If they insist, ask them to put their request in writing – if they are genuine they will already have your name and address so don't fall into the trap of giving it to them.

    - ➢ If they ask for your name or address refuse to give those details and ask them for their name, the company name, a telephone number and a contact address; if they are not genuine they will almost certainly hang up. If they do give company details, make a note of them, but tell them that you are not interested in what they are selling, promoting, surveying, and tell them you are going to write to their head office to complain about harassment. Be polite but firm and hang up.

- If they are persistent, consider asking to speak to a supervisor. If you are put through, complain about the way the company is operating. Explain that it is a breach of personal safety and security to pass personal details over the phone. Demand that they put any request in writing. Confirm the company name and address, and then write to their managing director, mark your letter private, personal and confidential and complain strongly about their methods, pointing out the potential risks associated with giving personal information over the telephone. I would also complain to the police and local authorities about the methods used by that company.

✓ Take care when formulating a message to leave on an answer phone. An obviously female voice saying, 'Hello, this is 256748. Sorry Susie Biggins isn't in right now so call again when she gets back,' gives far too much away.

- Your phone number is 256748 – you just told me that.
- You are probably a single female, you said you are 'Miss' Susie Biggins.
- You live alone – nobody else was mentioned in the phone message. If you lived with somebody else the message would mention them too, for example 'Susie and Mark are not at home.'
- I now have your surname, your first name and your phone number. Give me two minutes and a phone book and I will have your address.
- Be sensible – realise what you can give away. With a bit of forethought you could get your Uncle Bert to record a safe and bland message for you. For example, 'Sorry, I can't come to the phone right now, please leave a message or call back.' No clues in that but polite and to the point! An alternative is to make it sound as though several people live in the house. For example the message, 'Sorry, no one can get to the phone right now. Please leave a message or call back' will give nothing away.

Travelling

General advice on travelling safety applies to everyone, but there are some additional precautions that women may wish to take. One important point to make is that most sexual assaults are committed by men who are known to the victim, while assaults, robberies and thefts are committed by anyone.

When travelling, avoid wearing headphones. Listening to music may pass the time, but you are making yourself vulnerable because you can't easily hear what is going on around you. You could turn down the volume, or only use one earphone making it easier to remain aware of what is going on around you, or just not use those devices while travelling.

The Personal Security Handbook

If you have to walk anywhere after dark, make every effort to ensure that you are safe. Don't walk in dark and remote places alone. If you have to go somewhere, consider taking a registered taxi (not an unlicensed minicab), and asking if the taxi company has a female driver who could pick you up.

Travelling – countermeasures

- ✓ If you call for a taxi, ask for the make and colour of the car so that you know the car when it turns up.

- ✓ Give the taxi company a name, but as added security don't give your own name. Use the surname of your manager at work for example, you won't forget that. Don't forget that the driver is taking you home. If you give your name, it isn't hard to find out which house in that street is occupied by Miss or Mrs Biggins, but if you use your manager's name he won't find a Miss 'Wilkins' in that street!

- ✓ When the taxi pulls up, ask what name he is looking for. If it is a real taxi, the right make and colour and he gives the name (your manager's name) that is the car you booked.

- ✓ When in a taxi, always sit in the back behind the driver. Sitting next to him in the front passenger seat means he can easily reach you. Sitting behind him, he cannot see what you are doing. He cannot reach you to restrain you easily. He cannot stop you jumping out if he drives past your road or attempts to take you out into the country. Best of all if he attacks you, you can easily fight back. If you really have to, go for the eyes using keys, hairspray, a nail file – anything that comes to hand.

- ✓ If you are in a work environment, consider asking if a male colleague can escort you to your destination.

- ✓ If several people want to leave at about the same time, consider making arrangements so that you all go together.

- ✓ If you are going to a party or club, plan ahead. Make sure that you have arranged a safe way to get home. Book a taxi or have a nominated driver who is not drinking. Arrange for a brother or father to come to pick you up at the club or pub or party address. Do anything to stay safe, never take a lift with a stranger, and avoid trying to walk home alone.

- ✓ If you are waiting for your taxi and a man in a white hatchback, with no taxi plate on the back, no taxi sign on the roof, no radio or fare meter pulls up and says, 'Anyone order a taxi?' walk away. Take the number and make of the car, make a note of the description and report him to the police, but don't go anywhere near it – or him.

- ✓ Look out for each other. If a woman who has had too much to drink walks towards that suspect hatchback take her aside and tell her to share your taxi! She will hopefully do the same for another woman one day. Be safe not sorry.

- ✓ Remember, the drivers of licensed hackney carriages (taxis) have to be checked to make sure that they are suitable people to be driving potentially vulnerable people around. There are a lot of suspect people claiming to be mini cab drivers, who don't have insurance, are not checked and whose vehicle may not be safe. Avoid suspect mini cabs, and always use legitimate taxi companies. Though the fares charged by licensed taxis may be slightly higher, that small charge is an investment in your safety!

- ✓ If you get worried at any time during a trip in a taxi, for example if the driver starts making inappropriate comments or suggestions, wait until you are approaching somewhere where there are a lot of people and demand that he stop and let you out. If he does stop, get out and make a note of the company, car number and the driver and report him as soon as possible. If he doesn't stop, open the window and scream (you are approaching that crowded place you spotted so there will be a lot of people calling the police). Shout as loud as you can and be as clear as you can: 'STOP, STOP. HELP – CALL THE POLICE'.

- ✓ If you have any doubts about a driver just don't get into the car. If he wants to call the police and tell them you are wasting his time, let him. Don't be bullied into getting in, and don't feel you have to because he might make a scene.

Safety when walking

Select the safest route, not necessarily the shortest or quickest route. Use roads that are better lit with more traffic and people around. If the safe route is the long way around, take the long route. Attacks are more likely to happen in remote, deserted and badly-lit areas.

Safety when walking – countermeasures

- ✓ Buy an attack alarm and use it – they usually operate by withdrawing a pin or releasing a trigger. In an attack the alarm sounds and cannot easily be turned off, deterring the attacker and drawing attention to your distress.

- ✓ Know how to use it; you don't want to be trying to read the instructions if somebody is following you. Remember to test it so you know it works and you are sure how to use it. Some work on batteries, some work on a canister of compressed air. If in doubt – replace it!

The Personal Security Handbook

- ✓ If you have an attack alarm, carry it with you, it is no use leaving it on your kitchen table!

- ✓ When out, especially after dark, don't walk with your hands in your pockets. If you do you are at a disadvantage – you will not be able to fend off an attacker, not be able to balance very well, and won't be able to run as easily as if you have your hands free.

- ✓ If carrying bags of shopping in one hand, carry the bag in your weak hand. Keep your strong hand free in case you have to fend somebody off or punch an attacker. Use a rucksack if you can, then you will have two hands free!

- ✓ If you are carrying bags of shopping and you are attacked or fear somebody, drop the shopping and run. You can run faster and easier without the load of shopping, and with your hands free you have better balance and will be able to fend off attacks or punch and scratch at an attacker.

- ✓ If you are out walking and you think somebody is following you, check to see if they are. Cross the road more than once if you have to, and see what they do. The golden rule in these circumstances is to head for lights and people. A pub, a shop, a garage or even the reception area of an office block, anywhere there is light and people moving around is a safe place. Once there, explain your concerns and ask somebody to call for a taxi so you can get home. If no taxi is available, consider asking them to call a relative to collect you. If your 'stalker' is still hanging around, call the police and explain your fears.

- ✓ Make sure that you also have the keys that you need (house, office or car keys) ready to use when you reach your destination.

- ✓ A phone box could be the only place you can see with a light, but if you go into one, the attacker could trap you. If the phone is working you could dial 999, but only if it hasn't been broken by vandals.

- ✓ If you do use a public phone box, don't turn your back on the world. Put your money in, dial the number and then turn to face the door and anyone who is outside the box.

- ✓ Always use the busy route, which has good levels of lighting. Don't be tempted to take a dark deserted shortcut, where a dozen attackers could be hiding, even if it is cold, wet and windy and you are tired.

- ✓ Always walk facing the traffic. That way you can avoid being hit by a driver who comes too close. If you are facing the traffic, you will know if a car is slowing down or if anyone is leaning out of a car window towards you. Stay in control and don't let anyone creep up on you. They may just be trying to snatch your handbag or they may have something more serious in mind.

- ✓ When walking along a road, look for and pay attention to dark corners, doorways and alleys where an attacker could be hiding.

- If you are faced with a street that has a lot of doors, dark corners and side alleys you picked the wrong route home. Is there another way you can go even if it is a longer route?
- If there is no other route, consider going back to where you were safe and calling a taxi, a relative to collect you, or asking somebody to walk you home.
- If you can't avoid an occasional dark corner or side alley, keep safety at the front of your thoughts. Adjust your speed to pass that dark corner when the bus is stopped at the stop opposite (an attacker or robber probably won't come out with a busload of witnesses). Slow down or speed up so you walk past that risky place at the same time as a husband and wife or two workmen who are coming the other way.
- Be as safe as you can. The click of high heels will have announced that a woman is about to walk past that dark corner – could you change into trainers to go home?
- When you have to walk around a corner, go as wide as you can. By opening the angle of your approach you will get an earlier and better view of what is waiting around the corner. At the very least it will stop you bumping into strangers!
- When you walk past that dark corner, walk out away from the wall and try to walk as near to the road as you can. That means any hidden attacker would have to run out across the path, grab you and pull you right back into the corner. As soon as he appeared, you would shout, scream, sound your attack alarm and run to safety etc. Don't make it easy for them.
- Have an escape route in mind. If at any time you have doubts, go another way, any way that is safer. If you suddenly notice a dark corner, or think somebody may be hiding in a doorway, consider your options. If you are too close there is little you can do, so plan what you will do at the least sign of anybody lurking there. Have the attack alarm out ready, walk even further away from the possible danger, speed up or even run past to the next safe area, consider shouting telling 'Jason' to hurry up – if anyone is hiding there he now thinks some bloke called Jason is nearby. Do what you have to do to stay safe.

✓ If anyone threatens you make as much noise as you can. Sound your attack alarm, scream and shout at the same time as you try to get away and make for the nearest sign of life. If there is no pub, garage or shop around head for the nearest private house with lights on. Keep screaming and bang and kick on the door when you get there. Aim to get the whole street out to see what is happening – their descriptions of the attacker could be useful to the police, but usually at the first disturbance the attacker will have run off.

✓ Try to remember any details you can. If at all possible write down car numbers so that you can report them when the police arrive.

✓ If you are interested, ask the local police or council if there are any self-defence and personal safety classes for women operating in your area.

Using public transport

If you are waiting for a bus or train, use a popular bus stop or main railway station rather than using a remote bus stop or railway station. That means that there will be other passengers waiting with you so you should be safer.

Sometimes you may have to wait 15 minutes or even half an hour for a bus or train. If you find that you have to wait for more than say ten minutes for a bus or train, you can avoid waiting alone on the platform or at the bus stop. Consider waiting in a busy well lit place such as a shopping precinct or 24 hour garage, or a pub then going to the station or bus stop where you will only have to wait for your service for a few minutes.

Using public transport – countermeasures

- ✓ If travelling by bus or train, make sure that you don't fall asleep.
    - ➢ Somebody could take your bag or other valuables.
    - ➢ Somebody could give you drugs to render you helpless.
    - ➢ Somebody could surprise you, silence you, and attack you.
    - ➢ You could ride past your stop and end up at some remote terminus, or have to get off the bus or train at some unknown, deserted place.

- ✓ If you have to take public transport, try to sit near a member of rail or bus staff. When waiting for a train, stand near the barrier where the ticket inspector is standing. Sit near the guard on a train. Think of a way around a problem. For example, on public transport people tend to use the same service each day. If there are three people who always get off at your stop, you might find that Mr Biggins from 40 High Street is one of them. Could you talk to him or his wife and persuade him to walk home past your house and see you in each night? Think of a way to overcome a problem, but make sure that your alternative does not increase your risk. The person you ask to escort you must be safe!

- ✓ If you get on an empty bus or train, sit as near to the driver as you can. You can even consider telling him you are travelling alone and ask him to keep an eye on you. If you do, when you get off tell him you are OK and thank him. You never know, 10 drunken louts may get on at the next stop!

- ✓ If somebody pesters or annoys you while travelling, report them to a member of staff. Consider telling British Transport Police if a guy on the train keeps making lewd suggestions; they could put a plain-clothes officer on the train or they could send a uniformed officer to speak to the man. Resources are limited but they will respond if they can.

- ✓ Some public transport facilities are unmanned, lighting may be poor or broken and bushes overgrown. If they are, complain to the authorities, and point out how risky those conditions make using their facilities. Do it in writing and ask for an acknowledgement. If they do nothing write again and copy it to your MP, tell them that if there is an incident you will go to the press and tell the world that you warned them of the dangers but they did nothing. Perhaps even copy the letter to the local newspaper and radio station asking them to withhold your name and address.

- ✓ If conditions at your station are that bad, consider using another station or bus stop. Find one that you will be happy to use. It may be further away, but if the journey home is along well-lit roads with plenty of people around it would be a safer option.

- ✓ Beware of some men who use a crowded train or bus as an excuse to rub up against a female passenger. They often stand back waiting for crowded trains then walk along several carriages to see who they can stand by. Get your back to the partition and hold any bags between you and the 'pusher'. Ask them to move back – they often do because they don't want anyone making a fuss.

- ✓ When travelling by train and bus, be careful when using a mobile phone. By showing that you have an expensive phone, you may be making yourself a target for thieves. When using a mobile phone in public, you don't know who is listening. Any information you give out could be useful to a criminal. For example you might give your mobile or home number, give your address or other personal information. Even knowing that your name is Susie could help a potential attacker get close to you later, when he walks up and says, 'Hello, Susie, haven't seen you since . . .' Thinking you might know him because he knows your name you are off guard, but by the time you realise you don't recognise him, he is close enough to attack you.

- ✓ When you get off a bus or train, take a note of who else is getting off with you. If you don't like the look of people near your stop, or anyone who looks like they will get off with you, consider staying on the bus or train and travel to a main station or stop. Avoid putting yourself in an isolated place with people you don't like the look of. If you travel on to a main stop or station at least you can safely get a taxi home from there.

- ✓ Never try to thumb a lift, or accept the offer of a lift from somebody you do not know. Even if he claims to be a minicab, and has a radio and business cards, he might not be what he seems.

Driving – countermeasures

- ✓ If driving, remember to think ahead when you select somewhere to park your car. You may arrive in bright sunlight on what looks like a busy road, but after dark it may be deserted and unlit. Think ahead. Try to visualise what that parking place will be like at midnight when you come back to the car.

- ✓ Always lock your car and never leave the keys in it.

- ✓ Don't leave evidence in your car. A criminal could see evidence that a car belongs to a woman, which might make him wait to see who comes back to the car. Don't leave lipstick, a box of tissues, and a woman's magazine on the dashboard. Consider 'dressing the car' – for example putting an old pair of your brother's or boyfriend's football boots and some car magazines on the back seat. Anything that avoids making it look like a woman's car might be worthwhile.

- ✓ If you are attacked while you are in the car, lean on the car horn and don't let go until the attacker has gone and somebody has called the police. Attract attention in any way you can: turn the radio to full volume, switch the hazard warning lights on, and flash the headlamps if you can while you fight him off.

- ✓ If somebody seems to be following your car, find a brightly-lit public place, pull in and stop. Look to see what the car or bike following you has done. Try to see the car number if you can. If you do, write it down – for example: Saturday 19th 10.10 pm, High Street, dark blue volvo estate registration 123 ZYX, male driver, bald, thick-rimmed glasses followed me all the way from the office. If you write it down, at least you won't forget the details and if the worst happens there is something for the police to look at. If you do pull in to a busy place with bright lights make sure that the vehicle you think is following you has gone; he may have just turned his lights off and pulled in down the road to wait for you. Consider changing your route home so that you stay on busy main roads. Don't drive along any deserted dark country roads if you can avoid it. If in doubt, call the police and explain your fears.

- ✓ If you are driving, make sure that your car is properly maintained and is capable of making the journey. Fill up before you go, check the radiator and fill the windscreen washer bottles. Check the tyres and lights. Make sure you have a good torch in the car. You don't want to take all of these precautions and then break down miles from the nearest light or help.

- ✓ If you are driving a long distance or going to a place you don't know, buy a map, and make sure that you work out your route. You don't want to be lost or find yourself in the rough end of a strange town after dark.

- ✓ If you don't have a mobile phone, make sure that you have some change on you so that you can make a few phone calls from a public phone if you need to.

- ✓ If you are travelling any distance alone, make sure that somebody knows where you are going, what route you intend to take, as well as when you are leaving and what time you expect to get there. Call them when you do get to your destination, and agree that if you have not arrived and called to say you are there by a given time, they should raise the alarm and report you missing. At least to start with, Uncle Fred Biggins can drive back along your proposed route to see if you are struggling with a flat tyre or a leaky fuel tank!

- ✓ Especially in more remote areas, don't stop for hitchhikers, or anyone other than a police officer in uniform. Remember that somebody wearing a yellow reflective jacket isn't necessarily a police officer! Look out for a police vehicle or police markings on the uniform. Stop but keep the doors locked, and make sure they are police officers. If they don't look like police when you slow down or stop, drive off if it is safe and the road is clear and report the incident as soon as you can. Take care though, as road mending crews and breakdown drivers also wear reflective jackets and may need to stop you if there is a hole in the road or an accident or breakdown ahead. Be safe and take care – just don't assume anyone in a yellow jacket is a police officer!

- ✓ Never hitchhike yourself. You will *not* be able to tell by looking at the driver offering you a lift if they are safe or not. The biggest serial killers in history have been nice, wholesome, and pleasant to talk to. They have been just the sort of people who inspire trust and so persuade women to get into their car. Don't take chances. If you have to make a longer journey, by planning and booking far enough ahead you should be able to take advantage of discounted fares, so you won't need to hitchhike!

- ✓ At all times when you are driving keep the car doors locked, and keep the windows closed. Don't give anyone the opportunity to jump in at the first set of lights you stop at. (Consider following my advice and unlocking the car while you are on motorways and other main roads.)

- ✓ Put all valuables out of sight, under a blanket or under the seat if you cannot put them in the boot before you set off. Don't invite a broken window and an attack from an opportunist thief at the next junction.

- ✓ When you arrive after dark, select your parking spot carefully. Use somewhere that is well lit and near to your destination. Consider driving into the parking area and manoeuvring around for a while. Use your headlights to look down the path you will have to use. Light up the bushes, and turn the wheel so that the headlights sweep shadowy corners. Don't stop until you are certain that you are safe and there is nobody hiding nearby. Be prepared for the jokes about women drivers and parking ability – but ignore them. They don't know that with all that manoeuvring you parked safely *and* checked out the dark corners of the car park, the cars already parked there and the footpath leading to your destination. Think safety!

The Personal Security Handbook

- ✓ If you have a mobile phone, when you reach the car park consider calling whoever you are visiting to tell them you are there. If you ask they may come out to meet you, especially if you think somebody is lurking along the path.

Breaking down – countermeasures

- ✓ If you have broken down on the motorway, make sure you follow the advice below.
    - ➢ Pull as far onto the hard shoulder as you can, away from the high-speed motorway traffic. If possible stop beside an emergency phone.
    - ➢ Point the steering wheel towards the verge or the embankment so that if hit the car will move into the verge and away from the high-speed traffic.
    - ➢ Don't get out of the driver's door unless you have to. It is safer to slide over and get out of the passenger door.
    - ➢ The hard shoulder is a dangerous place – a vehicle could stray off the road and hit your car. If that vehicle is a lorry it will destroy your car and kill you, but even a small saloon can kill you if it is doing 70 miles per hour when it hits your car. Leave the vehicle and try to stand behind any crash barrier at a safe distance from the traffic, but near enough to get back to the car within a minute or so if you need to.
    - ➢ Leave the passenger door open. If anyone other than the police stops nearby, you can quickly and easily get back into the car and lock the doors.
    - ➢ You will probably have to use the emergency phone to report the problem. Familiarise yourself with them. The emergency phones beside motorways are only a mile apart. There are a lot of small posts in between which have a little picture of a telephone handset and an arrow pointing to the nearest one. (You can use a mobile phone to call for help, in which case you will need to report your location, and the little posts along the verge will tell you that. Stand beside the nearest post when you call as the police will ask what numbers are printed on that post.)
    - ➢ Make sure that you take any breakdown club membership card with you (for example AA or RAC), when you go to the emergency phone. Lock the passenger door while you go.
    - ➢ The emergency phones are usually connected directly to a police control room. You don't have to dial, just pick it up and speak to the police control room. Tell them that you have broken down and if you are a member of a breakdown service. Pass them the details of your car and membership number and they will summon assistance.
    - ➢ If you tell them you are a female travelling alone they will usually treat you as a priority call.

- ➢ The control room operator will already know where you are, because their systems will show which phone you are using and where it is.
- ➢ Go back to your car as soon as you can, open the passenger door again and stand back away from the traffic. Wait for the police or breakdown service to arrive.
- ➢ You might consider leaving a warm coat, tracksuit bottoms and warm gloves in a bag in the boot of the car. If you are broken down, the coat and gloves could be very handy. If it is cold, wet and windy, the tracksuit trousers may be welcome too.
- ➢ As you wait, keep an eye out. If a stranger stops, get back in the car and lock the doors.

- ✓ If you are going to have to unlock a door to get into the destination building, remember to lock your car and have your door keys ready and handy when you reach that building.
- ✓ If you don't already have one, consider buying a mobile phone. You don't have to sign up to expensive contracts or go for the ones with built-in camera, email and music. Shop around, tell the staff in the mobile phone shop that you just want a mobile phone to use in emergencies and rarely at other times, then consider the best offer.
- ✓ If you see a broken public telephone when you are out, report it and give the number and location to British Telecom! You didn't need it this time, but that phone could be the difference between you or another woman getting home safe or being attacked later tonight.

Cycling

If you ride a bicycle, most of the advice for pedestrians applies, such as using busy roads with good lighting, not wearing headphones to listen to music, never taking risky shortcuts, but there is some specific advice too. On the assumption that you may well be riding along country roads or through cycle paths and underpasses, you could be more exposed than a pedestrian and would be more exposed than a car driver.

Cycling – countermeasures

- ✓ Clothes and shoes. Wear decent walking shoes and trousers if you can. Heels and a skirt may be more elegant, but they won't make it easy for you to jump off the bike to defend yourself or run if you have to.

- ✓ Wearing bright fluorescent clothes with reflective stripes will make you safer in traffic, but they will also make it harder for somebody to make you vanish by dragging you into a bush. The fluorescent and reflective materials will mean you are clearly visible even among a few bushes.

- ✓ Wearing suitably warm and waterproof clothes will reduce the temptation to take that risky shortcut when it is cold, wet and windy. If you are warm and dry in suitable clothing, you should also be more alert to danger as well.

- ✓ Wear a cycle helmet, for road safety and also personal safety. An attacker cannot knock you on the head if you are wearing a helmet, and if you have to defend yourself, head-butting his nose with your helmeted head is very effective.

- ✓ Don't overload a bike with shopping, books, briefcases and other equipment and possessions. The more unwieldy you make your bike, the slower you are, the more exposed you are, and the harder it will be for you to avoid or evade an attacker.

- ✓ Don't forget that your cycle lamp is useful when you reach your destination. You can shine it down the path or check that there is nobody in the cycle sheds when you want to park your bike, and to check to see if anyone is lurking in the underpass, bushes or darkened doorways.

- ✓ When riding, be aware that an attacker could deliberately nudge you at a junction, or edge you off the road. Less than one in every million drivers will be a potential attacker, but by being aware that this is possible, you are alert to the dangers. You have to decide if a driver who comes too close or cuts in front of you is just a bad driver or a potential attacker. Take avoiding action – for example, stop somewhere that is brightly lit and where there are crowds of people.

- ✓ On a bicycle, you have a few advantages. For example, you can stop, get off and become a pedestrian if you want to. When riding you can probably outpace an attacker on foot if you need to, or divert and ride through a pedestrian precinct where a car can't go!

- ✓ When using a bike, many of the female car driver's countermeasures will apply to you too. Where will you park your bike? When you park and lock your bike, it may appear to be a safe place, but think about what the conditions will be like when you come back for your bike at ten that night. If dark and deserted with no CCTV coverage, find a safer place to park your bike. Remember that it is your safety you should be concentrating on, not the safety of the bike.

- ✓ If you are a member of a group using cycle parking facilities that are unsafe, consider asking the college, university or employer to upgrade or reposition them to improve safety.

- ✓ As with pedestrians, there is safety in numbers. If several people are arriving or leaving at the same time, or going in the same direction, arrange to travel together for mutual safety!

- ✓ When you buy a bike, take care over the lock you buy. Some are small and fiddly, and they need to be threaded through wheels and frames. Others are simple and can be snapped on and removed quite easily. Buy a lock that is easy to fit and remove. When you go back to release your bike, you want to stay aware of the people around you. You don't want to be kneeling in the dark, trying to fit a tiny key into a hidden keyhole that you can't see.

✓ For the same reason, be careful where you leave your bike. Given a choice between parking your bike in a dark corner near the bushes or in view of passing traffic and pedestrians on the main road under a street lamp, I would go for the main road every time!

✓ Perform a risk assessment before you use your bike. For example, if a meeting finishes late or you stay too long at a party and find that the streets are dark and deserted when you want to leave, consider the option of leaving your bike and getting a licensed taxi home – don't press your luck!

Shopping

Shopping is such a normal activity that sometimes people don't see any potential for threat in it. Some common threats are already covered elsewhere in this book, such as using public transport to get too or from the shops.

Bag theft

Keep your handbag on you. When you are not holding it, it is vulnerable. Later you will see a section dedicated to handbags; these reminders are shopping specific.

Most shops seem to be overcrowded. The way the racks are pushed close together is designed by shopping psychologists and marketing advisors. Lots of racks means a wide range to choose from. Not putting them in neat rows with a clear passage between them makes the prospect of exploring to see what is there a little more exciting. As they aren't in neat rows, you have to go around the shop three or four times to make sure you don't miss anything, and the longer you are looking, the more likely you are to buy things. It is all designed to make you come in, stay in and buy before you leave. Unfortunately the crowding also helps the thief.

Out on the high street, if somebody stood elbow to elbow with you, you would wonder why they were so close, because there is enough room for them to have their own space.

In a crowded shop, our notional 'personal space' shrinks. We expect to be jostled a little as we strive to find that bargain. If somebody else bumps into you around the clothes racks and then stands there for two minutes you probably won't even look up. If somebody says, 'Excuse me,' and pushes past in the narrowest gap you not only let them do it, you try to ignore them while you concentrate on the important business of looking at the details on the hem of that little black dress! The problem is that some of those people pushing past are thieves. While they are squeezing past, reaching over to get that top, or standing looking at the jackets on the rack behind you, they are actually dipping into your handbag and pockets.

A thief with a couple of dresses draped over her arm, conveniently hiding what that hand is doing, can easily brush past and dip into your handbag or pocket taking what she wants. She doesn't have to see, we all know what a chequebook, purse or credit card holder feels like. Yes, sometimes the dippers might get your bus season ticket or library card, but another bag will be along in a minute!

Shopping bag theft

When shopping you will also probably soon be carrying purchases. When you are in a shop and you put your bags down to compare two blouses, or hold that skirt up against you to check the length, who is keeping an eye on your carrier bags? When you take the blouse to the door to check the exact shade of blue in daylight, who is guarding the carrier bags you left on the chair? While you are out of the changing room checking what a new pair of jeans looks like in the big mirror, who is watching what happens to things that you left in the changing room? Many a shopping bag has 'walked' while a woman (or a man) has been distracted.

The beauty of stealing a customer's shopping is that any security tags have already been taken off in the shop where they were purchased. The stolen carrier bags look like 'normal shopping' so nobody takes any notice of a shopper (thief) with some shopping (yours) as they walk out and get lost in the crowd. The salespeople and security staff will be concentrating on keeping an eye on their own stock.

If a thief does get caught trying to pick up your carrier bags, all they have to do is look innocent and apologise saying they thought they were their bags. Staff and security probably won't want to get involved and chances are you will accept the apology and assume that it was a genuine mistake.

Shopping bag theft – countermeasures

- ✓ In any situation where your personal space is reduced, be particularly aware of the activity of thieves. In a crowded shop, at a sporting event, in a pub or club, don't take valuables you don't need, and be healthily suspicious of the motives of anyone who is getting that little bit too close!

- ✓ When in a shop, don't forget to keep an eye on your handbag and the shopping you are already carrying. You can't hold it all while you sort through the clothes on display, so you have to put something down. When you put it down, don't forget it. Try to go shopping with a friend, and take it in turns to guard the bags while you check out or try on what is on offer. Or put the bags down between your legs or between you and the rack so they are safer.

Back at the car

Thieves target cars. Thieves know that people don't want to carry a lot of bags around while they shop so they take them back to their car and leave them there, especially at Christmas. When your purchases are left in your car they are vulnerable.

There are other threats associated with returning to your car after shopping, which are more specific to women.

If you come back to your car and find you have a flat tyre, but a nice man conveniently appears and offers to help you change the wheel, be cautious. He may be an innocent knight in shining armour who happened to be passing by. On the other hand he might be a lout who just let your tyre down, to get close and gain your trust by offering to help fix that tyre!

If you are loaded down with arms full of shopping you are even more vulnerable. Add darkness and rain and a woman alone will almost certainly accept help with the tyre, so be careful.

Consider these options:

- Call your breakdown service. They will usually change a tyre, and will treat a woman alone as a priority.
- Go back to the shop, and ask a member of staff to come and help, or at least stand with you while you do it.
- Call home/a friend and ask somebody to come and help or to pick you up and get a garage to sort out the car.

Just remember to think security and be safe.

If a van with sliding side doors is parked close beside your car, consider the very, very remote risk that a criminal may be hiding inside that van waiting to slide the door open and steal your shopping, or worse.

If it looks like a van or other vehicle is blocking you in, think security. They could have stopped to pick up some heavy shopping or there could just be a more sinister reason. Stop at a distance and take a look. If you see anything you don't like, stay well away from your car. Rather than go and try to find a security guard, it may be quicker to wait in safety at the shopping complex doorway to see if that van drives off. Whatever you do, maintain an awareness of what is going on around you, and always think safety.

Back at the car – countermeasures

Follow the car jacking countermeasures. Also:

- ✓ If it looks like you have a flat tyre, look around. If the car park is busy with families walking back and forth, and you know how to change the tyre, do it. On the other hand if you can see any potential threats, think again. If you want to, watch for a while to see if the van behind your car drives off, or the guy with the crash helmet hiding his face gets on a motorbike and rides off. If it all becomes clear replace the wheel. If you have any doubts or fears, go and get help.

- ✓ If you are blocked in by another car, think security. If your car has been blocked in by ten shopping trolleys, think security. Stop and look: if the car blocking you has a family – mum, dad and the kids loading carrier bags – it should be OK. If it is a people carrier with heavily tinted windows so you can't see inside think again. Consider going back to the shops to ask for help.

✓ The most important thing to remember about cars in shopping situations is to check it out. Anything that would or could stop you from getting in and driving straight off needs closer inspection and more thought. If in doubt seek help.

Handbags

Handbag snatching is an opportunistic crime. Most handbag snatchers are male and up to about 18 years of age. They loiter in an area they know, grab the first available handbag and then run or cycle off to escape in alleys and underpasses. Usually the bag is rifled for valuables and then quickly discarded in a bin, some bushes or over a convenient wall.

Thieves target women and their handbags because there is little risk associated with taking a handbag. There are some things that you can do to reduce your exposure to this sort of crime.

Handbags – countermeasures

✓ Carry your handbag in a way that protects it. Carry it tucked under an arm, not dangling by its strap. Remember that some robbers like to swoop past on motorcycles or cycles and relieve women of their handbags.

✓ Consider using a rucksack, which will leave you with both hands free to defend yourself.

✓ If your bag has a shoulder strap, put the strap over your shoulder and hold it across your chest or stomach where you will see and feel any attempt to take something out of your bag.

✓ In winter at least, consider wearing your handbag under your coat. If it is mild you could put your coat on over the bag and wear your coat open.

✓ Where possible try to keep your house keys out of your handbag, so that a thief doesn't get your address and the keys in one simple theft.

✓ For similar reasons try to keep your cheque book and cheque card separately.

✓ Consider spring cleaning your handbag. This gives you a chance to:
  ➢ clean out the rubbish
  ➢ make it a lot lighter to carry

The Personal Security Handbook

> - remove things you don't need to carry
> - take out keys, diaries, addresses, passport etc, in case the bag is lost or stolen.

- ✓ If a bag snatcher tries to take your bag, scream and shout, but be ready to let them have the bag. If you do scream, shout words too: 'Stop, thief! Help! Police!' will be heard and acted on. Better to lose the bag and contents than to suffer an injury.

- ✓ Older women are more vulnerable because they cannot usually defend themselves and a simple fall can seriously injure them. An older woman may not have much of value in her bag, but cowardly louts are still willing to take them, even though they only get a few pounds and some change.

- ✓ Keep your handbag on you. Don't put it down and walk off, for example to go to the toilet or collect your coat in a hair salon. Given just half a minute, it is easy for a thief to flip open a handbag and grab the obvious purse and chequebook. A letter with your address and your house keys would be nice too!

- ✓ If possible consider not carrying a bag at all! Carry the things you need such as your car keys in your coat pocket or elsewhere.

- ✓ Don't attract attention: wearing expensive jewellery and flashing cash in a pub or shop will mark you as a target worth robbing.

- ✓ Try not to get too entangled in the handbag strap. Just in case, you may want to be in a position to release the bag rather than be pulled along or pulled over by a thief. For example, don't wrap a handbag strap around your wrist – if a snatcher tries to pull it off you, you could be severely injured.

- ✓ To reduce your exposure, don't carry more cash and valuables around than you need to. If you don't want to risk losing it, the easy rule is don't carry it. A fabulous diamond ring shouldn't be in your handbag unless you are taking it to put it in the bank vault – even then I would consider putting it in an inside zip-up pocket in my coat!

- ✓ When shopping, don't leave your handbag in the shopping trolley. In the shop nobody will notice if a woman takes a handbag out of the trolley, even if the woman was a thief. If it is your trolley and your handbag she walks off with, it's too late! Surprisingly people may not say anything if a man is carrying a handbag.

- ✓ In handbag snatches, most victims are attacked from behind. Most attackers run up, grab the bag and then run off. Beware of the sound of any running feet approaching you from behind, especially when it is dark, quiet or deserted. (If it is dark quiet and deserted, perhaps you shouldn't be there anyway.)

Mostly Women

- ✓ Know what you have in your handbag, which means having a regular clear out and weeding of the contents. That way you can remove things that should not be in there and you will know what has been lost if it is stolen so you can report the loss to the right people.

- ✓ If your bag is stolen, report it to the police and immediately cancel any credit and store cards that have been stolen. Inform the bank of any missing chequebooks. This will be easier if you have a list of all of your cards, account numbers and associated telephone numbers to call to report the loss – of course you shouldn't keep that list in your handbag! If the keys are missing change the locks. Knowing what was in the bag and therefore stolen, take any action necessary.

- ✓ If your bag is stolen, as soon as possible after the theft you should get friends and relatives to help you to search the area in the direction the thief ran, if it is safe. At the earliest possible moment he will have had a quick look inside, taken out any purse and visible money and probably have dumped the rest in a bin, into a ditch or bushes. If you have a look you may at least get the bag back.

Running/jogging/cycling/riding

Many people like to go running, jogging, cycling or riding. It may be something they like to do, it may be something to do with fitness and weight loss, but it does potentially expose them to additional risk. The following common sense advice should help to keep you safe. The advice could also be helpful to men.

Running/jogging/cycling/riding – countermeasures

- ✓ Don't attract attention by wearing expensive jewellery, watches and so on that you don't need while running or cycling.

- ✓ Wear appropriate clothes. Something loose that from a distance may look like a boy is best.

- ✓ Don't run with music or radio headphones or earphones on. You need to be able to hear what is going on around you, but with music blasting into your ears, you wouldn't know if an elephant was behind you let alone a car out of control or a suspicious male 'jogger'.

- ✓ If you have a dog, consider taking it with you. Women are very rarely attacked or bothered if they have a dog with them. You could even take your husband, brother, boyfriend, or neighbour out for a run.

The Personal Security Handbook

- ✓ Try to use a different route each day. Never ride, walk or canter along the same roads and track at the same time. Try not to let anyone who could be watching and stalking you see a pattern in your behaviour.

- ✓ Have a number of routes selected, and when you set off tell someone which route you will use that day. There is no need to give a lengthy explanation. List the different routes somewhere and give them a name. Then when you go you can say 'supermarket route' or 'road bridge route'. The list will show that the road bridge route is turn left out of the gate, down to the High Street, third left into Sutton Gardens and so on. In this way, if something happens, people will at least know which route you took.

- ✓ The route will also have a time limit associated with it. For example the supermarket route means that you will be back in 45 minutes. If you take any longer than an hour, people will call your mobile phone and start looking for you – probably limping home because of a twisted ankle or something else equally mundane.

- ✓ Never take short cuts while running, even if it does look like there is a storm coming. A shortcut down a deserted country lane or across fields could be a dangerous option. Get wet, rather than hurt!

- ✓ Avoid doing any exercising after dark, unless you have an athletics club nearby with good floodlights and plenty of people around.

- ✓ In case of an emergency, carry your mobile phone or a few coins. You might have a flat tyre on your bike, the horse could go lame, or you could sprain your ankle and need to call for assistance.

- ✓ If you are running on or near public roads, even if you do keep as far away from traffic as you can, wear light-coloured or bright clothes so that everyone can see you. Consider buying a fluorescent and reflective waistcoat, so nobody can miss you.

- ✓ Run facing oncoming traffic. You want to be able to see anyone straying towards you or stopping close by. Be aware and be ready.

- ✓ If you want to try a new route, or want to exercise in an area you don't know, only do it with at least one friend. You should seek advice from people who know the area, such as other members of your keep fit or running club. Always tell somebody which route you are taking and when you expect to be back.

- ✓ Always carry some form of identification just in case. Something with your name, a phone number and any medical history or problems.

- ✓ If you get the usual 'builders' compliments' – cat calls, wolf whistles and suggestive comments ignore them. (Do they really think any woman likes that sort of immature and pathetic behaviour?) Some women contact the building company and complain about this sort of behaviour. Larger national building companies now have a policy that forbids their building site workers from shouting stupid comments at passing women.

✓ Seriously consider carrying a security/attack alarm when you are exercising. As usual the aim is to make as much noise as possible, and noise and attention will frighten off an attacker.

The most important general safety rule is to trust your senses and gut feeling. If it doesn't feel right, be safe and get out of there. Make for a busy public place if you have any doubts about a person or situation. If you do, remember to phone home, tell them what happened and where you are. For example, if you took the road bridge route but you spotted a gang of drunks waiting under the bridge, you might call home and say you were coming back via the High Street, or that you are waiting at the petrol station for somebody to pick you up.

Attacks by strangers

No matter how alert you might be, no matter how many precautions you take, there is always the chance that you will be in the wrong place at the wrong time and be close enough for an attacker to try to harm you. Remember that the consumption of alcohol makes it more likely that you will be vulnerable to attack.

I think it is important to state that:

- Drunken assaults are usually made by strangers.

- Theft and robbery are usually committed by strangers.

- Sexual assault and rapes are usually committed by people known to the victim.

- Interfering with drinks is usually done by friends and acquaintances in pubs, clubs and at parties. Some just think it 'funny' to slip vodka into a glass of orange squash, while others have drug-assisted sexual assault in mind when they administer drugs.

Attacks – countermeasures

✓ Stay alert, and keep control of your life and yourself.

✓ At a party or in a bar beware of accepting a drink from a stranger, somebody you only met that evening or have only known for a few days.

✓ To be totally safe, go to the bar and order your own drink and watch them make it or open the bottle. Make sure that nobody slips in half a glass of vodka or anything else. At a party or in a bar, don't put your drink down and walk away. You never know what might be put into it.

✓ If you do have to go to the toilet, want to dance or otherwise lose sight of your drink, abandon it and get a new one. That is the only way you can be sure that your drink has not been tampered with.

✓ There are some strange effects to be wary of too. Mixing prescription and over-the-counter medicine can render you helpless very quickly. If the instructions on the packaging say 'do not drink alcohol', believe it and don't drink alcohol.

✓ Keep alert, so that you are aware of your surroundings – who and what is around you.

✓ Stay in well-lit areas, and with people you know. Be wary of trying a new club or pub if you are on your own, especially if it is in the evening and never on a Friday and Saturday night when they are so crowded you won't see what is going on.

✓ Remember that criminals often target people who are clearly lost, confused or otherwise vulnerable. Especially when you are out drinking, relaxing and having fun. Try to stay in places you know.

✓ Seriously consider what you would do if confronted and attacked. The law says you can use reasonable force to defend yourself, but criminals don't have that restriction!

✓ Be aware of conflict management warning and danger signs, as described in Chapter 3.

✓ Don't flash your cash, wear expensive jewellery, show that you are using an expensive mobile phone or do anything else that may mark you out as a potentially good target for a robber. Criminals are almost certainly watching!

If attacked

Don't spend too much time planning what to do if you are attacked. So far we have discussed various situations where you could lose control and be subject of an attack, and various countermeasures you could use to avoid them.

You should now have read and understood the conflict management section which teaches you to look for adverse signs, and to proactively take steps to avoid risk and danger, whether you are dealing with family members (domestic violence), acquaintance (social and work situations), or strangers. You should also now know and understand the three phases of acquaintance, sexual attack and rape.

You can take self-defence classes, but if you need to use self-defence classes you are already in deep trouble. I suggest that you put 95% of your effort into avoiding problems in the first place It is very difficult to give this advice, because circumstances vary so much. YOU are the only one who can decide what to do, but here is some advice to consider if you are ever attacked!

If attacked – countermeasures

- ✓ As usual, your first level of protection is noise. Attract as much attention as you can in any way that you can. Trigger your personal attack alarm. Shout, scream, call for the police, shout for help, and all the time, make every effort to stay out of his reach.

- ✓ If you have one, sound your attack alarm and shout 'HELP' 'POLICE' 'RAPE' to get help and distract him. DON'T just scream, a scream is usually ignored because people assume it is drunks larking around. Shouting HELP and RAPE will not be ignored or misunderstood.

- ✓ Run if you can, but make sure you run towards lights and people, not further into the darkness and bushes.

- ✓ If he says he wants your nice expensive mobile phone and handbag, don't be a dead hero – let him have them. It is a good price to pay for getting away safely, but beware of tricks – although sexual attacks by strangers are rare he could say he just wants your phone, calm you down and then grab and gag you.

- ✓ Try anything you can to put him off. Point and shout 'Police! Over here, this is him.' He will often be as scared and nervous as you are and might just run off if you say that or at least be distracted so you can run away.

- ✓ Fight him off in any way you can. He will have to get close to be able to touch you. That means he is close enough for you to get some blows in as well.

- ✓ Don't try to use 'reasonable force' – you may be fighting for your life. Smack him with your handbag, spray him in the eyes with deodorant, anything to keep him off you without resorting to potentially fatal measures.

- ✓ A martial art such as karate is more of a sport – the classes may teach you fancy moves, but unless you have had a lot of practice, a street fight is never the same as when you were practising those moves in the gym. I knew a karate black belt who was proud of his skills, but he was badly beaten in a street fight because the attacker didn't play nice!

- ✓ Self-defence classes assume that your opponent is out to get you, and the good self-defence classes concentrate on rule number one, which is to get away as soon as you can! If you can't get away, they teach you how to inflict pain and disable an attacker long enough for you to escape. For example, kicking below the knee joint. Contact the police or local authorities and ask about self-defence classes.

- ✓ Remember your objective is to get away, if you can. If you can make some progress towards safety, do it. Kick then run a few steps towards that pub or a family house where lights are showing downstairs keep shouting rape. If you see somebody looking out of a window, head for them. At least they already know you are there and in trouble, so make for them and scream for them to call the police.

- ✓ Your elbow is your strongest natural weapon. An elbow to the throat will stop a man just as well as a knee to the groin. Use your fists, nails, feet, knees and head. Do anything you can to fight them off. Don't let him get a firm hold – flail your arms and go for his eyes. He will be too busy not getting injured to concentrate fully on what he intended to do to you.

- ✓ As soon as you possibly can, call the police and report any sort of intimidation, stalking or attack. Remember that the man who has a sly feel of your chest on the tube today could be tomorrow's rapist. Report any assault.

- ✓ Remember also that people do not like to get involved. A man walking towards you when you are being attacked may walk on past assuming that he is witnessing a drunken lovers' quarrel. If you are attacked, make sure everyone knows what is happening. Continue to scream and call for the police. Unfortunately you also have to remember that even if he knows it is an attack, that man might still walk on past, not wanting to get involved or risk injury himself. Never let your guard down. Don't trust anyone in those circumstances until you are talking to a police officer face to face. I have heard of good Samaritans who stopped to offer help, but they only helped themselves by stealing the victim's handbag!

Mostly Women

- ✓ To clear up any doubts people may have, shout and make it loud enough for anyone to hear you. 'I don't know this man. Help. RAPE.' If you do that, everyone knows that it isn't a domestic disturbance or lovers' tiff. Carry on making that noise and trying to get away from him to safety. Remember safety is where there are lights and people.

- ✓ Another thing to remember is that most people are not used to functioning in a crisis. They don't know what to do. Psychologists say that in those circumstances people will obey direct instructions, but they are often incapable of responding to a general request. Given the chance, give them orders. Shout 'You in the red coat – call 999 and get the police,' and he is likely to do it, but if you shout, 'Somebody call the police,' nobody will. If you just scream people will probably ignore you.

- ✓ As long as you can fight, punch, kick, knee, elbow do so. Writhe, twist, duck, headbutt his face, scratch his eyes, push him over a wall, whack him with a branch, throw dirt in his face, pull away. If he has hold of your jacket, slip out of it and run towards safety, leave him holding the jacket. Most handbags weigh quite a lot; swing it on the end of its straps and it could knock him out. Pull his hair out in clumps if you can; it hurts and is absolute proof of his identity. Use the weapons that may be to hand. An umbrella, car keys, a stiletto shoe and your shopping can all be used to defend against an attacker.

- ✓ If he overpowers you, you may still have a couple of chances. You could talk to him. Tell him this is rape and he could go to prison for a long time. Tell him the police must be on the way. Tell him you have a period, tell him anything that may make him change his mind. All the time keep your eyes and ears open. If he has dragged you into a park, you may see people passing by, or people who responded to your early shouts. If they are close enough to hear and offer assistance shout again. Be clear and positive, 'Help! Rape. In the park,' he may get scared and run away or they may catch him. If you have the chance try to run towards them or to safety, for example run out of the park onto the main road. Keep shouting, 'Call the police! Rape.' Remember he will hear that too. It may scare him enough to make him run off and leave you alone.

- ✓ If he has somehow got you alone, in a place where you cannot see any signs of help, life, lights and people, but you still have a chance to get away, you may still have an opportunity to disable him. His groin, eyes, temples and throat are vulnerable. You could bite his tongue, ear or cheek. Pull some more hair out, try to kick and twist. If you get the chance your elbow in his throat will hurt. You could headbutt him on the bridge of the nose, or grab a fist full of dust, dirt and leaves, throw it in his eyes. You can clap your hands together over his ears or poke at his eyes. If you have a real chance to get away.

- ✓ If you have no real opportunity to escape, any further scratching or gouging by you could anger him, so he may retaliate in kind. At this point if you decide that you cannot get away, I suggest talking again. Tell him you have kids and a weak heart; appeal to him not to do it. Tell him anything you can to make him stop. Invite him back to your place so you can be comfortable! If he is stupid enough to accept, at least you will have a dozen more opportunities to summon help or escape on the way to your place. You of course will make sure you take him past places you know people will be to give you as many chances of getting away as you can.

- ✓ Try talking to make him realise the consequences of his imminent actions. This is rape, and the police will do everything they can to catch him. He could go to prison for a long time. What will his family and friends think of him? Tell him you won't tell the police (you will of course). He may suddenly realise what he is throwing away.

- ✓ If for whatever reason you cannot escape, he won't listen to reason and he intends to rape you, there is an approach called 'total submission'. The purpose of this method is to survive the attack and remember as much as you can. Don't provoke him; let it happen and be done with as soon as possible. One expert suggests that you should make yourself as limp and unresponsive as possible, even pretend to be unconscious – the idea being that it is less enjoyable for the attacker who stops and moves off quickly.

Sexual Assault

I couldn't write this book and certainly not this chapter without acknowledging the fact that sexual assault and rape happens. Any kind of sexual assault is a serious offence, which has long-lasting impacts on the victim, their family and partners.

Contrary to popular belief, most rapes can in some way be described as acquaintance rapes – that is the victim and rapist are known to each other. That may be through work, family or social connections, or more tenuous links such as use of the same club, sports hall or even just living in the same area. She may have known him for years or just a few days, but she knows him. It is very rare for a total stranger to commit rape.

There are a number of resources that concentrate on offering advice and support in this area and I cannot dream of matching their level of expertise, experience or resources, nor would I try.

It is quite easy to define ways to avoid strangers, but it is harder to describe ways to identify and avoid a potential acquaintance rape. Reading the whole of this book will give you a new insight into the concept of personal safety. The explanations and examples should help to show you how to generally look at your life, identify and avoid risks. In short, how to manage your own security.

Most people are quite careless with their own safety and security. There is a general failure to think ahead, to plan, as well as a failure to maintain a basic level of awareness about what is going on in the world around you. That allows you to make mistakes and give people an opportunity to attack you.

The critical element in your safety is **control**. Someone else can only take control if you lose it! There are a number of ways to lose control: for example failing to plan, failing to avoid possible problems that you can see, and taking a chance. Excess alcohol is a very common problem.

Alcohol mixed with something as simple as cough medicine can have strange effects. Mixing prescription and over-the-counter medicine can render you helpless very quickly. If the instructions on the packaging say 'do not drink alcohol', believe that it was put there for a reason and don't do it.

If you are female and you are only going to read and absorb a couple of pages of this book, make absolutely certain that the next couple of pages are the pages that you do study and remember.

Remember that rape is all about the two parts of **control**.

1) You losing control.
2) Him taking control.

How he gets control

In a worryingly high number of acquaintance and stranger attacks, a lack of caution and awareness on the part of the victim has allowed the attacker to take advantage of a situation. In one series of surveys it was reported that:

- over 80% of sex attack victims had consumed a quantity of alcohol and some were helplessly drunk at the time.

- over 50% of attackers were under the influence of alcohol or drugs.
- of 1,000 cases reviewed, only 21 victims had had their drink spiked with what is generally called a 'date rape' drug. These drugs might make the newspaper headlines, but alcohol is a far more important factor.
- over 30% of victims had taken illegal drugs, and some had mixed the drugs with alcohol.
- in nearly 75% of reported rapes the offender was an acquaintance, friend, relative, current or ex-partner of the victim.
- age, race, appearance and clothing appear to have little significance because 'being female' seems to be the only common factor among female victims.

It appears that by being careful with what you drink and avoiding the use of illegal drugs you are more likely to stay in control and stay safe.

Did you know that:

- alcohol affects different people differently.
- alcohol can have a different effect on men and women.
- alcohol has a stronger and quicker effect on women prior to menstruation.
- women taking birth control pills that contain estrogen often stay drunk longer than those not taking estrogen.

The whole aim of this book is to educate you, to show you where to look to identify threats and to remove those threats or protect yourself from them. We know that in most cases, the victim already knew the man who raped her or sexually assaulted her. Women should therefore think about their safety in social circumstances. As society changes and new practices such as speed dating evenings are arranged, you should know what to look for to maintain your safety.

Safe dating

Whether you know the guy or not, at the start of a possible relationship you should consider your safety and make any arrangements with safety in mind.

Safe dating – countermeasures

- ✓ *For your own peace of mind you should make sure you know at least some basic information about him before you agree to go out. If all he is willing to tell you is he is Bob from Manchester, be wary and ask more questions. For example, in conversation you can ask what his full name is, where he works and what he does. You can ask him for a telephone number in case there is a delay. If he won't tell you any more than that his name is Bob I suggest you make your apologies and tell him you can't see him again.

- ✓ Of course while talking to this stranger, you should avoid giving out too much information. If all he seems interested in is whether you live alone, if you've got a well-paid job, and he demands your address and home number, I would be very cautious in giving any of those details out. If he is a genuine guy he will understand.

- ✓ Whether you know him or not, make sure you know what the date will be. For example, if he wants to take you to a smutty film or club where there are lap dancers, you agreeing to go may make him feel that you are accepting a sexual element to your relationship.

- ✓ Similarly, if on a first date he seems to have roaming hands and you are not happy about it, slow him down and pull away. In his mind he may take your acceptance of early contact as a sign that you are open for sexual contact in the near future when you may not be. If he goes too far, too fast, pull away and tell him to stop.

- ✓ If he wants to take you away to a hotel in Brighton for the weekend it is your choice. But if you are expecting separate rooms and a lazy weekend on the beach chewing candy floss and soaking up the sun in a deck chair, make it very plain to him that that is what you are agreeing to.

- ✓ Avoid taking him back to your place at least for the first few dates, especially if you live alone. Make it easy to make a break from him if you want to. Making the break will be easier if he doesn't know your address or home phone number. If you want to give him some details, give him a mobile phone number – at least you can quite easily change a phone number if you need to.

- ✓ If he starts making suggestive comments or touching you in ways that you don't like, tell him! Push his hand away, move away and even tell him you are going home. Call a taxi and leave. Never accept intimate contact that you don't want or welcome.

- ✓ For the first few dates make sure that you go somewhere safe, a neutral and public place. Though it is a dated idea, meeting under the clock at a mainline railway station or at a shopping centre would be totally safe. Agree to meet at such a public venue and you can get to know each other with no risk. Still don't give out personal details, and make sure you stay in a public area.

If he becomes amorous or just plain abusive you can walk away. In that sort of venue if he tries to assault or attack you there is a CCTV camera to record the incident, people and security staff to come to your assistance or call the police, and plenty of safe places you can run to for help.

- ✓ If your date in the shopping centre or town centre burger bar goes OK, you can think about moving on to a more congenial setting, but pick one where there are plenty of other customers around. An amusement park, a cinema (be wary of the film that is playing in case he thinks he is getting hidden messages from you about your intentions). Go to a quiet pub or book a meal at a restaurant. If you don't know him, I suggest going to a modest restaurant, especially if he will have to pay by credit card, because that will leave an evidence trail of his bank details through which he could be traced if it ever became necessary.

- ✓ Be aware of the effects that alcohol can have on you and your personal control. If he goes to the bar and gets a drink, it may be just orange juice but it may be something else entirely if he slipped some drug into the drink!

- ✓ Similarly, if you are in the habit of taking and using illegal drugs be aware that those drugs are usually of unknown strength and purity, they can be so diluted that they have no effect at all, or may knock you unconscious. Note that there has been a recent increase in the level of drug-assisted sexual assault.

- ✓ As you come to know each other, you can decide if you want to move beyond friendship into a relationship. You don't have to interrogate him, but his honesty with you reflects his personality and intentions. Make a mental note of what he says. You don't have to interrogate him, but it should cause concern if last week he said he was from Manchester and this week starts claiming that he was born in Brighton. Maybe he has moved around a lot, or maybe he is simply dishonest. Don't be paranoid, but if his alleged pet dog Bonzo suddenly turns into a cat called Tiger I would start wondering why he is so dishonest and what else he is being dishonest about.

- ✓ As ever, the bottom line is trust your instincts and gut feeling. If something doesn't feel right, get out, go somewhere safe and terminate the relationship.

- ✓ If any relationship does end with arguments, talk to somebody about it. If you are being harassed by telephone, letters or email, or being stalked by somebody who won't accept that the relationship is over, record it and speak to the police. In the past, harassment has escalated to physical assault. Make an appointment to talk to somebody at your local police station. Explain to them what is happening, and take any evidence you might have. For example letters that have been sent to you, text messages on your mobile phone, printouts of emails or if possible recordings of messages from your telephone answering machine. You should also take some sort of diary to show that there is an ongoing problem. Buy a cheap diary and note incidents in it (you may have to hand it over as evidence so you don't want to use your usual diary, which contains all sorts of important and personal information). Your diary entries should be accurate and honest and show the frequency of the calls or visits and so on, their duration, what was said and so on.

Internet dating

The Internet is a powerful tool, but it comes with a significant danger, which is that Internet users can remain anonymous and claim to be anything they care to be. (See Chapter 7.)

Use caution when arranging to meet people via the Internet. While most people use it because it is readily available and fast, attackers use it precisely because they can maintain their anonymity, or at least build and use a false identity when they deal with you.

Internet dating – countermeasures

The countermeasures for safe dating apply. The following points are important too.

- ✓ Because an Internet user can claim to be anything, I would suggest that you should keep a note of any information relating to the person you are in contact with. A simple sheet listing name, age, place of birth, pet's name, job etc will suffice. Apparently, people who use false identities on the Internet often make it up on the spur of the moment and embellish it to make themselves sound more exciting and attractive a prospect. Your contact may claim to be an airline pilot to excuse a period of no contact, and then later claim to be a heart surgeon in an effort to sound worthy of your attention. With a note of the key points of what they have said before, a glance at your list will show you if they are lying or at least if their story is shifting. Of course just because he is lying it doesn't mean he is an attacker, but you have to wonder whether you can believe anything he has said.

- ✓ Keep copies of all emails anyway. If this person does attack you or harass you, the emails could contain evidence that would help the police. For example, people who create a fantasy existence over the Internet often use the same identity with several prospective dates or victims. The emails show for example, he calls himself Colin, works in an engineering firm near Heathrow airport, claims to have an E-type Jaguar car, and a dog called Boris. You never know, you could hear of an attack by somebody else who was called Colin, had an E-type etc, so you may be able to provide further proof to the police.

✓ Accept that in communicating by email you are only receiving and understanding a tiny proportion of the information available to you. Words account for only 15% of the information available to you. The other 85% is carried in stance, pitch, approach, tone of voice and what is often called body language. That means that when communicating by text, email or instant messenger on the Internet you are missing 85% of the information available to you.

✓ Beware of the email address you use. Never use your work email. For a start your employer may not like you spending your working day communicating with potential dates. More importantly with a work email address it is too easy to find the owner. For example if you are using the email address Sue.Biggins@NewCenturyPacking.com I can find you in a few hours. All I have to do is look at the web site, find the address, make a phone call or two to confirm that you are a secretary in the accounts department at their head office in the High Street. Now I have your work address and phone number. I could arrive at reception at half past four and leave some flowers for you with the receptionist. All I have to do then is wait for you to come out holding the flowers. I could soon know what car you have and follow you to your home address. To stay safe, always use an anonymous email address from Yahoo or Hotmail for example.

✓ Treat everything you are told over the Internet with a healthy scepticism. Don't assume that everyone is totally dishonest *and* a possible attacker. Just realise that you can only get limited information on-line. As above, you should swap a few long emails to express your views and see if you think you are compatible and if you want to go ahead and meet this person. Check their information, ask a few questions and see what the response is. If their emails rapidly get smutty and they start to demand a meeting on their terms, walk away. Generally, the signs are not so clear cut. Your contact may seem quite nice, but a few comments and ideas have made you uneasy, or indicate a darker side to them – test that. Ask open questions relating to that subject. If they really are only interested in grooming you as a sexual conquest with or without your co-operation you will hopefully begin to get a feel for it.

✓ Remember that when you are ready, make any date in a public place, so you can easily walk away if you feel you need to.

Speed dating

I believe that speed dating is an American invention, but it is certainly becoming more common and more popular in the UK. Single men and women join a club or pay a service to attend a speed-dating session. Sessions are held in bars or clubs, and the women sit at tables that have been set up around the room. The men come in and sit at one of the tables opposite one of the women and they have a short time to chat. Each of them has a notepad on which they can make a note to remind themselves of the people they meet. After a few minutes a bell rings, and all the men move to the next table where they get to know the woman at that table. The bell goes again and they move on, until everyone has had a chance to talk to everyone else.

At the end of the session, they can refer to their notes and make a decision on who (if anyone) they want to meet again. Some groups and clubs attempt to vet their male and female members to ensure that they are genuine. They may insist on checking a prospective member's passport, address or employment to ensure that they are honest and above board. However some clubs are just in it to make money, so their members may or may not be who they claim to be.

Speed dating – countermeasures

- ✓ As above, but in this case you may be dealing with an absolute stranger so use even more caution, particularly when leaving, just in case one of the rejected suitors has decided he needs to talk to you again – outside!

- ✓ Some predatory married and single men attend speed dating sessions because it is an easy way to meet and talk to a lot of women in a short time. They feel that they have a good chance of persuading at least one of the women present to go out with them, and hopefully to sleep with them.

- ✓ Be extra careful about drinks and food that may be drugged. They may try to keep you supplied with a constant flow of drinks or simply take you to a remote place and attack you.

Trusting

Trust has to be earned. Just because he says he is an army officer, doctor, police officer or bank manager, you should not necessarily accept it. Certainly don't give your trust to people just because they claim to be in those positions.

- Don't trust him because of the role or position he says he holds.
- Don't trust him because you think you know him now.

- If he 'accidentally' touches you for the second time don't accept it was another accident just because you 'know' him and after all he is a 'doctor'!

- Don't assume that just because it is Joe from the workshops or Billy from the big house over the road that you are mistaken when the signs begin to look like he is becoming more insistent in his advances. He may be working up towards an assault.

- Don't trust somebody to keep an eye on your drink. Don't trust a nice bloke to take you home from the office Christmas party when somebody has made and distributed some extremely potent mulled wine, which has left you unsteady on your feet and a bit giggly. Better still get a female friend to take you home, if not get a relative to collect you. Even better, lay off the alcohol at the party.

- Don't trust anyone, unless they have earned your trust over a period. Don't assume that the length of an acquaintance makes him trustworthy. Just because you have kind of known him for years, doesn't make him trustworthy. He has to earn your trust by more than just knowing you!

- Even when he has earned your trust, don't assume you are mistaken if he seems to be trying to take liberties. Those accidental touches that soon become deliberate cuddles and gropes should have started the alarm bells ringing. Tell him to stop and leave.

Offenders

A rapist may be the man next door, a boyfriend, a bloke at work, or in extremely rare cases a total stranger. Those who know him, usually report that a rapist had seemed to be a 'normal, average guy'. But there is no knowing how he will behave – he could be easily discouraged by a scream from his intended victim, or in extreme cases he might not stop until his victim is dead.

The law sees rape as a very serious crime. Even if minimal force or violence was used the maximum sentence is life imprisonment. The standard image of a rapist is that of a hooded stranger/maniac brandishing a knife, who drags a woman into the bushes. The problem is that in most real cases, the victim knows her attacker and the attacks happen in places where they think they are safe – at home, at work or on a date with the attacker.

Rapists are people. Don't expect to be able to tell if a man is a rapist. A lot of victims of acquaintance rape have said things like, 'But he was so nice', or 'He looked normal'. A survey of female rape victims, asked how they thought others would see the man who raped them, the most common description was 'a very nice man'. Any man could be a rapist; there is no pattern, no identifiable uniform or badge that they wear. You only know a man is a rapist when he attacks you.

Having said that, I would ask you to remember that not every man is a rapist. By all means treat everyone with a healthy level of suspicion, and learn how to avoid situations where you could lose control and become a victim. But don't become paranoid. If rather than just being careful you assume that every man around you is a rapist waiting his chance, life will be pretty dismal for you, and life for the men around you will be uncomfortable. Please remain aware, be careful and take precautions, but don't let the worry ruin your life.

Setting boundaries

Setting boundaries in a relationship is vital. It is a process that occurs naturally in a relationship. You don't treat a work colleague as your best friend, and don't treat a friend like a member of the family. Beyond that natural boundary setting you will subconsciously define boundaries for your relationships with everyone you know. In any situation where you feel that he is going further, expecting more than you want to give, going further than you want to go with physical contact, becoming aggressive or demanding sex, you *must* firmly establish, define, vocalise and stick to those boundaries.

Setting boundaries – countermeasures

✓ Think about your situation. Think ahead to the parties, outings, dates and other social occasions you are going to attend. Take a moment to consider the personal boundaries that will be appropriate for those occasions. When you are at that party or even a meeting at work, apply those personal boundaries. At a marketing meeting for work, you might decide that it is a work-related friendly meeting. If the head of advertising starts crowding you, leaning in and draping an arm over your shoulder, you know he is breaking your personal boundaries so you tell him to stop, or at least pull away and make it clear that you do not want him that close. In the pub, if a guy at the next table leans back and makes lewd suggestions to you, you are sure he is intruding and breaking those personal boundaries, so you might tell him to clear off, and complain to the pub manager! Take the time to define and know your personal boundaries in any situation so that you can easily recognise when a man is breaking those boundaries. Hopefully you should also stay in a state where you are capable of recognising and objecting if your boundaries are broken.

- ✓ As soon as you feel he is going too far, or getting over zealous, make it clear to him that you are not happy. At the first sign, pull back to regain some personal space. Stand up, become stern and even walk away. If you are in a bar or club consider leaving him and making it clear that the date is over.

- ✓ Even in a public place don't be embarrassed or scared to make sure he hears and understands that you don't want to be touched if you need to. Make it clear by using words that cannot be misunderstood, 'Stop touching me. I don't like that, stop it.'

- ✓ Make him realise that you are not playing hard to get or teasing him. Use simple, plain and clear words and actions. Say 'No – STOP. I want to go home now.' If it reaches that stage, don't waiver. Even if he does apologise – go home immediately.

- ✓ If you are in private and there are only two of you there pull away and make him stop and think about what he is doing. As you are alone you are in greater danger. Tell him to stop, get your coat and tell him you are going home. Don't accept a lift from him. If you have your own car drive yourself home. If you don't have a car, call a licensed taxi.

- ✓ If he is at your place, tell *him* to leave and make it clear that his advances are unwelcome. If he doesn't go you should consider leaving. If you have a mobile phone, go into the front garden or a public area of the flats and call the police. Don't stay in the house with what seems to be a possible attacker. Get out, get to safety and get the police to deal with him.

- ✓ If he persists pull back and say loudly 'No – STOP. I don't want to – I don't want this. This is rape.'

- ✓ Try to leave. Tell him to calm down. Tell him he will regret it in the morning.

Assumed consent

In the past where there has been an existing relationship, attackers have tried to use the defence that there was presumed consent by the victim, by virtue of marriage or other past or ongoing relationship.

There is no presumed consent. Any woman has the right to refuse sexual advances, whether she is single, married to the attacker, engaged, living together or in a long-term relationship. Courts now look for positive consent. Where it is absent there has been a sexual assault or rape.

Assumed consent – countermeasures

- ✓ If a man makes sexual advances that you do not want, make it perfectly clear that you are refusing those advances.

- ✓ Pull away, push him away say loudly and clearly 'NO. STOP. I DON'T WANT THIS. LEAVE ME ALONE. STOP. THIS IS RAPE!'

- ✓ Given those circumstances there can be no doubt that there was no consent – assumed or otherwise.

Sexual assault/rape – countermeasures

- ✓ If you learn nothing else from this chapter, learn that in most cases the victim knew their attacker. It is very rare for a sexual assault or rape to be carried out at random by a stranger.

- ✓ Accept that by consuming any alcohol or illegal drugs you could be relinquishing all or part of your control over your safety.

- ✓ Stay alert and be aware of your surroundings.

- ✓ Trust your gut feelings. If a place or situation doesn't feel right, make your excuses and get out.

- ✓ Define your boundaries and stick to them.

- ✓ If he is overstepping those boundaries in any way, pull back and consider telling him to stop what he is doing. Be prepared to leave or get him to leave.

- ✓ Be sensible and as far as possible plan for safety. Before you go anywhere, try to make sure that you have a safe way to get home. Book a taxi, travel with friends and go in a group. Do everything you can to ensure your own safety.

- ✓ Criminals often target people who are clearly lost or confused – so try to look confident even when you are not. If you are lost and, or nervous, head for the nearest bright lights and lots of people.

- ✓ Don't take shortcuts. Never use dark and deserted lanes or tracks. Never walk through parks, along unlit roads or down back alleys. No matter how late you are, no matter how cold it is, no matter how hard it is raining, *never* take a shortcut. Don't be in the wrong place at the wrong time even if using a shortcut is more likely to get you robbed than raped. Given the choice, take the long way around if it is well lit and busy with people and cars. Where there are people you should be safe.

- ✓ Seriously consider what you will do if confronted – you can use reasonable force to defend yourself but criminals don't have that restriction. Avoid a fight by staying aware.

- ✓ Where the rapist is known to the victim the most dangerous time is
    - ➢ soon after a separation or break-up
    - ➢ soon after a domestic violence assault.

- ✓ The real, fundamental and simple basis of rape prevention, or any attack or assault is awareness. Rapists rarely attack somebody on a whim. Often they will know the victim; they may have been observing for some time possibly looking for an opportunity or building up to the assault. Sometimes over-indulgence in drink or drugs will trigger an unplanned sexual assault by a male acquaintance.

- ✓ Rapists are often classified in a number of ways, for example 'anger rapists' and 'sadistic rapists'. The classifications tell you what sort of personality they are. Other rapists are classified because they are location specific, for example striking on footpaths, near railways or close to where they live or work. In nearly all cases, 'winning' and controlling the victim is more important to them than any sexual act.

- ✓ The very few attacks and rapes committed at random by strangers happen when the attacker finds a victim. A woman alone, drunk, fumbling for a car key, waiting for a train on a deserted platform, or jogging alone through a deserted park – anything that makes her vulnerable. The attacker is looking for an easy victim, so anything that you can do that makes you look nothing like a victim will make you safer. How do you avoid looking like a victim?
    - ➢ Most important of all, plan ahead so that you do not put yourself in a vulnerable position to start with.
    - ➢ Look confident, listen to what is happening around you, keep your eyes ahead and walk as though you have a purpose. Don't let people know you are lost, for example by constantly checking a map or an address written on a slip of paper. If you are lost, head for the nearest busy place with bright lights and a lot of people and ask for directions from an official or take a licensed taxi to your destination.
    - ➢ Look around occasionally, so that you know what or who is behind you. This also shows anyone watching that you are alert and aware of your surroundings. Don't look behind too often though, as that

will make you look lost and scared. Occasionally make an excuse to look around by watching a passing car or maybe stop and look in a shop window; use it as a mirror to see what is behind you.

- Don't lower your eyes or look away when you meet people. Making brief eye contact adds to the confident look. Be careful that your casual and passing eye contact doesn't stray into what they may think is a longer flirting or challenging look. Don't make problems for yourself.

- Believe in yourself but more importantly *believe yourself*. Millions of years of evolution have gone into your development, and a gut feeling that something is wrong is probably accurate. If it doesn't feel right, get out or tell him to get out!

- By constantly crossing the road to avoid people, you will look lost, weak and indecisive – just like a potential victim. You can adjust your path and speed to avoid coming into contact with potentially suspicious people. Walk past a husband and wife, or a group of school children by all means, but a furtive-looking guy who seems not to want to leave the gates to the park or the end of a back alley should be avoided.

- Don't let anyone get closer than six feet – keep them outside your personal zone. Any closer and they could grab you, knock you out or stab you before you can react. Remember an attacker may be a scruffy lout but he could also look like a bank manager or a favourite uncle! It is the behaviour and circumstances that should warn you, not the way he dresses or looks.

- Under no circumstances go anywhere that is clearly a high-risk area. Dark, dirty, deserted, overgrown, plenty of bushes or doorways and side paths to hide in means **keep out**!

Safe friends – PACTS

✓ If possible arrange to go out with a female friend or group of friends.

✓ Discuss this threat with them and make a pact that you will look out for each other when you are out.

✓ Arrange a signal that you can use to tell your friend(s) that you want to be taken out of a situation. The signal could be something like asking to borrow their lipstick, or mentioning a name such as 'I just saw Susie with Frank'. The signal should be recognised by everyone and acted on immediately.

✓ You should only invoke the pact when you genuinely think there is something wrong with your date or company, an unwanted pressure, or somebody who is too free with his hands and suggestive remarks. Don't invoke the pact just because your date is boring or stupid – your friends will become tired of ruining their evening just rescuing you from a boring date and when you really need rescuing they may not be there for you.

- ✓ Invoke the pact if you think you have recognised some of the indicators of a potential acquaintance rape or sexual assault, or if he really makes you feel uncomfortable. If he invades your space or gets progressively bolder in his actions, for example – it doesn't matter what is happening, the fact that you have real reasons to want out – even a gut feeling that he isn't 'right' – should be enough to bring your friend(s) to take you home (or for you to take them home).

- ✓ When a member of your group makes the agreed signal, take her home. Don't just put her in a taxi or take her to the bus stop. Take her all the way home and even consider staying with her that night in case he decides to call around 'just to see if she is OK'.

- ✓ If one of your group members does invoke the pact, don't forget any other members of the group. Don't leave one of the girls there alone; if you do she is without the backup, support and extra eyes of the group.

- ✓ The pact should also include watching your drinks. Keep an eye on what was ordered, and what was handed to each of you. Is that just a glass of lemonade or was a good measure of vodka slipped in there?

- ✓ Watch for small quantities of liquids or powders being slipped into a drink, or where somebody had the time and opportunity so could have slipped something in. Keep an eye out for strange behaviour, if he went to the bar, got the drinks and then turned his back on the group for two minutes before coming back with the drinks! Could he have done something to the drinks? What was he doing at the bar, apparently blocking your view?

- ✓ Beware of drinks that may have been marked! If there are three glasses or bottles on the tray but one has an umbrella in it, or all the bottles except one are in a group. Be even more concerned if he then insists that though there are three bottles on the tray *that one* is yours! In those circumstances I would claim a migraine, invoke the pact and be gone!

- ✓ If you see suspicious activity, even if the owner of a drink is not a member of your pact, I would talk to the drinker and ask how well they know the guy with the drinks. If it is her husband, OK. If she says has just just met him, I would discuss what I may have just seen with her, and leave it to her to decide.

- ✓ If somebody approaches you and asks how well you know a guy, listen. She may say that from what she saw he could have put something in your drink. Listen and even if it is your older brother, husband or other totally trusted guy, don't react negatively. Whoever told you that the guy might have added something to your drink had your safety in mind. Don't pick a fight because she just insulted your husband or your brother, thank her and make your mind up. Take a second to consider what you have been told, bearing in mind that in most cases the victim knows her attacker. Could Fred from the office have predatory desires? Could your drink have been interfered with? It's a horrible thought, but if you have any doubts at all you might consider accidentally dropping that drink or knocking the glass over.

- ✓ You can get stoppers to put in the top of a bottle. They have a hole where a drinking straw can be pushed through, and they make it exceedingly difficult to administer any drugs or potions. But a drug could be poured into the straw, or put into the drink before the stopper was inserted. The best way to keep your drink safe is still to watch it being opened, then hold it until you are finished. If you do let it out of your sight, abandon it!

- ✓ You may be looking for more information for yourself or a friend, and there are a number of web sites that offer advice and support. For example www.truthaboutrape.co.uk and www.rape-crisis.org.uk. www.crimereduction.gov.uk/sexual10.htm is the Metropolitan Police initiative to improve the care offered to victims of rape, and improve rape investigation.

- ✓ For any guys who have read this far, I doubt if you need this final little bit of advice, but make sure that your mates know it as well please. If she says no, it always, always, always means no. Challenge inappropriate behaviour around you, and if anyone furtively asks you if you want some date rape drugs, or tells you he uses them, report him to the police!

Drug-assisted sexual assault/'date rape'

When most victims know their attacker, this advice is probably relevant to a situation where drugs are not used. Very few acquaintance rapes are 'date' rapes. Rather, rapists/predatory men now target victims in social spaces like pubs and clubs, because women are there on their own or in groups in ways that they never were in the past. Though those involved are acquaintances, they are not necessarily 'dates'. In any circumstances, experts have identified a pattern of activity and escalation, which could help a woman to recognise them and halt proceedings well before a rape is committed.

An American study of date rapes showed that there were generally three phases of 'intrusion', which built up to a rape.

- Phase one – The man will openly invade a woman's personal space. For example he might move very close and openly put his hand on her knee, ignoring that they have only just met or that people were watching. In some pubs and clubs, because of the overly loud music you have to sit very close together to hear each other speak. For that reason such a touch may be thought of as casual or accidental. Phase one continues for a while, and the potential attacker may get bolder and make that 'accidental' touch more frequent or bolder.

- Phase two – If the woman didn't object to the invasion of her personal space and overly familiar touching, the man will go further. The woman may not be happy, but so close to him she may still be trying to persuade herself that there is nothing in it. She may be rationalising and even trying to justify what is happening in her own mind. She may not want to think that the way he has been pushing and touching, grabbing and holding can possibly be any more than misplaced familiarity, or that his boldness is due to him being a little drunk. On the other hand she may object but be reluctant to make a scene in such a public place.

  - By this time the woman may have recognised and accepted that her personal boundaries have been broken, by accident or otherwise. This is her first chance to leave – or ask/tell him to leave. If the woman hasn't reacted to the fact that her personal boundaries have been broken, the attacker may convince himself that the lack of reaction is 'permission' to go further.

  - Over time, his overly familiar touching could even de-sensitise her to his actions if she has been drinking too. Touching her knee at first, then her thigh. She could be enjoying the attention, but have no intention of letting it go further.

  - Again, she might object, but because of crowding at the venue she can't easily reclaim her personal space by backing off. If she reads his actions as a warning of worse to come she might leave then. If she stays unhappily and does what little she can to stop it, he will probably take that as a signal of her acceptance. His intention and actions are a form of grooming, by desensitising her, and easing her towards a situation where she consents to sex or he can get her somewhere he can rape her.

  - If she is unable to move because of the crowd and he has started groping her, she can shout at full volume 'Get your hands off me!' but she probably won't. In those circumstances, she may realise that she doesn't want to be with or even near the man, but doesn't want people to think she is a prude or the opposite. In many clubs and some pubs the loud music could drown out her comments anyway.

  - In a lot of cases, the victim reported that at this point she decided to get out of the club or away from the party, thinking that he would no longer have the excuse to invade her space and take liberties. Sometimes she has still been trying to rationalise the incident, trying to persuade herself that some of those touches were accidental due to the crowding in the club. If she hasn't told him she is going home she may look for somewhere that is quiet and less crowded, somewhere that will allow her to pull away from him. But the attacker wants to move to somewhere more private where they can be together.

- Phase three – Usually follows quite quickly. The attacker makes a move. She objects and tries to stop him but he attacks and rapes her.

Where the victim knows the attacker, this sort of three-phase pattern of 'date' is apparently common. Be warned that though all cases are different, the use of alcohol or drugs by both parties is frequently reported. Where it is used, inhibitions are reduced, which means each of the above stages is accelerated. In these circumstances a rape is considerably more likely.

Rape – countermeasures

✓ Recognise and remember the pattern of behaviour described above. Don't be paranoid, just be safe.

✓ If you think the man you are with is following this pattern, break the pattern.

✓ Tell him to keep his hands off.

✓ Tell him you don't like what he is doing and you are going to leave. If you are in your house, tell him to leave.

✓ Always have the number of a reputable taxi company on you or memorised and call for a taxi to take you home.

✓ If you want to let him down gently, tell him you are feeling ill. Make it sound as horrible as you can to put him right off. Tell him you are definitely going to throw up and you need a taxi home. (You don't want to go in his car because you don't want to risk making a mess in it.)

Drug-assisted rape – countermeasures

These drugs are easily available and are used in this country.

- ✓ Be wary if a stranger offers you a drink. He may be a nice-looking guy, a work mate or an old friend but the drink could still be drugged. If you are offered a drink, unless you see it poured by the barman, or see the container opened (like a ring pull can), don't accept it. If anyone touches it, or you lose sight of it, refuse it. It only takes a second to slip in a few drops of a fluid, or a little powder.

- ✓ Adopt the old nominated driver routine. One person in your group will stay sober, can drive the group and can keep an eye on what the group members are drinking.

- ✓ The drugs used in these circumstances are tasteless, odourless, and usually colourless. Rohypnol usually includes a blue dye but mixed in a red wine and cola for example, it may not show, and you won't be able to see it at all in a drink that comes in a coloured and patterned bottle. Rohypnol can be obtained on the black market in a clear form, because it is taken from the production process before the dye is added.

- ✓ Rohypnol dye may not show up in a drink for some minutes and in 'club' lighting may not show up at all.

- ✓ Beware of any blue drink – it might be drugged, or if it is supposed to be blue it could be a ploy to disguise a drugged drink.

- ✓ Given a choice, always drink drinks that come in bottles and cans. For a start the container is sealed and either opened for you or opened by you so you know it is not drugged. Secondly, it would be a lot harder for somebody to slip drops or other drugs into a narrow bottleneck or can opening than it would be to slip them into the wide top of a glass.

- ✓ Be warned that there have been reports of Rohypnol and similar drugs being given to victims in tea, drinking chocolate and iced water.

- ✓ How do you know if you have been drugged? You don't necessarily know, but it helps if you know yourself and your normal reactions and behaviour.
    - ➤ Monitor yourself. Everyone should know how they react to alcohol.
    - ➤ You should also always know how much alcohol you have consumed. If you lose track you have had too much. Leave and go home or somewhere else where you will be safe.
    - ➤ If your reactions seem to be out of line with the amount of alcohol you have consumed (you feel drunk), you may have been drugged. If you feel strange, sick, or simply too drunk for the amount of alcohol you have had, *assume you have been drugged*, and immediately find a place of safety. It could just be an unusual reaction because you are already coming down with flu, but it may not be. Be safe not sorry.

- If you are with your friends, invoke your pact and ask to be taken home. If you are alone find somebody in a position of authority and ask them to get you to a place of safety.
- Never ask the person you are with, and never accept assistance from a helpful stranger. It could be them who has drugged you. They may be innocent, but going with them would be walking into a trap.
- If your friend takes you home, ask them to stay until the next day to make sure you are safe. You may pass out from the effects of the drug so ask them to stay until the next morning when the effects of the drug or whatever caused it, have worn off. Don't stay alone – the drugging rapist may come around visiting when you have passed out.
- If your friend is male, are you really sure of them? Could they have administered the drug? If worried, ask them to take you back to mum and dad's place or a close female friend. Make them all part of your pact – if they will be your safe house you will be theirs. In the same spirit, if a female friend calls for help or arrives on your doorstep looking unsteady, offer all the help you can – it may be you next time.

Advice For Victims

First, I will admit to some bias in my approach, which comes from over 20 years of police service. My natural and professional desire is to protect people, to prevent crime and if it happens to gather sufficient evidence to bring the offender to court while supporting and protecting the victim and witnesses.

Having admitted that bias, I will support any decision that the victim of a sexual assault makes. You are the victim, it is your life and only you can decide what to do. Speak to independent advisors and take the course of action that is right for you. Do remember one thing, if nobody reports an attacker he will remain free to strike again.

All experts agree that the actual number of rapes committed far exceeds the number that is reported. Some studies claim that fewer than one in 10 rapes are actually reported. Which leaves nine in 10 rapists free to strike again.

This section contains:

- **Advice** – for anyone who is a victim of sexual assault.
- **General information** – on the basis that you have to understand a threat to beat it or avoid it.

- **Avoidance** – advice on how to avoid being in a position where you could be assaulted.

If you don't remember anything

With illegal drugs in circulation, it is possible that you could have been raped but not be aware of it. You could remember going out, being in a particular pub or club until, say, nine in the evening and then have no memory of anything until you woke up next day at home. The drugs used are intended to knock you out and have the effect of wiping your memory of the time in question. The following pointers may help you to understand if you wake up and can't remember what has happened.

- If you find that your house or room isn't the way you usually leave it, even if you do come in a little drunk. For example your coat is tossed on the floor, not on the hanger where you always put it and your underwear may be missing or on the couch. If you find any clues like this look further.

- If you have any physical evidence, for example bruises and bites, or sore genitals, you may have been raped while drugged.

- If you find physical evidence elsewhere, something as simple as the toilet seat left up and urine dribbled on the rim shows somebody was there. Don't wipe it or clean it; the police may want to see it. If you find something as definite as a discarded condom it's clear that something happened.

- If it looks like you had sex while drugged call the police. Insist that somebody take a urine and blood sample from you to check for the presence of drugs. (Most date rape drugs are apparently only traceable for a matter of hours.) If you think there is other evidence in your house, insist that they come to see and collect it as well.

If you have been raped

The first and most important thing for you to understand is that the victim is never to blame. You were attacked. You should now seek help, and there are some important things that you must know.

- **Go to a safe place** – a hospital, police station, women's refuge, anywhere that is well lit and has people around.

- **Call the police – go to the police as soon as possible or vital evidence could be lost**. It was a serious crime. Whether it was a 'boyfriend', somebody else you know or work with, or a total stranger. The police have special facilities and specially-trained officers who will support and advise you.

In some areas there are a number of organisations that offer help and advice to victims. For example in the UK there are some Sexual Assault Referral Centres (SARCs), which have facilities and counsellors available to support the victim through the evidence-gathering process, medical and forensic examination, police interview etc.

Whatever you do decide to do, a victim of a sexual assault or rape should get immediate counselling, help and support; the sort of support that can be found at a SARC or by going to the police or any other support group – *those who do suffer less emotional stress and recover a lot quicker than victims who try to cope alone.*

- **Preserve evidence** – don't shower or douche. If at all possible, avoid eating, drinking, smoking, cleaning your teeth, removing or washing the clothes you were wearing, or going to the toilet. This will allow the police to collect vital evidence, such as blood and semen. After the evidence has been taken and you have spoken to a police officer, the new police suites have washing facilities that you can use.

- **Get medical care** – even if you decide not to go to the police, you should seek medical care. Don't be embarrassed to describe exactly what took place. If the doctor doesn't know what happened, she can't check for injuries. You will need specialist help and support to deal with possible pregnancy, HIV, sexually transmitted diseases, or post-traumatic physical and psychological effects. This can be done anonymously at your local STD clinic, (often based in local hospitals), so your family doctor need never know or be informed.

- **Giving information** – you should be thinking about information. It has happened. It wasn't your fault. You are in shock but if you are going to report it you must try to pass on as much information as you can. During and after any assault, try to file away information that could help. If you know him you will already have a lot of information. If you don't know him very well or it is one of the rare occasions where the attacker is not already known to the victim you should try to gather as much information as you can. For example:

- Do you know his name?
- How do you know him?
- How old is he?
- Has he got any distinguishing marks?
- What was he wearing?
- Was he wearing any distinctive jewellery?
- How tall was he?
- What was his build: slim, athletic or fat?
- Was his skin greasy, spotty, white, oriental, black?
- What was his general face shape: oval, pointed, square etc?
- Did he have any facial hair, beard, moustache, sideburns etc?
- Was there any distinctive smell: aftershave, body odour, alcohol or maybe a work smell like paint?
- What was his hair like: colour, style, length? Did you see his eye colour?
- Any distinguishing points: scars, a limp, stutter, tattoo etc?
- What did he say; was there an accent?
- Did you manage to kick his left knee or scratch his forehead?
- Did he use a car or a van: what make, model, colour, markings etc?

The more information you can give the better.

Be ready to explain what happened to officers who attend the scene. If it was a domestic argument with pushing and shouting say so. But if it was more than that be ready to use the words that describe what happened; words like attack, punched or strangled. Later, you will be speaking to a specially trained officer, (you can request a male or female officer) they will need a fairly detailed description of what happened to you. It may be embarrassing, but you need to explain what happened, even if the language you have to use is difficult.

Be honest and give all the information you can, even if you are embarrassed talking about what he said or did, or if you had been drinking or had taken illegal drugs. Be honest even if you had trusted him and invited him into your home initially, or you had consented to kiss him before the attack.

It is vitally important that you are totally honest about what happened. Don't make assumptions, and don't try to cover things up because it could look bad for you. If you were drinking, say so. If you had taken some illegal drugs, say so in your first statement. Tell the police everything – if you don't and that truth comes out later, there will be doubt about your honesty and defence can claim that your changing description of the assault and circumstances is false as well. For example in your first statement you might leave out the bit about him asking for, and you agreeing to, a kiss. Later, under questioning when you admit that he had asked for a kiss and you had agreed, people might think that you have been caught out in a lie which could cast doubt on the rest of your evidence. Be totally honest.

Safety at Work

Women and men are attacked at work. The attackers can be visitors, customers, patients or sometimes just people who are passing through somewhere like a railway station or supermarket. This form of abuse and assault is increasing. The latest figures show that nearly 350,000 people were attacked at work in a single year. In a high proportion of those cases the attacker was under the influence of alcohol.

One trigger for such abuse is that the attacker feels that the victim or the organisation is deliberately keeping them waiting or treating them like a fool.

If you feel threatened in this situation then don't be embarrassed to ask a colleague for assistance. If the problem is regular, ask the employer to install protective screens, CCTV and personal attack alarms. Remember that if staff have to handle and retain money, the likelihood of an attack increases, so protective equipment should be supplied.

A full health and safety risk assessment should be carried out by the employer, and it should be fully documented. If unacceptable risks are identified, the employer should introduce measures to reduce or remove those risks and threats as soon as is practically possible.

At work – countermeasures

✓ Keep customers, passengers, and patients informed about problems or delays and the reason for them. I was told of one case where a doctor's receptionist was attacked. The attacker had waited for three hours past his appointment time, then the doctor buzzed reception and told the receptionist to move all remaining appointments to later in the week, because he had been very busy and had decided to take the afternoon off.

✓ Be reasonable and be fair.

✓ As a member of staff, don't let anyone jump the queue unless there is a very good reason. A medical emergency could be accepted, but only if you explain that to those who have been waiting.

✓ When you explain delays, tell them how long the delay will be. Try to be fair with them; if somebody has been waiting for four hours but can't wait any longer because they have to get back to work, offer to squeeze them in as the first patient tomorrow. Try to be fair and fit them in as best you can to suit their commitments. Make them realise that they matter.

✓ If at all possible make the working environment conducive to good behaviour. I know of an office where there was always trouble. The public waiting room had a cracked and smelly linoleum tile floor. There were a few wooden benches scarred with carved initials and insults. There was no real heating; it was far too hot in summer and too cold in winter. There was one strip light that flickered all the time. Everything was thick in cigarette smoke, and there were no toilet facilities for people waiting. Staff members sat in comfortable chairs in well-lit air-conditioned offices on the other side of a screen. One day somebody suggested that the people behaved like animals because they were treated like animals. Their HQ decided to throw some money at the problem when they found they had an under-spend at the end of the financial year. Some preparation work was done, then over a long bank holiday weekend the place was transformed. Air conditioning was extended to the public waiting area. Good lighting was installed along with a television hanging from the ceiling. The place was decorated in a light washable apple white colour, washable carpet was installed along with upholstered easy chairs. Large potted plants were strategically placed, and magazines were put out for the public to read while they waited. Result, they went from several fights and assaults per day to none in six months.

✓ If a confrontational incident arises, staff should try to calm things down.

  ➤ Deliberately use a calm voice and manner when confronted by somebody who is angry.

  ➤ Let them know that you can see that there is a problem. Listen to them. Don't be dismissive or condescending.

  ➤ Use words that indicate it is a joint problem. For example you could say, 'I can see that *we've* got a problem here, let's see what *we* can do to sort it out.' That makes them realise that you recognise it as a problem, and are not only willing to try to resolve it, you have actually offered to do it.

➢ As soon as they back off and lower their tone, invite them to sit down and explain exactly what has gone wrong.

➢ Make notes, and make it look as though it is important – it is to them, even if you can resolve it with one phone call.

➢ Stay calm, and speak slowly and clearly. Try not to interrupt unless you want to make a point or ask a relevant question, but don't patronise.

➢ If they stray right off the point and turn it into a session where they just want to complain about the world in general, bring the meeting back on track by taking an opportunity to ask a question that leads them back to their stated problem. For example, 'Oh that's bad, but how does that relate to your broken fridge?'

➢ If they are flowing in anger and rage, but you can't really understand what their problem is, you can try to concentrate their minds. For example you could say, 'I can see you've had a hard time, but how can the kitchen goods repair desk help?' (or whatever your function is).

➢ Sometimes, drink, drugs or mental illness mean that somebody is just out of control. In those circumstances, call for assistance, if you don't have security staff I suggest that the police are the only ones who can help.

✓ If you have been attacked or assaulted by a member of staff, a client, a customer or anyone, you have the right to call the police and report it as a crime.

✓ Work-related vulnerability extends outside the workplace. For example, shift workers have to travel home in the early hours when nobody is around. I would suggest that a good employer would make sure that facilities and services were in place to make sure female staff got home safe by, for example, providing a minibus service.

✓ Staff in those circumstances could arrange with each other to organise so that the husband of one woman could pick up his wife and three others and give them all a lift home. The husbands could do that in turns so they only have to do it once every week or so.

✓ If you are given a lift home, ask the driver to wait until they see that you are safely indoors. If they cannot see your front door, for example if you live in a flat, it would be nice if they could escort you to the door (unless they are a lone female – that would leave them exposed). You could call ahead and ask somebody to come out to meet you at the car park. Think your way around these problems and find a safe way.

✓ Insults and abuse in the workplace are a lot more common than actual physical attack, but you still have a right to be protected against the abuse.

Working outside the office

Some people spend time working outside their office. For example, health workers, social workers, community psychiatric nurses, estate agents and sales representatives spend at least some of the day visiting a variety of addresses. An office environment is usually managed and controlled, but there is often no management and control of the premises that will be visited outside the office.

Anyone, especially women who work away from an office, must take extra care with their safety and security. For example, a female health worker may be asked to visit a man with known mental health problems, who is supposed to be taking medication to control his problem. She is expected to go to his flat with or without an appointment and spend some time there assessing him, or maybe performing tests to see if the medication dosage is right. Social workers visit families where there is known, or there are strong suspicions of, violence and abuse. These are very dangerous situations. Making an appointment, he could lay a trap for her. Visiting without an appointment she might catch him involved in something he should not be doing which could trigger an attack.

In some professions, women make up an extremely high proportion of the staff – significantly more than 50% – in roles such as health visitors, social workers and community psychiatric nurses. In these jobs women are likely to be exposed to violence because they are dealing with disturbed and possibly violent people. They are required to visit those people in their homes; places where help is not immediately available.

Employers are not good at recognising the risks and introducing measures to remove or reduce those risks. For example knowing that attacks and violence are more likely when an attacker has recently been separated, or soon after an incident when domestic violence has been reported. The organisation should recognise the increased risk and take steps to ensure that their employees remain safe in those situations. In those circumstances the organisation could:

- Ask the police to make a low-key appearance to attend for safety reasons.

- Insist that when there is a higher risk of violence, or where there has recently been violence, that clients/patients are asked to attend the offices for interviews and appraisals.

- Possibly insist that in all such cases the employees who perform a home visit should be experienced and know how to handle disturbed patients/clients.

- Insist that in all such cases at least two employees should attend the home address. They should never allow the client to get between them and the exit door, and should withdraw at the first sign of trouble.

- The organisation could invest in technology that would help employees identify, plan for and cope with potentially violent people. For example the organisation could invest in IT systems that record and display warning signs about patients. Employees could be equipped with emergency panic buttons that track and report on the location of an employee to summon urgent assistance if they need it.

- Employers must accept that aggression and violence take many forms. An employee may be subjected to aggressive verbal abuse, swearing, threats and intimidation, before any violence is offered. The employees may need extra time to recover from these encounters, even though they were not actually punched or kicked. Employees may need counselling to help them deal with the stress of the violence they deal with and encounter in their role.

All employers and employees must ensure that they take basic levels of care, and that staff are properly trained and follow established procedures, using any equipment supplied.

Employee
Employees should take steps to ensure that they are safe.

- Make sure that your employer acknowledges your increased exposure to risks. Put it in writing and make sure that the employer takes steps to introduce training and support procedures to minimise those risks.

- As an employee you should follow all safety procedures strictly at all times. Don't break the rules. Arranging to attend a last-minute meeting that the office knows nothing about to try to reach this month's sales figures is not worth risking your life for.

- Use common sense. Meeting a client in his office at 10.30 am on a Tuesday, when he works for a large corporation, is probably safe – even though you should still follow the procedures laid down. If you are asked to meet a Mr Smith in a back street office, self preservation should be switching in as you don't have much to go on there. However, being asked to meet 'John' in the car park at the Oak Tree roundabout on the A435 (because he is really busy and is between meetings) is a huge risk.
- Where possible arrange to meet clients for the first time at your own office.
- Do your own checks on the alleged client.
  - ➢ Take time to visit their office address. If it is a vacant lot check the address you have been given against the place you are looking at. If it is a vacant site and you are not a builder who could be asked to build something on that site, consider calling the police – something funny seems to be going on.
  - ➢ If the 'office' is just a single shabby mobile cabin, be suspicious.
  - ➢ If it is an office building, is the company name you have been given prominently displayed? If it's a corporate headquarters things are looking good. If it is a shared building look for a smaller nameplate.
  - ➢ Talk to any receptionist or security staff. Tell them that you have to come there in a few days' time to meet Mr Biggins of Biggins Supplies and you want to make sure you are in the right place. If they say, 'Who?', be very careful. If they say, 'Yes, this is the place,' ask a few more questions – it makes business sense anyway.
  - ➢ What can they tell you about the company? How many staff do they have? How long have they been there? Do they have any other offices or buildings – if so what is the address (claim you are looking for another sales lead, even if you are just checking them out)? What do they do exactly? Do they have marked vehicles? What is Mr Biggins like? Is he based in this office?
  - ➢ Check the phone numbers you have been given. If you were only given a mobile number be careful.
  - ➢ Call the phone number given. See who answers. If it is a pub and the landlord asks who you want, be very careful. If it is a corporate receptionist ask a few questions and find out more under the guise of checking up about your forthcoming meeting – is there a parking space available? Where are they exactly? etc.

- Consider taking a colleague with you on your first visit. You don't have to say it was because you didn't trust them, or that their company looked a little shady. You could say that the colleague is a trainee, or part of a quality assurance scheme aimed at improving services to customers. Use any excuse you have to.

- Never give out a home address, home phone number or any other personal information. And remember that with a name and initials and a home phone number they can go to the library and look up your home address.

- If a client calls to change the plans, be suspicious. The closer to the meeting the call is made, the higher your suspicion level should be. They may have a genuine reason for changing the arrangements, but they may be attempting to get you alone, with no trace of what happened in your office diary.

- Gut feelings are based on thousands of years of genetic development. Gut feelings work. If it feels wrong, make your excuses and leave.

Employer

The employer must introduce systems and procedures that will equip a member of staff to work off site. They should also provide a support structure that will work to maintain employee safety and security.

- Employers should undertake health and safety risk assessment of all roles in their company, from the cleaner using powerful chemicals to the lone female who has to visit clients and or patients away from the office.

- Where risks are identified, the employer should introduce training, equipment and procedures to remove those risks or reduce their impact to an acceptable level. For example, visiting a mentally disturbed patient with a history of violence with a male colleague and police in attendance would be acceptable. It would not be acceptable if the employer didn't mention the mental health problem, and simply told the visitor that she should be careful. The employer should introduce a 'lone working policy' to protect vulnerable employees.

- Staff members should be fully trained to identify the possible risks associated with the business/organisation/agency/service (here called the employer) and their clients.

- The employer should supply staff members with any necessary protective equipment. That may be an attack alarm, a two-way radio, a mobile phone, or even a stab-proof vest. Employees should of course be fully trained in using the equipment issued.

- Employees should be able to feed back information where training or equipment needs updating.

- Employer guidelines, processes and procedures should be written so that they take account of possible threats. For example the human resources office could include a domestic violence policy in their induction, training and awareness campaigns.

- Where incidents have been reported, the employer should review their processes, procedures and equipment, and consider amending or upgrading it to counteract the newly identified threat.

- Where an incident escalates and violence is threatened or given, there should be a review of the training and procedures to confirm that they were adequate, and to identify any issues that came out of it.

- The employer should ensure that managers and supervisors are properly trained in how to check for risks, assign appropriate staff and check up at appropriate times to ensure that staff are safe and well.

- Managers and supervisors should review performance to capture any incidents where staff have become lax and have not followed established processes and procedures.

- Employers must introduce adequate systems to protect employees who work out of the office. For example:
    - A documented risk assessment of the role, identifying risks, threats and likelihood. It should identify the problems employees may face, how often the problems may occur and how severe the damage or injury that any incident may cause.
    - A list of the equipment and procedures that have been put in place to avoid or otherwise overcome these problems.
    - Appropriate training for employees that will teach them how to properly use the equipment, procedures and other safety measures that are in place.
    - A diary and reporting system that shows where each employee who works out of the office will be at any time.
    - A system where anyone an employee has to visit should be subject to basic security and safety checks, as described above. For example, employees

should not be sent to meet somebody when the only contact detail is a mobile phone number.

Domestic Violence

Don't let him or her catch you reading this if you are subject to any level of domestic violence. Domestic violence is surprisingly common. It is reported from mansions to leafy suburbs, tower blocks to private estates, newly weds to couples approaching their golden wedding anniversary, and wealthy stock brokers to unemployed road sweepers.

> **Victims of domestic violence say that the National Domestic Violence Hotline telephone number was the single most important piece of information that they found to help them to resolve their problems.**
> **The National Domestic Violence Hotline can be contacted on freephone – 0808 2000 247 (24 hour)**
> **Email – helpline@womensaid.org.uk**
> **Post – P.O. Box 391, Bristol, BS99 7WS**

One quarter of all cases of assault and violence that are reported to the police in the UK are classified as domestic violence.

About 25% of women have suffered, or will suffer from, an assault from a partner. When that violence becomes a recurring pattern and is connected to a range of controlling behaviours, it undermines self-belief and causes the victim to become depressed and over anxious in addition to any physical harm.

In about 50% of cases where a woman is murdered, it is established that her husband or ex-partner killed her.

Domestic violence is a difficult subject and I am not an expert, but the following information may help. There are many different forms of domestic violence and abuse, for example:

- physical – what everyone thinks about when discussing domestic violence, where the victim actually suffers physical assault.
- sexual – rape and sexual abuse is quite common in domestic violence.
- emotional/psychological – where a victim may be constantly humiliated, told that they are worthless, stupid and incapable.
- financial – where the victim may not be allowed to have any money, or the abuser may take charge of all resources just letting the victim have £10 a day to feed the family. The abuser may take her money, force her into prostitution, or force her to commit fraud.
- social – where a victim may be kept in isolation, refused permission to go out of the house alone, use the telephone, see friends or have a life outside the relationship.

Most victims of domestic violence are female, though there are some cases where the female is the abuser and the male in the relationship is the victim. It can also happen in same-sex relationships.

I have seen many cases of domestic violence and the immense strain it puts on the victims, especially when they are in love with the abuser. In those circumstances the victim almost resists admitting and putting a name to what is happening. They often hide what is happening from the rest of the world, maybe from shame or a sense of loyalty. They somehow feel that the abuse must be their own fault. At the same time they often keep the abuse secret from the people who know them best, neighbours, family and colleagues at work. Unfortunately that allows the abuser to carry on abusing.

Sometimes the abuser is in turmoil, and they know in their heart that what they are doing is wrong. If they have abused their partner, they can burst into tears, beg for forgiveness and claim that they will never do it again. In my experience the abuse never really stops, and all too often escalates to greater levels of injury and abuse. Often people who may see signs of the abuse minimise and excuse it, which reinforces the abuser's sense of entitlement and justification for the abuse.

As mentioned above, abuse can take many forms. A man might constantly accuse his wife of having affairs, refuse to let her go out alone and constantly call to check up on her. Any case an ongoing pattern of coercive control constitutes domestic abuse. A man who frequently humiliates his wife in shops or social situations is an abuser, as is a woman who does the same to her husband.

What the options are

Very often the victim feels that they cannot leave the relationship. There may be children and there is always a money worry, as well as family and religious pressure which can come to bear as well. But there is help and support available if you make that initial contact and ask for it.

As the victim, you should know in your heart if things will ever change. Look back, is the abuse getting worse or more frequent? Have you tried everything you can think of, including marriage guidance or counselling? I suggest that you seriously consider speaking to somebody about escaping from the relationship. Most important of all, where verbal and psychological abuse has escalated to physical beatings you should get out of the relationship as soon as you can. Though the victim may need to leave the family home to start with to find a safe haven and initiate the process, where possible the courts should remove the abuser, so that the victim (and any children) can remain in the family home.

The police have powers to deal with people who attack and abuse others, whether they are strangers, married, in a relationship or living together. Assault is a crime no matter what the circumstances. Judges can punish an offender, and jail him or her. By court order the victim can be awarded the family home and custody of the children. If necessary the court can also issue an order which can stop the offender harassing the victim, even barring the abuser from being inside a certain geographical area. Breaches of these orders can result in the offender being jailed. But, for any of this remedial action to happen, the victim has to summon the courage to speak to somebody to ask for help.

Am I a victim of domestic violence?

You will already know that the way you are being treated isn't right and your instincts will tell you that this isn't a healthy relationship.

When it has been a long relationship, or you started out being deeply in love, it can be hard to accept and name what has happened to you. The following questions may help you to confirm what you probably already know, or at least suspect.

You know the difference between a private joke and deliberate public humiliation. You know the difference between being frugal and keeping you from having any money. You should know the difference between an occasional bad day, and frequent temper tantrums. Answer the following questions honestly. Don't write in the book; somebody may see it. You will soon get a feel for the number of 'yes' answers you give.

- Does your partner make you account for every minute of the day and prove to him that you have not been with somebody else?

- Does your partner frequently accuse you of having affairs when it is clear to anyone that you were doing the laundry, out shopping or taking the kids to the dentist?

- Does your partner try to control the people you are allowed to meet, perhaps even trying to stop you from seeing your relatives?

- Does your partner refuse to let you use the telephone or sit and listen in if you have any conversations?

- Does your partner object to you having friends of any sort, particularly friends of the opposite sex?

- Does your partner refuse to let you out of the house alone?

- Does your partner criticise you a lot, making you feel that you can't do anything right?

- Does your partner get really angry over nothing that you can identify, then make you feel that whatever it was it was your fault?

- Does your partner get angry a lot?

- When your partner is angry and in a temper, are you scared that he might actually hit you?

- Has your partner ever used force against you, pushed you, slapped you or pulled you from one room to another?

- After hurting you, has your partner ever threatened you with greater violence and pain if you tell anybody that he has hurt you?

- If your partner does get into a temper, is that partly because he has been taking drugs or drinking alcohol?

- Does your partner keep tight control of the family money, insisting that the little money you are allowed to have is strictly accounted for in detail and that you produce receipts at the end of the day?

- Does your partner take or steal your money or take any child benefit money?
- Has your partner ever accused you of keeping money for yourself, hiding it or spending money on somebody else?
- Has your partner discouraged or prevented you from working or finishing your education?
- If you have a job has your partner embarrassed you or harassed you at work?
- Does your partner humiliate and, or embarrass you by making nasty comments in front of other people?
- Does your partner try to punish you by destroying or throwing away things that belong to you, perhaps favourite possessions from your childhood or family keepsakes?
- If you have children, does your partner seem to punish them unnecessarily as a way of getting back at you?
- Has your partner told you to make sure that the children and toys are cleared out of the way by the time he comes home?
- Has your partner ever threatened to kill himself, take, injure or kill you or the children to stop you from leaving him?
- Has your partner ever threatened you with a weapon? A kitchen knife or a walking stick? Or pointedly told you that you could easily fall down stairs or under a lorry and hint that nobody would know it wasn't an accident?
- Has your partner ever tried to, or made you, break the law in some way?
- Has your partner ever forced you to have sex against your will?

If you answered yes to more than a handful of the questions above, and it is in any way a common or regular occurrence, you are certainly not in a healthy relationship. If you answer yes to a lot of these questions, I think that you are being abused. As soon as you can, seek advice. If you and/or any children have been physically abused seek urgent assistance. The police can help and advise, even if it is only to put you in touch with a women's refuge. The National Domestic Violence Hotline **Freephone 0808 2000 247** is a very good first point of contact.

Physical abuse never goes away, it just increases in frequency, extent, duration and injury.

Preparing to leave

If you think you may have to leave the house to protect yourself and/or your children you should be ready to go. You don't want to walk out of the house at 2 am on a January morning with the kids and 42 pence in your pocket.

If you contact the hotline or the local police, they should be able to arrange for you and your children to stay in the family home, and for your abusive partner to find alternative accommodation. It may mean that you have to move to a women's shelter for a while.

If the abuse is serious enough for you to have to leave the house for your own or your children's safety, make some preparations. Don't make it obvious but quietly collect what you need. Below are some suggestions.

- Warm coats ready in the hall where they are kept anyway.
- Spare house and car keys held by a close relative or very close and trustworthy friend.
- As much money as you can find – enough for a taxi, or a few nights in a small hotel until you get the matter resolved with the local housing authority. A relative or very close friend could hold that for you.
- Collect the phone numbers for the National Hotline, women's refuge, social services, council housing department, relatives, police domestic crime team and so on – again possibly held by that relative or close friend.
- If possible, spare clothes for you and your children. They can still be in the airing cupboard or wardrobe, but stacked ready to take. You might not have time to sort out three or four outfits, if they are stacked ready you can just grab them and go if you need to.
- Documents that you might need: cheque book, benefit book, doctor's card, hospital appointment cards, birth certificates, passport etc. They are probably all kept in the same place, but if they were in a bundle with an innocent elastic band around them, they would be easy to grab if you had to leave in a hurry.
- If you have children don't forget to include a few special toys or objects for

them. Having their favourite teddy bear or red jumper will be a comfort to them in several ways.

- Take anything else that you might need. For example, make sure that prescription medicine is collected together ready to take in a hurry if you need to.

All of this will fill a sizeable bag or even a small case. Don't collect these items and then leave them next to the front door where they will be seen or found. Don't allow your preparations to trigger another rage or beating. If your cases are usually kept in a back room, you could leave the case there but start packing the things you need into it so it is ready to go. You may be able to take one or two items at a time and ask a relative or close friend to hold them for you. In confidence tell them what they are for and tell them why you might need them. They will have to agree to being woken at any time of the day or night for you to collect your necessities.

When assault happens

Many women stay in an abusive relationship for the sake of the children, but children see and know far more than parents think. They can feel the tension and often see the verbal and physical abuse or lie in bed listening to the arguments. If they do they will already be unhappy, anxious and even depressed. Faced with an ongoing abusive relationship it is better for them if you leave so you can all feel safe, rather than put up with the abuse to maintain the illusion of a family.

Especially where children are involved, you must not suffer in silence, because things almost always get worse. Find a safe way to call the hotline, or call the police to deal with the abuser. Domestic violence is an assault and the abuser will be arrested and charged. Don't leave any children at home unless your plan involves pretending to go to the shops but coming back with the police.

Seek expert advice and follow it. Many victims weaken when the abuser realises that their violence and abuse may have broken the relationship. Many abusers do love their partner, but they simply cannot control their suspicion, anger, temper and violence. If they realise that they might lose you, they often cry and declare that it will never happen again. Experience says that no matter what the promise, an abuser will abuse again.

Call the police. Explain the situation to trusted neighbours and even give them permission to call the police if they see or hear a dispute or fight; their intervention may stop a bad situation from getting worse.

What Men Can Do

I am hoping that men will have read this chapter and have a tiny bit more of an insight into what it is like to be a woman. Perhaps they now realise how worrying it may be just walking home from the bus stop after dark. Men should see how upsetting it could be to a woman or even a couple of women if a group of lads are 'just having a laugh' on the train.

I am hoping that men will see how what they see as innocent behaviour can make a woman feel threatened. There are things that men can do which will make women feel safer.

- Men should accept that under some circumstances a woman may be intimidated by, concerned about, or actually scared of an innocent man or group of men.

- Men must maintain their own awareness to avoid muggers, for example. At the same time, use that awareness to recognise the circumstances where a woman may be intimidated simply by your male presence. Where possible modify your behaviour to put her mind at rest, or at least reduce her fear.

- When you are in a group, with your increased understanding of the vulnerability and possible worry a woman may be feeling, be aware. If there is a woman or group of women in the vicinity and you and your friends are a little too lively, calm your group down. If they are drunk and beyond calming, get them talking about something that will take all of their concentration, something important like who will win the match at the weekend, or the far more weighty pizza or kebab question. Acknowledge the woman/women with an apologetic nod or shrug and go on your way.

- If you are walking in the same direction as a woman on her own or after dark, you know that she may be worried that a man is following her. Don't walk behind her; cross the road and walk on the other side or even consider taking a different route home.

- When getting on a train or bus, unless it is the only seat available, don't select the seat opposite or beside a woman. By sitting near a woman on an otherwise empty bus or train you will be invading her 'safety zone'. Sit a few seats away and even if you think she is attractive, don't keep looking at her or trying to talk to her.

- Realise how threatening simple actions can be. Staring/ogling, whistling, passing comments and jostling can be threatening to a woman, particularly when men are in a group. Actually, while we are on the subject, don't shout crude comments at passing women at all; only losers do that.

- If you are thinking of chatting to a woman alone, for example at a bus stop or railway station, remember that she won't know you mean no harm, so think again. On the other hand, if you sit silently staring at her, you will worry her more than if you said something. Try an innocent, 'Have I missed the number seven?' If she clearly doesn't want to talk, don't push it.

- If you are in a vehicle and are driving past a lone woman, remember that you can easily scare her. If you slow down and stop behind or beside her she will probably be worrying that you might want to attack her. If you need to stop, be courteous and stop some way behind her so that she won't feel threatened.

- If you see a woman in trouble, don't run up to her. The sight of a strange man running up could really scare her. By all means offer assistance, but do it in a non-threatening way. For example:
  - If she is being attacked, run to help but shout to make her aware of what you are doing and why. Repeat her call to somebody to call the police, and make it clear that you are coming to assist her not to assist the attacker. Shout something like, 'Hey you! Leave her alone! Help! Call the police' so she knows you are on her side.
  - Your intention should be to chase the attacker away before he can cause harm.
  - Have your mobile ready to use. Stop a few paces away from the woman outside her personal space and ask if she is OK. Hand her your mobile phone making sure that any locks are released and tell her to call the police. People in shock don't react well to advice, so give her an instruction: 'Dial 999 and get the police.'
  - If you do tell the woman to call the police, make sure she knows where she is – tell her the location.
  - If other assistance is coming consider chasing the attacker. If you don't want to risk it or the attacker has already run off, stay with the victim and

call the police yourself. If you think she may need an ambulance ask for one at the same time. Be ready to give police a description of the attacker, what he wore, and which way he went. Tell the police that the offender ran off, and a dog may be able to track him if the area is quiet.

- ➢ Protect any evidence at the scene and don't let other people contaminate it. For example a police dog will be able to track the offender as long as dozens of passers by haven't been walking back and forth where the offender made off. Don't let a spectator stand on the tissue he dropped, or pick up the bottle he was holding.

- ➢ Stay with the victim, and protect her from further assault or attack. It has been know for a light-fingered bystander to take a victim's handbag while she lay waiting for an ambulance.

- ➢ Allow one woman or person she knows to comfort her, again to minimise contamination of evidence.

- ➢ Stay with her and keep talking calmly, keep saying things like, 'He's gone', 'You're OK', 'The police are coming, don't worry.' Reassurance is important now.

- ➢ If other people are around, send two of them to the main road or junction to flag down the police and, or ambulance when they turn up, so that help arrives as soon as possible.

- ➢ Depending on who was around at the time of the incident try to keep potential witnesses at the scene until the police arrive. If somebody looks like they are going to walk away, speak to them yourself or assign somebody to go and talk to them. Say something like, 'What did you see? The police want to talk to you.' At least get their name and address, but if possible keep them at the scene.

- ➢ Remain until you have spoken to the police and the victim has been safely taken away.

• As a male, and with your new insight to the problems and worries a woman alone may have, be more considerate of female friends, colleagues and family members by giving them a lift or walking them home when you can. If you do, make sure they are safely indoors before you leave.

• Lastly, challenge the loutish, crude, and stupid actions, comments or behaviour of other men. You know that it isn't mature, clever or funny. Make sure that they know it isn't acceptable at all.

7 Mostly Your Children

This book has been written for adults. I assume that many of you will either have your own children, or have some input into the guidance and development of a niece, nephew, godchild or other young relative. I have included this chapter to discuss some of the threats facing young people, and to propose a few countermeasures that you or the child can take to avoid the relevant risks and threats.

I have assumed that children will not read this book. I assume that you as an adult will learn from this chapter and teach them what you think they need to know in a way and at a pace that is suitable to you both. I use a very simple definition of child – and that is anyone who is not an adult.

As an adult, you can be as security conscious and careful as you like, but children can ruin your security by losing keys or going out to play and leaving doors and widows open. When they are small they have no sense of fear, so they can wander off, talk to strangers or otherwise cause you distress. As they get older you have to start letting them explore the world and build their own character. Older still and they may want to experiment with glue sniffing, tobacco, alcohol or illegal drugs.

All of these activities have an impact on your life and security, peace of mind and happiness. You can lock your valuable watch in a safe to keep it secure, you can immobilise your car to stop thieves driving it away, but children present a unique problem. You have to help a child to grow into an independent person, which means that they have to be allowed increasing freedom to find their own path in life. You can still guide and advise them, but there comes a time when you have to allow them to go out into the world to take their own chances and hope that the life skills you have given them will keep them safe.

Child care experts have written many books and papers but this book simplifies and summarises some key points for you, offering common sense precautions that you can take to protect you and your children from harm.

Not my child!

Most parents will be thinking that their children would never be allowed to come to harm or cause any harm. We all think that, but you only have to read a few newspapers to see that it is happening all the time all over the country to somebody's children. Therefore there has to be a risk that it could happen to *your children*. The more you know about the vulnerabilities, threats and risks the more you can do to make sure that it isn't your children.

Do you really know what is happening among the children in your street? Could it be that the little angels are not as pure and innocent as your think? As an eye opener, read the following points.

- When asked, nearly 75% of parents stated that drugs were not available in their area. They were wrong; drugs are quite readily available everywhere in the UK if you know where to ask – and kids usually know where to ask!

- In one survey, nearly 30% of all children asked stated that they had on occasion carried a knife as a weapon.

- In the same survey, nearly 60% of children who had been excluded from school admitted that they frequently carried a knife as a weapon.

- Among children who had been mugged (been a victim of a street robbery) about 45% admitted that they now regularly carried a knife as a weapon to defend themselves.

- In England and Wales, 176,000 young people between the ages of 10 and 17 were found guilty of, or cautioned for, serious crimes including burglary, assault, robbery and fraud.

- By the age of 19, nearly 40% of UK children admit that they have tried illegal drugs.

- By the age of 15, nearly 50% of children say they drink alcohol regularly.
- In 85% of cases of child sexual abuse the attacker is known to the child and the family.
- In 2002, statistics show that 142,900 juveniles were cautioned by police for crimes ranging from theft (54,000), drug offences (45,000), to violent assault (23,000).
- Statistics seem to show that at least 20% of children who come to police attention go on to commit more crimes.
- In traffic accidents 12% of casualties are aged 15 or under. 12% of casualties are pedestrians. 4% of casualties are cyclists.
- More pedestrians are injured in road accidents between 3.30 and 6 pm than at any other time of the day.
- Nearly 26,000 children are on child protection registers. They are registered under different categories. For example, 34% are held under the neglect category, 17% physical injury, 7% sexual abuse and 13% emotional abuse.
- Half of all crime committed in the UK is committed by people who are under 21 years of age.

Don't get too tied up in the statistics. I included them only to show you that in every sense, crime by and against children is a bigger problem than most people realise. One final thought – no matter how grown up you think your child is – a child is by definition immature and irresponsible. As an adult, you have a duty and responsibility to protect your child and raise them to be responsible citizens.

Bullying

There have been some horrific cases where bullying has been the cause of a child or young person taking their own life. For a long time, schools denied the existence of bullying or stated that if it existed there was nothing they could do about it.

Luckily, things have changed, and there is something that can be done. The problem has been identified and every education authority, school and council are actively supporting schemes to defeat bullying. When bullying is reported, there are defined procedures that should be followed, teachers and schools should no longer ignore or dismiss complaints.

What is bullying?

I have seen a number of definitions, all much the same, but none seemed to me to be complete. They describe actions that could be termed bullying, but by defining a list they exclude other actions that are just as bad.

I would define bullying as any action or inaction that repeatedly causes a child to suffer loss, distress, emotional or physical harm, injury, pain or worry. A bully can do this in person or sometimes by mobile phone, telephone call or text message, email or any other means. That includes any of the usual bullying activities:

- Name-calling; picking on somebody because they are tall, skinny, fat, have a disablity, have a prominent mole or birthmark, unusual hair colour, wear inexpensive and unfashionable clothing, have unusual parental circumstances, appear to be of lower intelligence, in fact anything!
- Stealing, damaging or destroying the victim's things. For example, hiding school bags or throwing them off a train or bus while it is moving, pouring salt onto their dinner, taking their pocket or dinner money, stealing football boots or other equipment, letting the tyres down on a bike.
- Ganging up on a child and forcing him or her to do things against their will, for example beating them up, pushing them into the stream or a bramble patch, tearing a school uniform, or spraying ketchup on them at lunchtime.

How do I know?

The easiest way of finding out if your child is being bullied is if they tell you. Unfortunately, children rarely confide in parents or any other adult, though that is beginning to change. Admitting to being bullied is embarrassing to a child, an admission of defeat, an inability to cope when they are trying hard to prove to you how grown up they are. There is also the chance that the bully has threatened them with even worse treatment if they report the bullying.

When a child is being bullied their mood and behaviour can change quite radically, so there are usually clues to the fact that everything is not right. For example a child may display some of the following:

- Suddenly not wanting to go to school at all, sometimes pretending to go but spending the day in the local town centre or library, or even pretending to be too ill to go to school.
- Begging for a lift to and from school (especially if the bully picks on them on the way to and from school).
- Coming home with missing items, or torn clothes, and cuts and bruises for which they offer no explanation or an obviously false one. When you ask how it happened, they might become more even upset and evasive.
- Appearing to be withdrawn, depressed, not like their usual self. You may think they are sickening for something, or avoiding a maths test, but the state continues.
- Changing behaviour. For example, a boy might change from an active lad who plays football as long as there is light to play, to refusing to leave his room.
- Taking things. Some children are bullied into giving things to the bullies, so you may find money missing from your purse, a mobile phone or chocolate and cans of drink etc missing from the kitchen. If anything goes missing and you ask the child about it, they may become angry or run to their room crying.
- Getting a bad report. School work may suffer, and a child who usually gets good reports may suddenly get a report saying that they don't concentrate on their work, are failing to do homework, and the quality of their work is failing.
- Not being able to sleep. Some may start wetting the bed. It is even possible that some will start to sleep walk, or have bad dreams and scream or talk in their sleep.

What can I do?

You know your child so you can take the action most appropriate for them, bearing in mind that they may be in an unusually fragile state because of the bullying, worry, stress and lack of sleep.

Bullying – countermeasures

- ✓ Talk to them. Ask what they did at school today. Ask if they enjoyed it, what their best lesson was, and if they did art today. Did they have any problems? Because they can always talk to you about any problems that they have. By talking about the day you give them the opportunity to ease into the fact that they aren't entirely happy at school.

- ✓ If you don't get the information volunteered to you, the experts advise that you make a direct approach. Ask the child directly if anyone is bullying them, making sure that you remain calm and show that you want to support them and stop the bullying. Stress that you will not march up to the head teacher during assembly and demand to know 'who is bullying our little Jimmy'.

- ✓ Explain to the child that you know that bullies exist and assure them that there is something that can be done.

- ✓ When they do talk to you, reassure them that they are doing the right thing. Most children want to avoid telling on somebody else. Many children don't like breaking the secret by admitting what has been happening, especially if they have to admit that they have been taking money from your purse or dad's pockets to pay off the bully. Be understanding, and make absolutely sure that they know that they can talk to you about anything at any time. No matter what they tell you, you will still love and respect them.

- ✓ Find out what has been going on. When you know, make a note of it and approach the school. The school should want to know if Bobby Biggins is picking on the smaller kids and taking their dinner money. Start by talking to the class teacher or head teacher and talk to anyone else she may bring in. Explain what has been happening, how often it has been happening and where it is happening. If the head teacher knows that Bobby Biggins is robbing little kids at the back of the games hall at lunchtime, she can make an appearance and bring his criminal career to an abrupt halt. The teachers can keep a special eye on your child and on Bobby Biggins to stop him finding a new target or venue for his activities.

- ✓ Write down what happened. Include specifics such as names, places, dates and times. Memories can fade and stories change and discussions between a child and their parents can alter beyond recognition from the comfort of a child's bedroom to the formality of a school office.

Keep records of ongoing problems. A diary is a good way of retaining information in a formal and organised way. (That diary may have to be copied or handed over as part of your evidence so don't use your own diary, but a diary you use just for recording incidents.)

- ✓ Make sure that you and your child stick with the facts. You and the child have to be honest and accurate. You may be tempted to say it happens every day, to pressure the teachers into doing something. If at a later stage any lies or exaggerations are discovered in what either of you have said, everything you have claimed and said will be viewed with suspicion. Be honest; that's all you have to do. Even if it only happened once. Tell the truth.

- ✓ When you talk to the head and other teachers:
    - ➤ Stay calm. You have only just found out about it, so they might not know that they have a bully in the school.
    - ➤ Explain what you have found out. Give the head teacher the bullies' names; explain what they have been doing to your child; describe incidents and any other children who may have been involved as either victims or bullies.
    - ➤ Ask what the school anti-bullying policy is and ask to see a copy of it.
    - ➤ Ask what they will do to stop the bullying and help your child. For example they could agree to look out for bullying when they know who is responsible. They could offer to keep a careful watch over your child. They could give a special anti-bullying assembly to remind bullies and victims that bullying will not be tolerated in the school.
    - ➤ Make arrangements for another meeting, or telephone contact to discuss progress. Be specific, not just 'sometime in a couple of weeks or so.' Make a specific appointment, for example 9.30 am on Tuesday 27th November, which will be attended by you, the head teacher and the class teacher. Formalise this by sending a letter, confirming the appointment and the purpose of the meeting. Consider copying your complaint to the school board of governors if it appears that the head teacher is not doing all they can to resolve the problem.
    - ➤ If the school will not co-operate, refuses to accept that there is a problem, or does nothing about it when you have reported it, take it further. Give the school a final chance. Warn them that unless they take action you are going to take it to a higher authority. Write a letter which includes details of what the bully has been doing. Give dates, circumstances, threats, injuries etc. Include in that letter names of the school officials and teachers who you have contacted, give dates and time scales, including any broken promises and failure to make contact or attend meetings. Copy the letter and send it to the last person who failed to take action. Escalate it further by sending a copy to the school governors.
    - ➤ If they don't act in a reasonable time scale, update the letter with the most recent failures, copy it to the head teacher and governors and . . .

- the chief officer of the local education authority – if he doesn't take action in a reasonable time scale, update the letter with the most recent failures, copy it to the head teacher, the governors and the chief officer of the local education authority and repeat the process sending it to . . .
- your local MP . . .
- the child protection office of the local police force . . .
- the national press.

✓ When you have spoken to the head teacher, make sure that your child has a point of contact who has been informed of the situation, who they can go to and report any bullying when it happens.

✓ If the bullying is happening outside school, the head teacher will still like to know, so that they can do all they can to stop it. You can help by taking the bullies' opportunity away, and arranging to take and collect the child from school. Even if you can't because of work commitments or other problems, you can always explain the circumstances in confidence to a trusted neighbour or relative, so that your child is escorted and beyond the reaches of the bully. Depending on circumstances, the child can possibly be escorted by an older brother, sister, cousin or even (with the knowledge and permission of neighbours) a neighbour's older child.

✓ When one child stands up and speaks out about a bully, others often find the courage to do so and evidence of bullying can become easier to collect. The more evidence there is the more chance there is that something can actually be done.

✓ Make sure that your child knows that they can help themselves by staying where there are lots of other people. If they go to some quiet corner of the school field at lunchtime, they will give the bully a chance to intimidate them. If they stay in the playground near the buildings where teachers and other school staff are watching they will be safer.

✓ Don't isolate your child. By escorting them to school and back, you may accidentally isolate them from their friends. If at all possible, talk quietly to the parents of your child's friends. Don't identify bullies, just explain that there have been incidents and what you have done about it. Explain that you don't want to isolate your child and ask them if it is OK for their child to come to and from school with you and your child, or if they will agree to take your child with them. Ask them if their child can come to your home after school to play. Allow them to play in the garden and anywhere near the house, where they can come home for protection if a disgruntled bully turns up. Do what you can to make life normal for your child.

✓ If the bully does try to make trouble out of school, make a note of what they do and report it to the school. If the bully throws stones at you or your child, spray paints the garage door or sends text messages threatening revenge for the trouble they are in, report them to the police.

✓ Never fight back with violence. That could leave you in a lot of trouble.

✓ Never join them. Some children are tempted to join the bullies to pick on another child to stop the bullies picking on them. Remind them how bad it felt when they were being bullied; talk it through so that they realise that they don't want to impose that on another child.

My child is a bully

If you are being told that your child is a bully, don't panic. There are some things that you can do. The first reaction of most parents is that the accusations are wrong, because their child could never be a bully. They loudly deny the claims and become determined to ignore the false claims they feel are being made.

Step 1: Listen. Don't dismiss such accusations, but don't accept them at face value either. Don't become defensive, keep an open mind and listen to the accusations that are being made. Remain calm and ask the accuser:

- to describe what happened (it may be that an overprotective parent is describing normal playground rough and tumble as bullying).

- to explain where any incident happened (if an incident happened on a rugby pitch it may just be over-exuberant play).

- to describe the source of the information (if the source of the information is a teacher or playground supervisor there is a level of validity to the information. If the only source of the information is another child, it is *possible* that that child is a bully and trying to get other children into trouble).

- to describe the alleged bullying behaviour (it should be clear from the circumstances and description of the behaviour if it was acceptable or not).

- to explain the cause of the alleged bullying (depending on the age of the child, the cause may have been the sharing of a toy, jealousy about a new bicycle, a confrontation between rival football supporters, name calling about a disability or physical characteristic, an argument about which boy is interested in which girl, or any number of causes).

- to describe the alleged victim(s) (most bullies pick on easy targets: younger, smaller, weaker children, those with a disability, poor children who don't wear the latest designer clothes and don't have the latest must-have gadget. It is highly unlikely that an eight-year-old boy is bullying a 14 year old – though it isn't unheard of where the older child has a mental or physical disability, or other health problem).

- to explain if this is a single incident or part of an ongoing problem (if there are sketchy reports about an alleged single incident, there is scope for monitoring the situation at least. If there is evidence of ongoing bullying of a number of younger and smaller children, possibly connected with stealing money or property, damaging clothing and property, and humiliating the victims, something has to be done).
- Listen calmly to the answers to your questions and, if necessary . . .

Step 2: Make a decision. You have heard the evidence and seen the proof. Review it and try to decide if the three elements of bullying are present.

- Bullying can be defined as any action, inaction or behaviour that repeatedly causes a child to suffer loss, distress, emotional or physical harm, injury, pain or worry.
- The victim actually feels threatened and upset by the bullying.
- The victim fears that the bullying will continue.

If the accusations seem to point to a single argument and resulting name calling, or over-ambitious tackles in playground football, don't dismiss them. The accuser is genuinely concerned and only wishes to protect the alleged victim, just as you would want to protect your child.

Appease the accuser; try to find common ground, and to look for a mutually acceptable solution. For example if your child does tend to launch into over-aggressive tackles in playground football, talk to them. Remind them that playground football is just a friendly game and though you admire their spirit and commitment, under the circumstances they should probably not play so hard! For a while monitor the situation, make sure that their natural skill, exuberance and enthusiasm doesn't make them go back to hard tackles.

On the other hand, if there is genuine bullying, you need to address the issue.

Step 3: Discuss with the child. If you have accepted that there does seem to be evidence that your child is or has been bullying other children, you have to find why they have been behaving in this way.

The easiest way to do that is to speak to the child. Find a quiet time and place to sit and talk. Don't start making accusations, don't lose your temper and don't threaten the child. Remember that it is just possible that they are being bullied and forced to do it.

Discuss the matter openly and calmly. Explain and describe the bullying actions that have been reported. When confronted many bullies either blame the victim or act like the victim themselves. Many cry and claim that the victim provoked the incident or that it was an accident. In some cases it may be true, in others it is not; you have to resolve the issue.

Make sure that the child understands that bullying is wrong and unacceptable. Explain that the victim is really scared, intimidated and upset then ask the child what they would feel like if they were being bullied. Talk it through and try to get them to consider what they would feel like if they were being bullied.

Don't demand a confession. Don't make the child feel as though he or she is on trial. When you have described the alleged incidents that have been reported to you, ask them to describe the incident in their own words. The victim may have exaggerated the incident, or mistakenly identified your child.

When the child describes what they did and said, pick up any actions or behaviour that could intimidate or scare another child, but still avoid accusations. For example you could say, 'I see, a little child could be scared if somebody runs off with his school bag. If you play like that with your friends they might laugh, but the juniors are probably scared about that.' The child may not be deliberately bullying another child, they may just not have recognised or considered the effect their actions could have on the other child. It may be that the parents of a child have spoiled them by giving in to everything they want, so they have little concept of sharing; if they want something they take it.

If that is the case you must show them how to join in with other children, to share and wait their turn. Point out that pushing, taking, demanding, name calling and so on are not acceptable. You know the child; use the best method you have to explain and/or demonstrate what you mean. If your child considers him or herself to be mature, you might get a better result by casually mentioning that such behaviour is rather childish or better still that the more mature approach would be to share or step back and 'let the little kids' take a turn.

The best approach is to make sure that you teach your child about good manners, co-operation and waiting their turn so that sharing comes naturally to them. Praise them when they play and share with other children and if there is any sign of selfishness or bullying, intervene gently.

Step 4: Talk to the school. Whether you accept that your child is a bully or not, you have to talk to the head or form teacher, or head of year at the school. Either to explain that you think the accusations are a misunderstanding or a form of bullying themselves, or that you accept that your child's behaviour could be considered to be bullying. Some children accuse others of bullying as another form of bullying and intimidation.

If you genuinely think your child is totally blameless you have to talk to somebody at the school to resolve the issue. You would have to pass on your child's explanation of the incident. Accept that realising that they may be in trouble with you, your child may have understated their involvement or the nature of the incidents.

Keep one idea in mind. If your child is participating in bullying in any way, you want to know as soon as possible so that you can take remedial action. Allowing a child to develop into a bully will certainly create ongoing problems for you and your family. Allowing the child to be a bully will create major problems for the child in family life, social situations, relationships and future work scenarios. Having said that, don't forget the stress that a bully will be inflicting on their current and potential victims.

If you accept that the child is a bully or is at least exhibiting some behaviour that is selfish and intimidating you need to stop it.

> *Billy Basher has been accused of bullying. In computer class, Quentin Quiet was always slow with the answers, and when the teacher wasn't listening Billy told the children around him that Quentin was stupid. Later in the class Billy Basher sent a computer message to everyone in the class saying Quentin Quiet was stupid and had fleas in his hair. After class, other children wouldn't walk near Quentin because they said he had fleas. Billy laughed and said Quentin was stupid and dirty. By lunchtime children from other classes were asking if Quentin really did have fleas. Quentin tried to resolve the problem by chasing Billy across the school playground. He caught up with him at the toilet block where Quentin Quiet held the front of Billy's shirt and demanded that Billy Basher should tell everyone that he didn't have fleas. By this time other children were gathered around but they were laughing at Billy this time. Billy didn't like being held against the wall by Quentin so he kicked Quentin in the legs, then punched him several times to make him let go. Other boys were excited and cheering. Billy Basher then chased and hit Quentin a few more times amid applause from other children. Then a teacher came over and took them both to the head teacher.*

- Make sure that the child knows you still love them, but at the same time that the bullying behaviour is unacceptable.
  - Name calling of any kind – picking on somebody who is less able in some way.
  - Spreading lies about somebody – such as saying they are dirty and have fleas.
  - Hitting and kicking; chasing somebody and hitting or kicking them just to play to an audience.
  - Isolating somebody by spreading lies and making other people avoid that person.
- Discuss the incidents that have been reported with your child and point out precisely the actions, words and behaviour that are unacceptable.
- When pointing out what is unacceptable, describe and discuss more acceptable responses. Stay calm. Don't lose your temper. Try not to make the child feel 'stupid' or abnormal.
  - Is Billy better with computers than Quentin?
  - Is Quentin better than Billy at other things, for example in Maths classes or sports?

- Make the child understand that some people are good at one thing and not so good at another. Somebody who is a good football player may not be good at long distance running. Somebody who gets high marks at mathematics may be at the bottom of the class in art.
- Ask Billy how he felt when Quentin chased him and held him against the wall. Ask Billy how he felt when the other children came and started laughing at him. When he says he didn't like it, ask him to describe what he didn't like about it. Listen to what he says, and make a note of a few key words or phrases. For example Billy may say he felt humiliated, helpless or stupid.
- Discuss those feelings, and now ask Billy if he thinks that Quentin may have felt humiliated, helpless or stupid when Billy was picking on him because he wasn't very good with computers, or when Billy told everyone Quentin was dirty and had fleas?
- Make sure that Billy understands how badly Quentin probably felt in those circumstances.

* Talk through how the situation developed. Show how the possibly innocent comment about Quentin and his ability with computers could have upset him. Show how further name calling and accusations about fleas could have made Quentin feel really bad. Make sure Billy knows that friends can make jokes, but a joke can be taken too far. Try to make Billy accept that he should consider the effect of things he says and does and how they could easily hurt the feelings of somebody else. Remind him how badly he felt when the other children were laughing at him.

* Take a look at your own behaviour; is it possible that you are sometimes rather overbearing? Could the child think that bullying is OK because you are a bully, intimidating neighbours, shop staff and other customers and relatives to get what you want?

* Talk through how different situations can be handled.
  - Watch for the reaction of people around you. The rest of the class may think comments about being stupid or having fleas are funny, but what about the reaction of the person you are picking on?
  - Join in with general joking and play, but don't pick on one person or group of people. Realise that words can hurt just as much as being kicked. Know when to stop.

- Be mature enough to realise when a joke is going too far and be big enough to stop it and apologise if necessary.
- Be mature enough to recognise and challenge inappropriate behaviour in others. Don't stay in the crowd and run with the pack just because it is easier to do that than to stand up and say no.
- Don't retaliate and either pick on somebody else or resort to physical violence if you are cornered.
- If you are being bullied, or you know that somebody else is being bullied, use the school procedures to resolve it. Most schools and other children's and teenager groups and clubs have defined programmes and procedures for handling bullying. Ask a teacher or visit the school library and ask what the policy and procedures are for bullying. Follow the procedures, talk to the class teacher, any teacher you know well, talk to your parents. Talk to anyone, but talk to someone.

Step 5: Define a solution. Whatever the incident, frequency or accusation, something has happened to make you work through this process. You must now define and work towards a solution.

In the over-ambitious playground football tackle example above you might agree a two-part solution.

- First, persuade the child to be less aggressive in playground tackles.
- Second, ask the school football coach if there is a possibility of the child joining a team and being coached in football to channel that winning spirit into the game as opposed to unwanted aggression.

In the example where Billy Basher was verbally and then physically picking on Quentin Quiet there might be a multi-step solution.

- Discuss the situation with Billy to make him realise that name calling can humiliate and upset somebody. Make Billy realise that by saying Quentin was stupid and telling people he was dirty and had fleas he was making Quentin very upset, worse than the way Billy felt when the other children were laughing at him. (Or remind him how upset he was on some other occasion, such as if his pet rabbit died, or his new bike was stolen.)

- Discuss the physical assault with Billy, and make him realise that physical attacks are never acceptable.

- Make peace with Quentin and his parents, possibly inviting them around. The parents can have a meal, and Billy can use some of his computer skills to help Quentin with his computer lessons and homework so he does better in that class.

- Include the school in the process so that they know what is being done. At the same time the families should sign up to the concepts and goals of the anti-bullying programme in the school.

- With their first-hand understanding of the effects of bullying, Quentin and Billy could become pupil ambassadors for the anti-bullying programme in the school. Some schools actually run pupil forums, which deal with conflicts and disputes on an informal level.

- Bullies often have poor social skills. They lack the ability to understand another person's feelings. They need to learn to be kind, caring, and compassionate.

- Don't protect a bully, or by inaction encourage bullying. By stopping the bullying you will benefit the victims, you and your family and the bully.

Step 6: The long term. With the incident either resolved or on the way to being resolved, you should make sure that your child understands what to do when they encounter bullying.

- Ask them what behaviour constitutes bullying to make sure that they understand the concept.

- If there is a group, ask them to role play different situations to describe bullying.

- Ask them who they would go to in school or their youth group or club if they suffered from, or identified, bullying.

- Have a copy of the school bullying policy handy and make sure that everybody knows and understands the serious consequences if bullying continues.

- Work on the child's social skills. It has been found that bullies can seem to be quite popular in school. This is often because other children are being friendly because they are too scared to shun or avoid the bully, not because they like the bully or seek their company. Generally, bullies have poor social skills and as part of that they lack the ability to identify and associate with another person's feelings. They need to learn to be kind, caring, and compassionate.

- Some researchers claim that bullies have difficulty in reading body language and understanding how people around them feel and are reacting to them. Bullies are therefore selfish, only caring about how *they* feel. They can't empathise with the victim or understand how upset they may be. Bullies may need to be taught how to read non-verbal signs in other people, possibly by role play. Make it a game. Say, 'I like you, I want you to be my friend,' try it in several ways. Use a bored voice and turn away in an absent-minded way. Use an angry voice and clench your fists. Use a laughing, mocking voice and sneer when you say it. Try to get the child to look beyond the words; help them to practise reading the bigger message instead of just what is being said.

- Bullies need to be taught and encouraged to identify and consider the feelings of those around them. They need to be taught about sharing, friendship, consideration and empathy.

- In some cases, the parents may need to create a less aggressive and angry atmosphere at home. Children copy the behaviour patterns of their parents. Make sure you are not inadvertently teaching them hostility and aggression. Parents should not be aggressive towards each other, by not arguing, not losing their tempers and not fighting with each other.

- Don't allow the child to watch violent films and programmes on television or play violent computer games.

- Don't use physical force as a punishment for the child. Is the message you are giving them that the bigger person gets what he wants, that strength wins, might is right, violence is acceptable?

- In some cases, giving a child responsibility for a pet will help them to learn appropriate attitudes, caring and nurturing. Taking care of a helpless pet rabbit or hamster could help.

- Consider getting a child interested in groups or clubs that encourage sharing and learning. Cubs and scouts are usually good, but school groups and clubs can be just as valuable especially if they relate to an interest the child already has. For example astronomy, stamp collecting, bird watching or swimming.

- If the child has any particular skills you should encourage them to help others. By volunteering to help younger children to make model aircraft, or by raising money for charity by participating in a sponsored cycle ride, your child will benefit from a selfless act. You can then play up their accomplishment in, for example, raising £75 towards special equipment for disabled children.

Child Abuse

No matter how much you don't want it to, child abuse exists, and very often someone the child knows who is doing the abusing. Abuse frequently causes severe problems for the child when the cumulative effects of the abuse surface in later life.

Child abuse can be physical, sexual, and emotional, and also abuse from neglect.

Possible signs

The longer the abuse has been allowed to continue the more signs of that abuse there will be. When viewing the possible indicators of child abuse listed below, I urge you to use *extreme caution*.

One indication of child abuse is that a child could suddenly be very reluctant to visit their Grandpa George, or Uncle Harry. **Don't jump to conclusions** if this happens, because there are a million other explanations, which have nothing to do with abuse. For example, if Grandpa George fell asleep on the last visit and the child doesn't want to go again because he was bored silly while Grandpa was sitting in the armchair snoring. Similarly, Uncle Harry may have told the child off for breaking a window, or stopped them from playing near the river on their last visit, so the child would simply prefer to go somewhere that they can do what they want to without Uncle Harry spoiling their fun! Don't assume that the presence of any of these indicators means that somebody is abusing your child.

Remember that these indicators should *never* be taken in isolation. If one or two seem to apply to your child, take a closer look. If several of them seem to apply to your child, I suggest that you take them seriously and look into the matter further, but never, never, never jump to conclusions.

Mostly Your Children

- Physical injury, unexplained bruises, cuts, scratches.
- Inappropriate use of words or actions with a sexual or violent content.
- Possible comments from school about words or behaviour; sexual or violent drawings in art class.
- Withdrawal in both personality and actions, dropping friends and favourite pastimes, withdrawing to their room, spending a lot of time alone.
- Dislike or avoidance of normal hugs from mum or dad.
- Nightmares, bed-wetting and other sleep disruption.
- Refusing to eat, or demanding certain foods.
- Refusing to go to school, or leaving for school but never arriving, or staying as long as possible at school.
- Fighting, temper tantrums, destructive behaviour.
- Threatening to or actually running away from home.
- Sudden character changes, becoming disruptive, starting arguments or fights.
- Signs of stress at certain times – for example when Uncle Harry or Cousin Mary is mentioned (women can abuse children too).
- Self injury, self harming.
- Attempts at suicide which may be a half-hearted cry for help or a genuine attempt.
- Possible aggression towards others, becoming a bully, abusing smaller children.

Remember that any actions or behaviour that are out of character, and which reflect or mirror the sort of behaviour described in this list *might* indicate that the child has been abused. It might also be a sign that they are being bullied at school or that they have learning difficulties, or a number of other possibilities.

If in doubt, speak to the child. If you get nowhere seek expert advice.

Perhaps you may have concerns about a child at a house nearby, or one you see on your way to school with your child. If you have any evidence or concerns that a child is being abused, make a note of the circumstances and then report your concerns to the police, social services or the NSPCC.

General Child Protection Advice

Bullying or abuse will hopefully not be an issue for most children, but there are still some significant topics that a parent or carer must know about and try to teach the children in their care.

Stranger danger

Every parent and carer must teach their children about the possible dangers that they face from strangers. Just getting smaller children to understand the concept of 'strangers' is quite hard. There is no need to scare them, or make them feel that every single person in the world is a homicidal maniac! But you do have to make them understand that 'strangers' might be nasty.

Perhaps you could describe a stranger as somebody you do not know. No matter what they look like, no matter if they are friendly and helpful, and no matter if they say they have a puppy or that mum sent them.

- Teach your children that they should avoid talking to strangers, especially when there is nobody else around.

- On the other hand you want to teach them that if they get lost or in trouble, they are allowed to talk to some strangers. Make them understand the difference between talking to a guy in a raincoat lurking in the bushes, and talking to a husband and wife in the high street, or the lady behind the counter at the sweet shop. If you achieve that, you know that they will be happy to approach somebody safe to ask for help if they do get lost or hurt.

- Teach your child how to recognise somewhere that is safe. You can make it a little game with smaller children. While walking to school, or going shopping, talk about safe places. Point out standing with the school-crossing lady as a safe place. Point out the library as a safe place and go in to see where the person in charge sits so that the child knows that it is OK to go there. Make it a little game; get the child to guess which are safe places and which are not. Praise them if they get it right, and educate them if they get it wrong. Make a point of finishing on a high note – after they have picked two safe places in a row.

- Teach children about their personal safety zone. If you want to, tell them to imagine that they are in a big bubble, and that if strangers reach out towards them they will pop that bubble, which is something that they must avoid at all costs. Make the child realise that they are safer if they stay six feet away from people on foot or in vehicles. If the stranger comes closer move back to protect your bubble. If the stranger keeps coming run to somewhere safe!

- Teach them not to get into a car or any other vehicle with strangers, and not to get so close that they could be pulled in.

- Teach them that nasty people might try to trick them into coming close by asking for directions, saying they have a puppy in the car, or saying that mum or dad has asked them to come. Teach them that nasty people might even know their name, but whatever the nasty people do to trick them into going with them they should say *no* and run to a safe place.

- Teach your child that they own their body, and that nobody can touch them in a way they don't like.

- Teach them that some people, including people they know, may want to do things that they want to keep secret. Teach them that they have a right to say no to anyone, adult or child, who wants them to do something they don't want to do and that nothing has to be a secret from mum and dad.

- When they are ready, teach your child the difference between private and normal parts of their body. Teach them that normal areas of the body such as hands, head, shoulders are sometimes touched by other people when teaching them to write, playing or guiding them where they have to go. At the same time teach them which areas of their body are private, and explain that usually nobody should touch these areas. Explain that doctors and nurses sometime have to look at normal and private bits of the body to make you better when you are sick, but nobody else should be allowed to look at or touch them, or ask the child to touch their private areas.

- When the children are old enough, you can expand on the reason nasty people are nasty. You know your children, and you could take an opportunity if you have just read a book or watched a film with the nasty 'child catcher' in it. When they are ready, and when you feel it is right, you can explain that some adults are sick so they like to hurt children or take them away. Don't go into inappropriate details about paedophiles, just make them understand that a nasty man or woman could harm them badly.

- Teach your children that you can't always tell if somebody is a nice person or a nasty person. Teach them that they should suspect everybody, except those safe people you have practised picking out. For example, they can trust teachers they know, police officers in uniform, the school crossing guard, and the lady behind the till in a big shop.

- Teach your child to say no to anything that they don't like. For example, if a man says he is a teacher and wants the child to come into the bushes where somebody has left a toy. Teach the child that they don't necessarily have to obey any adult, no matter what authority or position they claim to have.

- Teach the child that if somebody does grab them, they should shout and scream, kick and bite, punch and scratch – anything to get away. That is going to surprise the one in a million people who do grab a child to stop them running under a bus, but they will understand.

- You are teaching your child to behave and obey teachers, and crossing guards, and the leader at the play centre, and the swimming pool guard and the referee, but sometimes they *can* disobey a grown up. Explain to them when they are able to really understand that when a teacher says, 'Stand still' or 'Come here', they should obey. But, if that nasty man or lady or bigger boy in the park tells them to come here, they are allowed to run away to a safe place, and they won't get into trouble for it. Then teach them that even some teachers do naughty things, and if a teacher wants to touch them, or wants the child to touch them, they can say no and tell you all about it.

- As soon as you can, teach your child how to use the telephone, so that they can call for help. They should know how to pick up the phone, dial 999, ask for the police, tell the operator what has happened, what their name is and where they are. They should hopefully know their name, address and a phone number where mum or dad can be contacted.

- Teach them that they should only trust a police officer in uniform, especially if they are in a marked police car or van. They should never trust somebody who is in normal clothes who pretends they are a police officer.

- Never ever make a police officer out to be bad. I have lost count of the times when I have been on duty and a parent has seen me approaching in full uniform and said something to their child like, 'If you don't behave the policeman will take you away.' Don't do it! You should want your child to think of a police officer in uniform as a safe haven from any problem or worry, not as a possible ogre who will take them away from mum and dad.

- Where a child has been abused, often the parent and/or child knew the abuser. Parents must be aware of stranger danger too – according to reports taken when children have been abducted or abused, the parents sometimes had an inkling that the person who did it was 'not quite right', 'a little strange', 'too good to be true' etc. A single man who offers to babysit, a couple who seem to take more interest in your children than you do. You have gut instincts – trust them!

- Teach your child that if anyone does ask them to go with them, try to touch them, offer them a ride in a car, ask them to look for a lost puppy etc, they should refuse. They should go and tell mum or dad, or a teacher or other safe person as soon as they can.

- By the time the child understands all of this, they will probably be old enough to be looking for a little bit of freedom. For example, wanting to go to the playing field with their friends or go to the shop to buy a comic. Now that they know about nasty people who they may or may not already know, they should understand and accept your request that they should always tell you where they are going, agree when they should be back and tell you who they are going with before they go anywhere.

- If you go anywhere new, especially if it is big, crowded or unusual, as soon as you arrive agree a meeting point in case you are separated. Look for a landmark at the venue and agree that if you are separated for any reason you will all immediately go to that place and meet up again. You may want to give all small children a card with your name and mobile phone number, as well as writing a description of your meeting place so that if they are found a 'safe' person can call you and arrange to meet up at the meeting place.

- If the child is lost at a large event or venue, seek help from the staff, stewards and marshals as soon as you can. The more people who are looking the better. As soon as you can involve the event managers, they can request all staff, particularly those manning exit gates, to look out for the lost child.

The Personal Security Handbook

Stranger danger – countermeasures

✓ In these days when most parents take their children to school and collect them by car, there is a chance that a stranger could tell a child that mum or dad has sent them to pick the child up. Tell the child that that is extremely unlikely, but that if they ever did ask somebody to pick them up, that person would know a code word that you have agreed. If the person offering the lift doesn't know the code word, the child should run to a teacher or other adult with children nearby and tell them. If the parent and child agree a code word now, that unlikely situation is catered for. Make the code word something that you will all remember and which will not arise in normal conversation and cannot be guessed. For example the code words 'Niagra Falls' might do if you had a really enjoyable holiday there.

✓ Make sure that where possible children always play in groups and are careful not to play alone in isolated places.

✓ Make sure children agree to come home at a certain time. Make them agree that no matter what time they have arranged to come home, if there are strong winds, thunder storms, heavy rain, or it gets dark earlier than expected, they should come home immediately. Unless they are with a friend in their house, and then the friend's mum or dad can call you to say where they are and how and when they will get home.

✓ Very few children are abused by strangers but they should realise that strangers, adults and big boys should never be allowed to join in with their games. If one of them hangs around and shouts or watches from a corner they should all go home and tell mum and say what the stranger was doing.

✓ Make sure that you talk to your children, and listen to what they are saying. They may not be able to put into words what they are thinking. They may not want to tell tales on somebody else. They may want to complain about what somebody has done to them or in front of them. Get into the habit of taking some time to talk to them and actually listening to what they have to say.

Knowing who the abusers are

Usually the police and other agencies will only inform members of the public if a known sex offender or other dangerous person is living in the area in rare and exceptional circumstances. The police and other agencies will be aware of their presence, and will monitor them bearing in mind any court orders and curfews.

Parents could ask any club or organisation that their child belongs to (such as kick boxing, brownies, children's summer camp) what their child protection policy is and the extent to which staff are trained and police checked. At least that will hopefully reassure them that all members of staff and volunteers have been checked and have no record of sexual abuse or violence.

Any properly-run organisation should have a written policy on staff checks and employment, which should be available to the parents. Having a policy is not enough though. Parents should satisfy themselves that the policy is adhered to. For example is the gym club teacher letting her teenage son (who has not been checked by police) help out on busy weekends? Be suspicious of any organisations that exclude adult spectators during sessions, particularly acting/modelling assignments. Take note of what is happening at training sessions. For example, have you given permission for your child's picture to be taken during swimming lessons? Who is taking the pictures and what will they be used for? Is the child's private piano/maths/whatever lesson occurring strictly behind closed doors – if so why?

Be healthily sceptical. Take an interest in what your child is doing or learning at the club. Drop in for an unannounced visit occasionally. Talk to your child, and ask them to explain what the lessons were today. Get them to show you what they had to do. If you have any suspicions take it further. If you have cause for concern follow it up; don't assume that that nice Mr Biggins couldn't possibly be doing anything wrong. He may have run the club for 30 years without complaint, but you might be the first parent in all that time to question what he is doing and discover that everything is not as it should be.

General advice to parents

- **Know where your children are**. As far as is possible try to know where your children are at all times. When they are babies you need to have them in your sight every moment, but as they mature and prove they are worthy of your trust, you can allow them more freedom. You don't have to keep track of them minute by minute, but even as they become teenagers, you should broadly know where they are and who they are with.
- **Know who their friends are**. If you take an interest, without quizzing them under bright lights, you should know who your children's friends are, where

they live and what they are interested in. Knowing that, you may need to impose some reasonable and explained restrictions on which houses your child can visit without you. For example, an eight year old may not be able to go to Jason's house alone, because he will have to cross three main roads to get there.

- **Get involved in your child's life**. By getting involved you will know what they are doing, what their moods are, what they like and dislike. All these things are critical to their safety. You have to know what normal behaviour is so that you can spot abnormal behaviour, which may be an indication of a problem.

- **Listen to your child**. Get to know how they talk and express themselves. When you know that, you will be in a better position to spot clues and nuances of speech which may indicate that they are trying to talk to your about something difficult. That 'something' may be bullying, illness, drugs or any number of important topics. Really listening will be worthwhile.

- **Watch what people do with your children and their reaction to them**. An abuser has to get close to a family and a child to make the opportunity for the contact that they crave. By being aware of how people approach your child, you can form an opinion as to how appropriate that might be, especially if the child is showing reluctance.

- **Teach your child that he can say no, or run away to protect himself**. We try to teach children to behave, to obey adults and to be polite, but we must also find a way to teach them to be clever! They have to obey mum and dad, they must do what a police officer or crossing guard tells them to do, and they must obey a teacher. They should also respect and obey other adults – usually. What if the teacher or babysitter is an abuser? What if the policeman is a kidnapper? Teach your child that their first priority is to stay safe.

- **Never leave a child alone in a car**. There are too many risks. The car may catch fire, the child may start the car or release a brake, the child could choke on a sweet, the child may be abducted or could suffer heat exhaustion and die in very hot weather. There are other risks; just don't do it.

- **Let everyone know if plans change**. You want your children to tell you if they decide to do something different, to go somewhere other than they said they were going, so I suggest that you return the favour. If your plans change or you are running late due to train cancellations or whatever, let the kids know. In that way, you inform them when you will be in, and prove that letting people know if your plans change is an acceptable and normal thing to do, not a rule you impose on them to humiliate and embarrass them in front of their friends.

- **Train them to be safe**. As soon as they are old enough, train them and reinforce that training by playing educational games when you are out. Get them to point out safe people who they would go to if they are ever hurt or in trouble. Praise them if they pick crossing guards or police officers, but be patient and explain why they are wrong if they pick strangers. Similarly, get them to pick safe places, police stations, hospitals, libraries, large supermarkets etc. You could also get them used to how a public telephone works so that they at least know the principles and can dial 999 if they need to. Make sure that they know their name and address, a telephone number where mum or dad can be contacted, and that they start getting to know the places you travel to. If they are lost but know where they are, at least they can say it is Tesco in Bracknell, rather than just 'a shop'.

Children and the Internet

The Internet is an amazing tool that can help children with homework, inspire them, stretch their minds and make them actually want to study and learn. The Internet also allows global communication between people to exchange ideas, chat and expand their horizons. Unfortunately at the same time the Internet has the potential to be a cesspool of crime, pornography and evil.

As a parent or carer, you can monitor and control access so that your children reap the benefits of a global library and communications device, but avoid the darker side of the Internet.

You and the Internet

I have heard many parents complain that when they were at school, computers were only just being introduced into the school secretary's office. Back then the children were never allowed near them or taught anything about them. Now it seems that children are born computer literate, and parents don't know what they are doing when the kids are sitting at their computer screen for hours on end.

You should learn how to use computers, so that you can check to see what your child is doing and monitor what they have been up to with the computer. Many parents are worried that computers and the Internet are beyond them. Though some people do their best to make using a computer sound difficult or clever, with a little teaching and practice anyone can learn how to use a computer and find their way around the Internet.

If you can read, you can use a computer. All you need is somebody with a little bit of patience to slowly introduce you to the power and pleasure of computers.

Your and the Internet – countermeasures

- ✓ Don't be scared. Anyone can learn how to use computers and explore the Internet.
- ✓ Find somewhere locally where you can get training. The local library, school and college often give classes. Some people find trainers through adverts in newsagent windows, others find younger relatives who will teach them the basics.

Email

It didn't take people very long to realise that because the computers were connected by 'telephone lines', we could send typed messages to each other too. You type a message, press send and the message flies down the telephone wire to the recipient and appears on his screen in seconds, where sending the same thing by post would have taken days. He might be in the room next door or in a hotel in America, a farm in Brazil or a school in Australia. Thus electronic 'mail' – email – was invented. Your friend can read the message and reply, so you can get a reply immediately.

Chat rooms

People realised that if it was that quick, they could actually hold 'conversations' with each other by typing the conversations into the computer. For example, I type a question *Are you coming to my birthday party?* and send it. A few seconds later you get that message and send a reply *OK. What time?* I reply to you *Meet at the station at 8*. The whole interaction has been done in real-time, just like we were talking face to face or on the telephone, except we typed our conversation.

So the chat room was born. Instead of me talking to you direct, I set up a place where anyone who is interested in talking about football for example, can chat about the game. I can make up a chat nickname such as 'BigRed' and start chatting, real time. Everyone in the room can see what I am typing and saying, and anyone can reply. If you want to have a private conversation, we can switch to a one to one conversation where only you can see what I am typing and I am the only one who can see what you are typing.

The problem. It is easy, fast, and because it uses 'screen names' it is anonymous. Children love to text each other on their mobile phones and use chat rooms, and certain criminals like to join in and try to take advantage of some of those children.

It takes a minute or two to log into a chat room and create an identity, which means that I can very easily become:

JetPilot – I am an RAF fighter pilot, based in America as a test pilot on a joint space mission with NASA. Does anyone want a date?

Bobby12 – I am a twelve-year-old boy and I hate my mum coz she just said I can't go down the park tonight. Does anyone want to sneak out and meet in the bushes behind the cricket pavilion tonite?

SarahJane – I am a nine-year-old girl, having problems at school. Aren't boys horrible? Does anyone want to meet in Richmond Park to talk about boys? I can bring cans of drink and loads of sweets because my mum runs a shop.

It is as easy as that. I can become anything I want to become. I might just want to hide the fact that I am a fat, balding divorcé by claiming to be a jet pilot. Sad but no harm done! On the other hand if I was a paedophile enticing girls and boys to come and meet me the outcome could be very different.

Moderator. Some chat rooms have a moderator; an adult or two who are supposed to monitor what is happening in the chat room. If somebody introduces off-topic conversations, starts talking smutty, giving out personal information or trying to arrange a meeting, the moderator is usually expected to delete that conversation, warn the guilty party and even bar them from any further conversations in that chat room. The problems with that are:

- Some chat rooms don't seem to be monitored. (If they are monitored many moderators don't seem to be very effective).

- By the time a moderator spots a banned conversation, such as disclosure of personal details or arrangements being made for a meeting in Richmond Park, it may be too late.

- If I am JetPilot and I am barred from a chat room for trying to meet children in the local park – I can come back in five minutes and be FighterPilot, or LionHunter, Millionaire, RollerCoasterBoy, or PopStar. In fact I can be anything and anyone, because it really does only take a couple of minutes to create an entirely new identity.

Computers/Internet/chat rooms – countermeasures

✓ Learn how to use a computer and know your way around the Internet so that you can see and understand what your child is doing.

✓ Beware of letting a child have a computer in their room where they could be viewing pornography, or communicating with undesirable people when you will know nothing about it.

✓ Teach your child that they should never disclose or share their Internet passwords with anyone other than you. A friend could log on and use your child's identity to buy things, access porn, send threatening messages etc.

✓ If possible try to keep the family computer in a family room. You can turn the television or radio off while the child does their homework, but with people coming and going it is unlikely that the child will connect to anything or anyone that could cause harm or distress without somebody noticing.

✓ Try to give them a sense of privacy while they are using the computer, emailing or messaging each other about horrible teachers and cruel parents. Don't make them feel that you are looking over their shoulder all the time or they might go to a friend's house or an Internet café where nobody will be watching what they do. You could take a close look now and then as you pass by, taking an interest and praising their skills, for example 'Gosh that's clever – how do you make it do that?'

✓ Keep personal details private. Just as you will never give out personal details over a phone or in a street survey, make sure that your children never give out any personal information. Use a computer nickname if you want to, but never give out home address, phone number, which school you go to etc. Whoever they are they don't need any of that.

- ✓ An extension of the chat room is the use of a 'webcam', which is a cheap little camera that connects to the computer and allows the people chatting to send live pictures of themselves, and even speech too via microphones and speakers, to their friends. Consider disconnecting webcams, and banning children from using them, or accepting images sent to them unless you are in the same room.

- ✓ Make sure you talk to your child about what they do on the Internet. They might not be alert to dangers but you will be. If they start talking about a new kid they are talking to who keeps trying to get them to meet at the railway station, or at the back of the shops, terminate the contact or consider calling the police and explaining your worries. Sit in on a few chat sessions and see if you think that this kid is other than he claims to be?

- ✓ Make sure that your child avoids making one-to-one connections with their on-line friends. There is no need to hold private conversations if they are just talking about homework, the maths teacher or how horrible their mum and dad are. By staying in the main chat rooms, if there is a moderator present, there is some control over content and participants.

- ✓ Just as you should never give personal details out over the Internet or through chat rooms, anyone should be wary of meeting people they only know through a chat room. Of course, not everybody is a homicidal maniac, rapist or paedophile, but just in case, if there isn't an acceptable reason to want to meet, don't even talk about it. If there is a reason (and it will be one that mum or dad agree is a real reason), then any meeting should be arranged with mum or dad, and then held (in a public place away from home) with mum or dad.

- ✓ You have been careful about giving out your name and address over the Internet and through chat rooms; don't slip up and give details now. You might have decided that Bobby12 can come around and swap his computer games with your son. You give out the name and address but Bobby12 doesn't show up – because he is a 49-year-old lonely man, who now knows where you live so he can hang around outside with a trial copy of the latest computer game and be pretty damned sure that your son will want to go with him to try it out. Never give personal details, whatever the circumstances.

- ✓ When connected, a child should always call an adult if they think that a conversation is a bit strange.

- ✓ When you buy your computer, ask the people in the shop to install a firewall, nanny software, pop-up blocker and put a password on the computer. The firewall will stop people connecting to your computer and doing things to it that you don't agree to or know about. The nanny software is set to automatically block connection to porn and other suspect sites. The pop-up blocker will automatically block files that some people and web sites sneakily download onto your computer. You don't have a choice – they just pop up on your screen, and they can include anything from nice to nasty. Putting a password on the computer that you keep to yourself means that the child can only use the computer if you are there supervising. If he or she is at home sick and granny is keeping an eye on them by being fast asleep in the armchair, without the password they can't access anything nasty even though they have the chance.

✓ Make sure that your child knows that they should not open attachments or accept downloads. Attachments are sent with emails, and they can contain adverts, pictures, private letters or viruses. Downloads are often small and sometimes large programs that are sent down the telephone wire and loaded onto your computer (downloaded). As with an attachment they can be an update to your nanny software, an advert for a new computer game, a virus of one sort or another, or a hardcore porn film. If they know never to open unknown attachments or download anything, they and the computer should remain clean and safe.

✓ Most important of all, be interested in your child's Internet existence; what they're doing, and who they are chatting to or emailing.

Children and mobile phones

In chapter 3 I gave some general advice on mobile phones. Mobile phone crime is a major problem with children and young adults. The following statistics show you how big a problem it is, which means that teaching your children how to own and use a mobile phone responsibly, will make them less likely to be the victim of crime.

- Just over 50% of mobile phone crime involves teenagers.
- Teenagers and children are five times more likely to suffer a phone-related crime than an adult.
- In 33% of mobile phone robberies the offender is aged 15 or 16. 90% of offenders are male. 80% of victims are male.
- In an average year, 2,000 phones are stolen every day which makes a total of almost three-quarters of a million phones a year.
- In 66% of phone thefts, the phone is stolen by a gang of offenders, not a single thief or robber.
- In London, 28% of all recorded street crime was to steal just a mobile phone and 49% of all street crime included mobile phones.

- Nearly 50% of the victims of mobile phone crime are under 18 years of age.

The figures might also be slanted by fraud. Well, the children involved might not see it as fraud, and it might be you who is unknowingly committing that fraud, but it exists. As manufacturers and suppliers compete for a shrinking market, they introduce new mobile phones, which are smaller, have built-in cameras, music players and any number of other gadgets.

Unfortunately when their mobile phone gets to be a month or two out of date, it seems to be becoming common for children to throw it away. They then claim that their phone has been stolen and ask mum and dad to claim on the insurance for a replacement. Of course the replacement will be the latest model with fashionable extras. Unfortunately, mum and dad are then making a fraudulent claim on their insurance, because the phone in question was not lost or stolen.

Mobile phone – countermeasures

✓ Teach your children that their mobile phone is attractive to thieves, so they should take care of it.
  - Take the IMEI number and details as described in chapter 3.
  - Mark your phone (under the battery pack where it will not rub off) with your postcode and house name or number using a UV pen (available from some shops or your police local crime prevention officer).
  - Keep the phone with you at all times. Don't leave it in a bag, locker or desk etc. It is a lot harder to steal if you have it with you.
  - Don't show off. If you let the thieves know that you have the latest model phone, they will probably target you.
  - If phone thieves attack you, don't fight them. Let them have your phone rather than risk injury.

✓ If your phone is stolen:
  - Remember as much detail about the thieves as you can.
  - Report the theft to the police. Give them the make, model, serial number of the phone and also report anything you can about the thieves. Did you recognise any of them – do you know names? Can you describe them – were they wearing school uniform? If so which one, etc.
  - Report the loss of the phone and the IMEI number to your mobile phone service provider as soon as you can so they can block it and stop anyone from using it.

- ✓ If it is a genuine theft report the theft to your insurance company as soon as possible to arrange for a replacement.

- ✓ When you get a replacement, take the advice given in chapter 3, and take the IMEI number for the new phone.

  - ➤ Don't make it easy for the thieves; never show or lend your mobile phone to anyone, especially a stranger.

  - ➤ Most mobile phones have a keyboard-locking function. The locking works when you press a few keys in a special order, and it locks the keyboard so that the phone cannot be used. If anyone steals the phone while it is locked they still cannot use it. Learn how to lock your keyboard and lock it when you are not using it.

  - ➤ Take extra precautions if you go into a particularly risky area, where there are crowds of strangers. For example at a station, a sports match or pop concert, in a crowded shop or on a very busy street. Make absolutely sure that your mobile phone is safe by putting it in an inside pocket.

- ✓ I understand that there is a new service being offered that can track where your child is by reading the signal from his or her mobile phone. You may want to look into it!

Cycle helmets

I know a lady who lost her son when he fell off his bicycle and suffered a massive head injury. I promised I would include a reminder in this book.

Most children have a bike. Roads are too busy, traffic moves too fast, and road surfaces are often rutted and full of potholes. It is all to easy to fall off a bike.

If you fall off a bike when you are not wearing a helmet, you could be lucky and fall on a convenient stretch of long grass and bushes. Unfortunately it's more likely that your head will come into violent contact with tarmac roads, concrete kerbstones, a street lamp or something else equally hard and equally damaging.

Drugs

Drugs are quite readily available all over the country and teenagers, if not school kids, nearly always know who is using, who is dealing and what the prices are locally.

Don't try to fool yourself into thinking that your child cannot be entangled in the drugs scene. It has been known for pushers (people who sell drugs) to give 'free samples' of drugs to young people to get them hooked. They will soon be back with a craving for more, but this time they will have to pay. It isn't unheard of for a pusher to seed a marijuana cigarette with crack cocaine, to trap a young user into addiction to harder drugs, and so expand his customer base and profits.

Young people often give in to peer pressure. Some young people just want to see what all the fuss is about, especially in the club and rave scene where ecstasy tablets are so inexpensive and so readily available. They try just one tablet. Unfortunately it has been known for that first tablet to kill.

If they survive and they enjoyed the rush of the drugs they used they may want the same feeling again, so they become a frequent and possibly addicted user. Some young people don't notice any effects from their first drug experience, which may be because they were conned and what they swallowed was aspirin or baking soda. In some cases the drugs they took were so diluted that there was no effect. Those young people may decide the experience isn't worth the money, risk, hassle and never take drugs again, but some may move to other more powerful drugs to experience the high they hear and read about.

The bottom line is that drugs are out there, and your child is at risk of trying them one way or another.

I won't preach about drug taking. The facts are widely known, and there are a number of resources available to explain the potential threats drug use brings. Most school authorities, colleges, libraries, youth clubs, local authorities and even the local police can advise and make presentations to groups on the problems and risks of using illegal drugs.

Signs of drug use

The signs of drug use are not always clear. They change with the age and health of the person concerned, the drugs that are being used, the strength and frequency of the drug use and even with the way in which those drugs are used.

There are some signs that may indicate drug use. If you see somebody you know who is in a drugged state, you will be able to see that something is wrong with them. If they hide away while using drugs, you might only see them when they are not actually under the influence of drugs, but eventually you will see changes even then. Generally the changes are in behaviour, appearance, health and character. For example, they may become withdrawn or violent, they might start stealing or committing other crime to get enough money to feed their habit. You might not be able to see any signs that a loved one is using illegal drugs, or you may see some of the following signs.

- Their character changes and they may
    - go from lively to withdrawn
    - go from shy to wild child
    - switch moods suddenly
    - become ill-tempered and even violent.
- They may lose interest in, or ignore, school or college work, and their marks start to slide.
- They may skip school or college quite often (it is worth checking with their school if you see other signs to check if they are attending).
- They may abandon their favourite hobbies, sports, friends and stop watching their favourite television shows.
- They may start spending time with a new group of people, who you find scruffy, rude and lazy. That is if they don't hide these new friends from you!
- They may lose interest in food and start skipping meals, making silly excuses.
- They may seem unable to concentrate, unable to hold a conversation and unable to get anything done.
- They may make things up to excuse themselves. Because it is easy to see through the lies you may challenge them and find that they become angry and storm out, or even resort to destructive violence.
- Their sleeping patterns may change. They may be out until the early hours and then sleep from 8 am until late afternoon for example. When they wake they may be edgy and go straight out.
- They may lose interest in their appearance, not bothering to wash, brush their hair, bathe, change their clothes etc.

- If they have developed an expensive drug habit, money and small valuable objects may start to vanish, but they will deny all knowledge of the theft.
- You may find clear evidence of drug taking:
  - unknown pills, powder or herbal material in little packets or bags.
  - vials of medication, hypodermic needles.
  - burnt tin foil, smoke-stained spoons, funny-looking smoking pipes.
  - smoking an obviously hand-rolled cigarette.
  - little black or brown knobs of cannabis resin.
  - needle marks on their arms, legs, and feet.
  - you may find them in a drugged coma, or so far gone that they appear to be in a coma.
  - they may come home with valuable property, and you don't know where it came from, and next day it is gone.
  - they may have large sums of money that seem to go as quickly as they appear.
  - you find bags of 'used' glue, a lot of empty solvent or lighter fuel cans in their room, or the bins.

Widely-available drugs

Below is some information on the names, street names, use and effect of some common drugs.

Name: Cannabis. The leaf of a plant.

Street names: marijuana, weed, draw, grass, hash, ganja.

Use and effects: Usually smoked. Effects include:

Behavioural: Feeling relaxed and talkative. Anxious and paranoid. Confusion. Perceptual and conceptual changes. Lack of concentration. Giddiness. Euphoria. Heightening of senses. Disorientation. Short-term memory loss. Affects co-ordination increasing the risk of accidents. Heavy use by people with disturbed personalities can bring on temporary mental disorders.

Biological: Increased pulse rate. Reddening of eyes. Dryness of mouth. Increased hunger ('munchies'). Sedation. Nausea. Change in blood pressure and blood temperature. Impaired driving skills. Increased risk of respiratory disorders (lung cancer).

Name: Cocaine. A white crystal powder or small 'rocks'.

Street names: Change frequently and include – blow, coke, charlie, rock, crack.

Use and effects: Usually snorted, smoked or injected. Effects include:

Behavioural: Feelings of well being. Alertness and confidence. Sometimes feelings of anxiety and panic. Frequent use can cause restlessness. Confusion and paranoia. After-effects can cause depression. With regular use feelings of happiness are replaced by an uncomfortable state of restlessness, excitability, nervousness and suspicion.

Biological: Reduced hunger. Tiredness and indifference to pain. Feeling of great physical strength and mental capacity. Can cause hallucinations. High doses can cause death from breathing failure or heart attack. Weight loss and sickness. Confused exhaustion due to lack of sleep. Snorting cocaine can damage nostril tissue.

Name: Heroin. A powder with a bitter taste that varies from white to dark brown, can come as a tar-like sticky liquid.

Street names: smack, brown, horse, gear, h, junk, skag, jack.

Use and effects: Usually injected, smoked or snorted.

Behavioural: Feeling of great happiness. At higher doses calmness takes over. Usage creates a relaxed detachment from pain, desires and anxiety. Feelings of drowsiness, warmth and contentment. Relieves stress and discomfort. When physically dependent, pleasure is replaced by the relief of getting the drug.

Biological: Pain-killing. Impairs brain activity, affecting reflexes such as coughing, breathing, and heart rate. Widens blood vessels. Constipation. Overdose results in unconsciousness, coma, and death from breathing failure. First-time users often feel sick and vomit. Withdrawal causes uncomfortable side effects such as aches, tremors, sweating and chills, sneezing, yawning and muscle spasms. Weakness and loss of well being may last for several months. Repeated injection causes damage to surrounding blood vessels. Use of dirty needles increases the risk of contracting diseases such as HIV and AIDS.

Name: Ecstasy. Distributed and used in small tablet form, where each tablet is usually imprinted with a symbol or logo.

Street names: XTC, E's, disco biscuits, hug drug, fantasy, burgers, echoes, love doves, and sometimes names drawn from the symbol imprinted into the tablets.

Use and effects: Usually swallowed; can be crushed and snorted or injected.

Behavioural: Calming effects. Heightened perception of colours and sounds. Anxiety, confusion and paranoia. Feelings of alertness. Emotions seem more intense. Euphoria.

Biological: Bodily co-ordination can be affected. Energy buzz causes people to dance for hours. Users may feel a tightening of the jaw. Nausea and sweating. Increase in heart rate. Usage has been connected with 60 deaths in the UK alone. Causes damage to the brain cells and liver. Can cause insomnia.

Overdose: as illegal drugs are not made to any standard, it is easy for a user to take an overdose because they don't know how strong each one will be. Ecstasy seems to be commonly used on the club and rave scene. An ecstasy overdose is characterised by 1) rapid heartbeat 2) high blood pressure 3) faintness 4) muscle cramping 5) panic attacks 6) in more severe cases, loss of consciousness or seizures. Because one of the side effects of the use of ecstasy is jaw muscle tension and teeth grinding, users will often suck on sweets to help relieve the tension. In extreme cases, ecstasy may cause hyperthermia (severe overheating of the body), muscle breakdown, seizures, stroke, kidney failure, heart failure and possible permanent damage to sections of brain critical to thought and memory.

Name: Methamphetamines and amphetamines. Methamphetamine is more commonly used. Typically a white powder that easily dissolves in water, or a clear crystal referred to as crystal meth or ice. Also distributed and used in the form of brightly-coloured tablets, sometimes called Yaba which is the name used in Thailand.

Street names: meth, speed, uppers, sulphate, wizz, billy, poor man's cocaine, crystal meth, ice, glass.

Use and effects: Injecting, snorting, smoking, swallowing.

Behavioural: Some people become tense and anxious or paranoid. People may have very bad mood swings. Gives feeling of self-confidence. Psychological dependency can occur due to people becoming addicted to the high/buzz. Hallucinations, delusions and feelings of persecution with regular, high doses. This can lead to mental disorders.

Biological: Breathing and heart rate increase. Pupils widen. Appetite is suppressed. Comedown includes tiredness and depression, which can last for as long as two days. Tolerance can occur, therefore a higher dose is needed to create the same effects. Long-term use can lead to damage to the heart and blood vessels. Overdose can be fatal. Can cause insomnia and mental confusion. Sleep, memory and concentration are affected in the short term.

Name: LSD (Lysergic Acid Diethylamide) is the most potent hallucinogen known to science. Usually sold as small squares of impregnated blotting-style paper, where the squares are printed on sheets with colourful designs. LSD has been known to be used as tablets (microdots), thin squares of gelatin (window panes), impregnated sugar cubes and rarely in liquid form.

Street name: acid, trips, tab, blotters, dots.

Use and effects: Consumption of an amount equal to a few grains of salt will produce vivid hallucinations. An average dose will have hallucinogenic effects for up to eight hours, and 12 hours is not unknown. Flashbacks are quite common, that is where a user reports LSD-type effects days or even months after taking the last dose.

Behavioural: Depression, dizziness, disorientation and sometimes panic attacks. More likely if user is unstable, anxious, or in hostile/unfamiliar surroundings. Long term effects include acute anxiety or brief mental disorders. Brain function can be permanently affected, which can trigger long-term mental illness. Flashbacks can occur years later without warning. Although they can be short-lived, they can be intense and confusing.

Biological: Effects often include strong colours and distortion of vision and hearing and senses – users report 'hearing' colours and 'seeing' sounds. Reactions may include heightened self-awareness and mystical or ecstatic experiences. A trip may cause hallucinations that can last for hours. Users have little perception of time, space and danger.

If you want to know more, approach your local authority, doctor, library, college etc, and ask about presentations, pamphlets and help in identifying and combating illegal drug use.

Drugs – countermeasures

- ✓ Teach your children about drugs.

- ✓ When they are young start by teaching them that aspirin and other household medication, which you always lock safely away, are not sweets.

- ✓ When they are old enough teach them that there are other drugs that silly people take, but which hurt them and can even kill them.

- ✓ When they are ready, expand their education. Be honest and tell them about the effects drugs can have on the human body. Describe HIV and AIDS, sores and ulcers that can result from illegal drug use.

- ✓ If they are old enough to understand it, don't be afraid to point out some horror stories in the paper where illegal drugs have been involved.

- ✓ Remind them that illegal drugs are illegal and that they can go to prison for having, buying, selling and using them.

- ✓ Explain that illegal drugs will destroy the family and their life.

- ✓ If the child is a member of a group, talk to the group leader and ask if they have arranged a drugs talk. Sometimes the police, education authority or local health authority can arrange to give a drugs talk to groups of young people.

- ✓ Make sure that your child knows that they can always talk to you whatever the subject, no matter how bad or embarrassing they think it is.

- ✓ Make sure that your child knows that they can and should *always* say no to any drugs of any kind.

- ✓ Make sure that your child knows that if they ever want to get away from a situation where drugs are available, for sale, being used or discussed that they can call you. If they call, no matter what the time, weather, location or reason, you will either collect them or arrange for a taxi to bring them home.

- ✓ Make sure that you keep an eye open for some of the signs of drug taking. If you see anything, talk to your child and don't give up until you get to the bottom of the problem.

- ✓ If your child does start taking or using drugs, you have to decide what to do. Personally I would call the police and report the matter.

✓ While you are teaching your child about illegal drugs and the adverse effects they can have I suggest that you should point out that tobacco and alcohol have similar effects to some drugs and can be addictive and dangerous in their own ways.

Young Adults

You are clearly old enough to be reading this book yourself, and I will assume that you have read the whole book up to this point and will continue to read it all, and that you have achieved a level of maturity where I can speak to you as an adult. You will have realised that in my view the basis of security and safety is common sense, caution, planning and awareness. I have tried to point out vulnerabilities, threats and risks, and then suggest ways that you can avoid them and so stay safe. By reading this book you will learn more than you need to know, which will put you in a position to advise and protect those who are younger than you, are not so mature, or who have not read this book.

Having said that I think that there are a few basic guidelines that young adults need to follow.

Young adult – countermeasures

✓ Realise that no matter what you think, you are still young and inexperienced in the ways of the world.

✓ Realise that there are some particularly vicious people out there who might attack you, get you hooked on drugs, steal from you or do anything else they care to do to you and your family.

✓ Realise that you have achieved and displayed an advanced level of maturity by picking this book up and reading it, especially if you have learned from the warnings I have given.

✓ Realise that people around you may not be as mature as you are and may mindlessly follow the crowd rather than stand up and say no. They probably won't have the maturity to call a halt to a silly game that is going too far, whereas you have the maturity to say 'Stop this, it isn't funny any more.' You can bring common sense into your group and protect yourself, members of your group and innocent people around you by being brave enough to be the voice of reason.

Mostly Your Children

✓ You probably realise that your parents and guardians have your best interests at heart and accept that they will worry about you. I expect you are therefore mature enough to do them the courtesy of letting them know where you are going and what you are doing. You don't have to report in like a child, just keep them in touch with your activities. For example, a young adult might conversationally tell mum that he is going to go to Brighton with Jake, Sue and Jennifer and doesn't expect to be back until Saturday morning.

✓ It may not be cool for a teenager to phone 'mummy and daddy' to say where they are going, but if you send a text message nobody needs to know who you are contacting or what you are saying. So, remain cool but send a text to your parents telling them what you are doing, particularly if you said you would be home by two but have decided to stay at a friend's house. Teach your parents to text so that they can send a text to you rather than call to check that you arrived at the party safely.

✓ Accept that it is in the job description of parents to worry about their children. Accept that even when they are 97 and you are 64, you will still be their 'little Benjamin'. So, if you said you would be home at midnight but you missed the last train, give them a call to say you are walking and won't be back until 3 am. You never know, you might get the offer of a lift. Even if you don't, at least they won't be sitting worrying and calling the hospitals to find out where you are.

✓ As young adults (particularly females) if you do go anywhere try to go in a group. You are more vulnerable when you are alone. With friends you can watch each other's backs.

✓ When using public transport for a big night out, try to make sure that you know when the last service departs. If your service is anything like mine, aim to get the second to last service, because our last service is frequently cancelled. At least you have another chance to get home on the last bus or train if you run late and miss that second to last service or it is cancelled.

✓ If anyone gets ill or injured, make sure they get home safely. They may say, 'I'm OK, you go on.' If they are suffering from concussion, they might fall under a bus or collapse in some bushes. Be a real friend and make sure that the whole group or at least one male escorts them all the way home – even if you do miss the party.

✓ I suggest that you have a talk with your parents about emergency taxi fares, again particularly if you are female. Agree with your parents that if you are out and for any acceptable reason need to get a taxi home in an emergency, mum or dad will pay the fare. You don't want to find yourself alone outside a concert, your handbag stolen and only 38 pence to your name. If you have made the agreement you can get a taxi home to safety where mum or dad will pay the fare. (If you are as mature as I think you are, you will of course agree to pay that fare back as soon as possible.)

- ✓ Accept that illegal drugs are widely available, and that people take them. They might give you a buzz – but more often than not the results of drug taking are
  - ➤ being violently sick, collapsing and waking up with dried vomit all over you. Worse still you aren't sure if the vomit is yours or not.
  - ➤ feeling really scared about nothing you can put your finger on.
  - ➤ having hallucinations, which alter your perception so even your best friend can seem to be a scary monster.
  - ➤ picking fights that you know you shouldn't, know you can't win, getting hurt and not knowing why you are doing it in the first place.
  - ➤ looking and acting like a total, absolute jerk in front of everyone, totally destroying any cool that you ever had.
  - ➤ picking up serious and fatal diseases.
  - ➤ being open to sexual assaults and robbery.
  - ➤ increasing your chances of having accidents and getting hurt or killed because you are not really in control of yourself.
  - ➤ suffering long-term mental health issues. Latest research shows that even sampling illegal drugs once can cause flashbacks to those hallucinations over the coming years. Not something you want to happen when you are pulling out to overtake a lorry. There are also risks that drug takers who only smoke a little dope will develop something like Alzheimer's Disease (the medical term for being senile).
- ✓ You may not have a car yet, and a bicycle is way too un-cool, but avoid hitchhiking, taking a lift from a stranger or taking a lift from anyone who has had too much to drink or taken drugs. You know how valuable your life is – look after it.
- ✓ If looking for part-time work, be aware of the law. Be aware of health and safety, training, safety equipment and clothes. Be aware that you could be injured in a number of ways, or lured into a position where you could be assaulted. Even something as simple as an early morning paper round could put you at risk with nobody around, with dark and isolated roads and houses.

Apply my concepts of awareness, common sense and caution. Look out for yourself and those around you and you will have a very pleasant and happy life.

8 Mostly Older People

There isn't much I need to tell you. What I am trying to teach younger people by writing this book, you have probably already learned from your experience of life. Perhaps some of the earlier sections may have been a refresher, or maybe the description of computers and the Internet have inspired you to get a computer to start exploring the world. I know one thing, I don't think I will ever stop learning! There are a couple of topics I would like to present for your consideration.

How Vulnerable Are You?

The answer is probably not as vulnerable as you might think in some ways, but probably more vulnerable in other ways. There is one important lesson to take away. Although crime in general and violent crime is rising, the likelihood of an older person being a victim of that crime or violence is very low. If you learn from the advice given in this book, maintain a level of awareness and implement as many countermeasures as you can, you won't become a victim.

You may like to read *The Home Security Handbook* for advice on home security.

General safety – countermeasures

If you are elderly, how can you stay safe?

✓ Make sure you are safe when you are out.
  ➢ Use the pelican crossings and underpasses. Don't try to make a dash across a busy road at a dangerous junction. Accept that your reactions are slowing down, and adjust your pace of life.

- In colder weather, wrap up well. It is surprising how cold it can be waiting for a bus that never comes, especially when town centres seem to be designed to funnel arctic winds right through the only bus shelter you use. Wear multiple layers indoors too.

- Make sure that you lock the house whenever you leave. Don't assume that you will only be two minutes – a long conversation with a friend or relative that you haven't seen for years might keep you chatting for hours.

- When you leave home, don't take any cash or valuables with you that you don't really need. You don't want to risk losing that gold pocket watch to some opportunist pickpocket; if you don't really need to have it with you leave it safely at home.

- If you do have anything of value with you, keep quiet. Hide it away securely in an inside pocket; never talk about it or wave a wad of cash around in the bank or post office. There are thieves out there; no need to advertise.

✓ I don't think anyone keeps their life savings under the mattress any more, but don't keep large sums of money in the house. You don't need it, and in these days of credit cards, cheques, debit cards and credit transfers you shouldn't need cash.

✓ Avoid paying substantial bills with cash if you can. If word gets around that you pay by cash some low-life thief will get it in his head that you have a mattress full of money waiting for him to come and collect. There is another benefit too. If you are pressured into paying for something by cash, once he takes the money he will be gone. If you pay by cheque, you have a chance to stop the cheque if he turns out to be a cheat and a swindler. If you pay by credit card, many cards insure their cardholders against fraud so you could get your money back under some circumstances.

✓ Many local authorities, charities and crime prevention panels provide signs that people can stick on their front door. Signs that read something like 'I do not buy anything at the front door. I do not want to take part in any survey and I do not discuss religion or politics with strangers.' Hopefully that will stop the 'knockers' from calling on you.

✓ Never, ever believe any workmen who come to your door and tell you the roof needs to be repaired, the gutter needs replacing, the trees need pruning or anything else. Remember you *never* buy anything at the front door, including products or services. Most of these passing workmen are crooks. If one knocks at your door and tells you that some work needs doing tell them to go away, then later get a younger relative to check to make sure that the workman was lying and that there are no loose slates or broken gutters etc. If there is a problem you can get three quotes locally and get a respected local tradesman to do the work properly at a reasonable price.

- ✓ You do have a door chain and door viewer don't you? If not, get one installed and use it. Make sure that you have read the section on bogus callers, and be aware that they often try to target older people. The basic rule is never open the door unless the door chain is on. Don't let anyone into your home unless you are 1,000% happy that you know them, can trust them, and that they are not conmen trying to steal your money and valuables.

- ✓ Make an agreement with your neighbours (young or older) that you will keep an eye on each other. If you live alone, you can make a pact to call somebody who lives next door every morning just so they know that you are awake and OK.

- ✓ You can also watch each other's houses in a formal or informal neighbourhood watch scheme. If you see strangers going into their house, call them, and have a prearranged code. For example, if they say it's OK it's my nephew from Brighton and his sisters, then it is OK. But, if they use the code and say something like 'Sorry, wrong number, Mr Constable,' that could be a code for you to call the police or send younger relatives around to see what is going on.

- ✓ Consider getting a personal attack alarm for use at home or when out. Criminals don't like noise because it attracts attention, and if they are seen there is a greater chance of them getting caught.

- ✓ Realise that some clues will tell anyone passing by that an elderly or infirm person lives in a house. For example, stout handrails built around gates steps and paths, wheel-chair ramps and electric mobility buggies or chairs parked outside all indicate that an elderly or infirm person lives in that house.

- ✓ Consider 'dressing' your hall to make it look like there may be a young man living with you. A few items from the charity shop could help, for example a young man's coat, a pair of used trainers and a baseball cap left on the hall table would do. Any visitor looking into your hall could see them and should assume that a baseball cap and trainer-wearing young man may be elsewhere in the house. At least you then have the chance to say something like, 'My grandson George will be back any moment,' if you want to make people think they may be interrupted.

- ✓ Consider contacting your local council and the local police. Some councils operate schemes that help to subsidise the installation of decent locks and door chains for elderly people.

Driving and the elderly

Advanced age does not mean that you are incapable of driving safely. Unfortunately, it is an inescapable medical fact that hearing, eyesight and reactions gradually get worse as we grow older. The average teenage boy-racer probably takes more risks and causes more accidents than his grandpa, but his age doesn't make him a bad driver either. Unfortunately as we age the quality of our driving skill does diminish and some older drivers should not be driving.

Driving skills can start to fade any time after the age of 60, but generally people don't suffer any appreciable change until about the age of 75. Statistics show that the number of traffic accidents, driver and pedestrian deaths attributable to older drivers increases sharply after the age of 65. To some extent this could be due to the frailty of the drivers themselves, but failing eyesight and slower reactions must be a major contributory factor.

Unlike a drunk driver, an older driver should be able to recognise that time when their skills and abilities don't equip them to drive on our increasingly overcrowded roads.

While failing eyesight, poor hearing and slow reflexes can reduce driving ability, illness can also be to blame. Diseases such as the early phase of Alzheimer's disease, heart disease, alcoholism, diabetes, effects of a stroke, arthritis, sleep apnea, and Parkinson's disease can all make a driver dangerous.

On top of that, some prescribed medication can make a driver unfit to drive. Antidepressants, some antihistamines, glaucoma medications, some anti-inflammatory drugs (painkillers such as aspirin and ibuprofen), and muscle relaxants can all affect a patient's driving ability. Mixing even a glass of sherry with some medications can produce the same impairment as drinking ten pints of beer.

Though the above diseases and medications do not mean that you are definitely unfit to drive, if you suffer from any of those diseases or take any of that medication, you should arrange for your driving skills and safety to be assessed.

Driving and the elderly – countermeasures

✓ Have your eyes checked regularly. You may be suffering from poor vision, lack of peripheral vision, distorted vision or cataracts. The effects usually come on slowly, so you will not necessarily notice them. Only an eye test will accurately indicate how well you can or cannot see.

Mostly Older People

- ✓ If you have poor night vision and are bothered by the glare of oncoming headlights, consider only driving during the day to maintain your mobility.

- ✓ With reduced vision, don't drive in bad weather and always make sure that your car windows are clean and clear outside and inside to give yourself the best view you can get.

- ✓ Remove distractions by turning off the radio and not chatting to passengers. Older drivers generally need to use more of their concentration on driving safely.

- ✓ If you have a disability such as arthritis in the neck or shoulder, you may not be able to turn far enough to let you see to reverse safely. If that is the case, get your passenger to get out to see you safely back when you need to reverse.

- ✓ If other drivers always seem to be stopping suddenly in front of you it may be that you are not seeing or reacting to their brake lights quickly enough. Accept that and pay extra attention to the vehicles in front of you; leave a bigger gap, brake earlier and get an eyesight test to make sure.

- ✓ If other drivers seem to be going far too fast around you, check that you are not going particularly slowly or being hesitant. Check your speed against the posted speed limit. If the limit is, say, 50 miles per hour and you are not comfortable or happy going faster than 20 miles per hour, it is probably time to sell the car and get that bus pass.

- ✓ If motorways seem to be too busy, too congested and too rushed and you can't cope, stay off them at rush hour, and try using side roads.

Driving warning signs

You may not be able to see some warning signs, and a relative or passenger may have to warn you about some of them. For example:

- Driving though red lights and junctions without realising that they were there is a common problem with elderly drivers who are unable to see properly, who cannot concentrate on driving, or who have very slow reactions. If you are always being flashed by angry drivers at traffic lights and road junctions, that may be why. Arrange for your driving skills and safety to be assessed:
  - ➢ If you stop at green traffic lights for no reason.
  - ➢ If you come close to hitting cars and objects but don't realise it.
  - ➢ If you switch lanes or merge into traffic flows without looking.
  - ➢ If you drive the wrong way down a one-way street.

- If you get confused or lost on roads that you know.
- If you confuse the brake and accelerator.
- If you try to drive off and forget to release the handbrake.

Warning signs elsewhere

- Research has shown that a person who has trouble walking up stairs or doing heavy housework frequently has a reduced standard of driving. It is only an indication, but there is a common link between the two.

- If your doctor tells you that you should not be driving.

Driving assessment

- If you want an unbiased assessment of your driving skill and ability, you could contact a major driving school. Explain your concerns to them and ask if they would arrange for you to pay for a driving assessment.

- You would of course have to pay for the 'lesson', but peace of mind and safety are worth the investment. To avoid embarrassment, a driving instructor could discreetly meet you away from your home address, assess your driving, give you feedback and then drop you back where you were picked up so relatives and nosey neighbours won't ask why you were seen getting into a driving school car.

- Remember something as simple as getting more rest, an eye test and new spectacles, waiting until a course of medication is completed, or even a few discreet refresher driving lessons could be all that is needed to put you safely back on the road.

The bottom line is that if you aren't safe, stay off the road. I spoke to one old gent who had cataracts in both eyes, when I pointed out how dangerous it was he said he was 'willing to take the risk' because he wanted to get around. The problem was that his driving was putting everyone else at risk! If you are driving a car, remember that it isn't just you that you put at risk, it is all other road users. And other road users include your wife or husband, your daughter, grandson, nephew, neighbour, old Mrs Biggins from number 42, and the world in general.

When it is time to stop driving, recognise it, accept it, and sell the car.

9 Terrorism

The next book in this series of Security Handbooks will be *The Holiday and Travel Security Handbook* and it will include information to help people protect themselves from acts of terrorism. However, publication is not until Spring 2006. In view of the terrible bombings in London I felt that readers would benefit now from some of the information that will appear in the next book.

Terrorism – countermeasures

In reality, there is little that the average person can do and probably little that the vast majority of people need to do, to protect themselves from terrorist attacks.

A new good quality bullet proof vest will cost you at least £800. But that vest only fully protects your torso from a frontal or rear assault.

A bullet can hit your head or neck, arms or legs and they could maim or kill as well. If hit in the arm or leg by a bullet, without prompt medical attention blood loss and shock will kill you anyway. A shot or injury to the groin, which is not protected by a ballistic vest, is notoriously hard to treat in the field. As vital organs are in the lower abdomen and major arteries run through the thighs and groin, unless you get immediate attention, after being hit in the groin area you will probably die.

So a bullet proof vest isn't as protective as most people think they are, and they won't protect you from a car bomb, a nail bomb, a blast bomb, virus release, poison dust or gas, etc.

Try not to panic though, as a member of the public you are extremely unlikely to encounter terrorists. Unless you work for a defence contractor or news station in a war zone, you shouldn't lose any sleep about the protective quality or otherwise of ballistic vests.

Nobody can guarantee to protect you from terrorist atrocities. However, you can protect yourself and help to protect society by remaining alert.

General

✔ Human beings have nervous systems, which react according to our genetic programming. That means that we have automatic and natural functions that we cannot control. We breathe, sweat and shiver when the body decides that conditions are right. When we are scared, we are genetically programmed to prepare for 'fight or flight', to fight the threat that has scared us or to run away from it. That means that when we are scared, the body automatically prepares itself for one of those actions. Our heart rate rises and adrenaline is squirted into our systems making us more alert, which also makes us visibly more nervous and apprehensive.

A suicide bomber will be nervous. Unless they are heavily drugged, and you would probably be able to see that in their behaviour anyway, you will be able to see that somebody is on edge, hyped up and ready for action.

If a person was hyped up and nervous while waiting for a job interview, or about to run a race, you would expect that, but you wouldn't expect somebody walking into your government office to be like that! Anyone who is hyped up and nervous just walking into a government office should raise suspicions. If the bomber is that close, it is probably too late but these are potential clues that somebody could pick up.

✔ If the suicide bomber isn't carrying a bag or case, they have to strap the device to their body. If they do that they would have to hide the bulk of the explosives, and the wires and trigger device from general view so they would probably be wearing a coat or bulky garment. If it is a hot day, they will stand out because of their clothes, but also because they would be sweating from the heat as well as acting nervously and on edge. That will make them stand out from the crowd. Are they carrying a briefcase with a strange wire going to a switch in the handle? There are some signs if you look for them and can identify them.

✔ Suicide bombers are single minded. Once they set off on their mission they have increasingly tunnel vision and can only see their goal. This means that they can appear to be rude, they push and shove to get to that office door. They might push to get to the front of the queue, then pause a moment before purposefully striding in to kill and be killed. That might make them stand out from the crowd too.

✔ A person who pauses when he sees uniformed security staff, or turns away when he sees that visitors have to go through a metal detector has to be suspicious. A visitor who is nervous but appears to be waiting for something unknown, may be waiting for a bigger crowd to gather in reception or might be waiting for the Chairman of the company to arrive before doing his or her dirty deed.

✔ Even simple clues are available. A person who does not have a company pass, or doesn't know that staff use the right hand access gate and only visitors use the left hand gate. Somebody who just doesn't fit into the normal scene should be watched.

✔ When driving a vehicle a suicide bomber has the same tunnel vision. Approaching their target they will only see that office door, or the entrance to the underground car park. They may wait, illegally parked ignoring car horns and insults, so that they can follow somebody through the entrance barrier, or they may be preparing to ram though it. They might cut through traffic and appear to be oblivious to it, or to the rules of driving as they concentrate on getting the vehicle to the target. After all they aren't worried about parking fines or court appearances for driving the wrong way up a one way street!

At Home

✔ Keep up to date with the news, so that you pick up any information available on terrorist threats, plans and trends. If they announce on the news that terrorists are thought to be targeting an airport, and you live next to an airport, you should become more vigilant for yourself, your family and the rest of the world!

- ✔ If you work in a government building or work for any 'capitalist' or other official organisation, be aware that you are more likely to be selected as a target than Mrs Biggins who works as a cleaner at the local supermarket.

- ✔ Familiarise yourself with the alert states, so that you know when the risk level is rising. (Most organisations have a system to show the threat level. For example Green means there is no real threat, Amber threat levels have increased, and Red a significant threat exists).

- ✔ You will know if you are in a role or position that is a potential target. If you are, check with your security people and familiarise yourself with the ways to check your car for any suspicious devices attached to it or placed around the house and garden.

- ✔ Get used to checking around your home for potential or suspicious devices and packages. Terrorists have been known to set explosives under items in the garden of a target individual. For example they may rig a shed door with explosives or, arrange for a device to explode if the garden hose is moved.

- ✔ Familiarise yourself with emergency evacuation or terrorist alert procedures relating to your building.

- ✔ Be particularly aware of potential devices such as unattended bags, cases and vehicles.

- ✔ Be aware of the threat of letter or package bombs – check your security procedures to establish how to spot and deal with them.

- ✔ Be aware that chemicals and infectious agents have been used in postal attacks. Check your mail handling procedures.

- ✔ Be aware of what is happening around you. Terrorists do not wear a uniform or carry membership cards. You could for example be suspicious of a lot of late night activity in a lock up store, or different people constantly coming and going at odd hours from a flat across the road. By being aware of it and reporting it to the authorities you could save the lives of a lot of innocent people if the activity you reported is a terrorist cell preparing to make an attack.

- ✔ If you have any suspicions, make some notes. This will help you by reinforcing your suspicions and give you something concrete to report. By making some notes you will see if that suspicious late night activity boils down to a group of students going out and coming in drunk every Friday and

Saturday night, or if it really is a random pattern any night of the week. By making notes of numbers, descriptions and vehicles, you could talk to the police and give them those details.

- ✔ If people regularly come and go and you don't know their names it makes it difficult for you to refer to them. For the purpose of your notes identify individuals and make a name up for them. For example, make a note, 'Harry is the "30 something man" drives white transit A123BCD, short blond hair, always drives the white van and walks with a limp because of something wrong with his left leg'. You may also for example have identified 'Male "Big Nose" comes on foot has sometimes left with Harry in his white van. Big Nose has dark hair that is trimmed very short, he smokes small cigars'. In that way you will simplify your notes on the activities, you can simply say Tuesday 2 a.m. Harry arrived took heavy box into flat from van, left at 6 a.m. with Big Nose. With that the police could do some discreet checks, they may find that you live opposite a brothel, or that the people who live there run a night express courier service. If that is the case then nobody is hurt, but if there is a more sinister reason for the activity, the sooner the authorities know about it the better.

- ✔ If you do make notes:
  - ➢ Don't let the suspects see you watching and making notes.
  - ➢ Never try to get closer, or take photographs or go up and look through the windows of the house or any vehicle. If they are terrorists you could quickly end up dead, and anyway, your information will be more valuable to the police if the bad guys don't know that they are being watched.

- ✔ As soon as it looks to you like something is going on, talk to the police. Don't wait until you see somebody deliver dynamite to the house. Report it and then step back.

- ✔ If you do report something that turns out to be significant, the police may want to ask if they can use your spare room to keep an eye on what is going on. Be ready to answer them.

- ✔ If there is a report of a threat to a passenger aircraft, or American business interests, keep that in mind. When you go about your daily life you might not want to avoid buying a burger, but you could postpone your plans to fly to New York for an anniversary weekend with your wife!

Travelling

Transport systems are a favourite terrorist target. Because people have easy access to public transport, the terrorists can easily get in to plant their devices. Stations, ports and airports are a hub of activity, which means that any explosive will almost certainly kill and injure a lot of people no matter when it goes off. Stay alert.

✔ Be aware of any unattended bag, case or package wherever you see it. They have been left on seats, in luggage stores, under seats, in luggage racks, on platforms or on the concourse. If you do see something unattended, report it to a uniformed member of staff. Make sure that they know exactly what it is and where it is, then move away. It is probably just an innocent bag that someone has forgotten, but it might be something more sinister.

✔ During a high alert, if you see an unattended bag on a train or bus and you are between stops, I would loudly ask who owns the bag. If the owner stands up to claim it – no problem. If everyone denies all knowledge I would ask again. If it's still not claimed I would consider voicing my suspicions and suggest that everybody move away from the bag to another carriage then I would report it to a member of the crew immediately. Again making sure to say exactly what it is and where it is. Describing a 'red rucksack with the word *HIKER* sewn in large blue letters on the top, left on the rack above the third row of seats on the platform side of the train' is a lot better than 'a suspicious bag'.

✔ Listen to announcements, and obey any instructions that are given, the staff should now know what they are doing.

✔ When flying, where possible, book yourself onto direct flights, because airports are a potential terrorist target. So direct flights will reduce your exposure to risks at and around airports. Direct flights also mean that you take maximum advantage of British airport security, if you have to wait for hours in some remote third world airport and then fly on one of their aircraft, they may be no security protecting you.

✔ Avoid going to, stopping at or transferring to different aircraft and carriers at high risk destinations as defined by the Foreign & Commonwealth Office.

✔ When at any airport get away from the potentially risky public area of an airport as soon as you can. Check in, book your luggage in and then go through to the departures lounge. Strict controls and security procedures in

Terrorism

force there, mean that the departure lounge should be one of the safest places for an ordinary citizen, in any country in the world.

✔ When you arrive at your destination, try to leave the airport as soon as you can. The airport is a potential terrorist target and therefore a high-risk area, so you should leave it without delay.

What to do after an attack

If there is an attack, be it by bomb, rifle or anything, everyone who was at the centre will probably be dead or severely injured.

Everyone who was in the immediate area will be injured to some extent. If it was a bomb they will be deaf, suffering from shock and concussion, confused and disoriented with their eyes full of dust and grit. They may have been injured by debris, office and shop windows for streets around may have been shattered by a bomb and falling glass will have caused a lot of injuries.

Anyone further out will be scared. Though they heard the incident, due to the way noise moves in built up areas, they will not know what has happened and probably won't know where it has happened. You may find people running towards an incident thinking they are running away!

There will be people running in every direction, some wanting to get away, and some moving towards the incident to locate loved ones or to offer assistance, some just running in a panic!

The immediate threat is that when bombs are used, terrorists often place secondary devices at the scene. Secondary devices are placed to cause maximum death and injury to the emergency services, police and officials who attend to deal with the initial incident.

Your main responsibility is to not become a casualty because you will only be adding to the problem. If you stay in the area, you are at risk so in this book the advice has to be to go to a place of safety and get home as quickly as you can.

If you insist on offering assistance some actions are priorities.

- ✔ Somebody has to make sure that a report has been submitted, if you are not sure if the incident has been reported, contact the emergency services and calmly explain what has happened. For example if there has been an explosion, it may be a gas leak – don't assume it was a bomb unless you know it was.

- ✔ Call 999 (or the local equivalent) and explain what has happened. For example 'There has been an explosion in The Whisky Bar, in Bogtown High Street, on the junction with Lower Road'.

- ✔ Now give details. For example: 'The Whisky Bar has been destroyed, the building has collapsed and is on fire'.

- ✔ Tell the operator how many casualties you can see so that they know if they have to call one ambulance or invoke the emergency medical response in the surrounding towns. You should also try to indicate the type and number of injuries. For example: 'I can see five people who I think are dead. There are another 15 with serious injuries, one man has lost both legs, there are a lot of burns and facial cuts, several broken arms and legs. Looking around there are at least another twenty people who are bleeding from smaller injuries'.

- ✔ If you know the area, you may be able to help the emergency services by telling them if there is an obstruction that will prevent them using an approach. For example: 'Lower Road is blocked because the end wall of the bar fell on a lorry which is completely blocking that road'.

- ✔ You may be the only coherent point of contact at the incident. The emergency service operators may want to keep you on the line to ask further questions. Ask if they want you to stay on the line, if they do not they may want to call back to check to see if you have any more information.

- ✔ Protect the scene. Send somebody to the end of the street to direct traffic away from the incident and try to keep it clear for ambulance, police and fire engines. Where possible send two people, the first to do the job and the second to come back and tell you it is being done. When you get the report that traffic is being stopped you can cross one problem off your list, and send the second person back to help the first unless you have another job for them. Use common sense in where you stop traffic. If you stop it half way down the road, it will have nowhere to go. If you stop traffic at the junction at the end, any vehicles can turn around or turn left and right so traffic will continue to move away from the area.

✔ With a major incident there may be gas or petrol spilled. Smoking can cause further injuries so insist that people do not smoke, shout at them if you have to. When you give any instructions or advice to people for the rest of the incident tell them nobody is allowed to smoke, no matter how much they claim it will calm their nerves. Tell them they will blow everything up because of gas or petrol leaks and do anything you can to make them understand.

✔ When in shock, casualties may wander off, they should be collected together so that they can be watched as they wait to be treated. Usually by this stage people are beginning to want to help, but often they are not sure what to do. Remember that you are also in a potential crime scene. If it was a bomb you are at the scene of at least five murders because you can see five dead people. Anyone around may be a witness. If they are not injured, get them to stay and help or at least wait to be questioned, then they will be available to talk to the police when they arrive.

✔ Keep your ears open and listen to what is being said. If anyone seems to know what happened insist that they stay with you to talk to the police when they arrive which they will very shortly. Try not to let anyone who knows anything go, keep them around or at least insist that they give you their contact details.

✔ A major incident is entirely outside the experience of most people. They are lost and do not know what to do. Many want to help but are in shock. Most people will take sensible orders from somebody who seems to be calm and seems to know what to do. To start with you may be the only person at the scene who can organise assistance for the casualties.

✔ With a major incident, normal first aid skills and abilities are usually overwhelmed. The average first aid trained person will not know what to do with an amputation, serious burns or crush victims. Don't try to be clever. The one part of basic first aid training that works in a major incident is that the noisy ones can usually look after themselves. Stop to look at them, staunch bleeding, reassure them and offer them support, tell them that they will be OK but move on to the more serious injuries. Stop bleeding as best you can. If somebody is not breathing clear the airway and if necessary give mouth to mouth resuscitation. If at all possible instruct somebody to carry on with it while you do something else. People in shock can follow orders but may be in no fit state to decide what to do on their own.

✔ Look for anyone who is trapped, at risk from fire or further collapse. Make best efforts to rescue them, without putting anyone else at risk, and without causing additional injuries to the casualty.

✔ After the first shock, more people should be arriving to help, I would direct them to moving the walking wounded to a safe area, where paramedics and ambulance staff will have the space to set up and treat them. A supermarket car park would be ideal for this. You will be updating the emergency services all the time, so you should have told them that 25 walking wounded are now sitting on the wall outside Tesco car park waiting for treatment. Get the new helpers to stay with the walking wounded to reassure and support them.

✔ If you have any time left, you should go back to check on the seriously injured, make sure that their helpers are still with them, and make sure that the two key actions are being done, keep them breathing and stop them bleeding.

✔ When the emergency services turn up, go and talk to them. You possibly know more about what has happened than everyone else at the scene, update them, then hand over to them so that they can do their job. Each emergency service will have their own incident control for a major incident, there will be a senior police officer, senior fire officer and senior ambulance officer.

✔ Though any explosion and fire should be self evident point them out to the police and fire brigade. Explain what you know about fires, gas and petrol escapes, dangerous walls and other dangers and leave them to it. If you are still in telephone contact, tell the emergency operator that the fire brigade (or whoever) has arrived and pass on other similar details as long as they want you on the line.

✔ Tell the paramedics where what you consider to be the serious casualties are and if you have any idea explain which you think should be the priority cases. Point out where you have sent the walking wounded. Explain that for example you picked that area because it has vehicular access, plenty of space for turning and parking, with direct access back out onto the main road (if you are lucky enough to have that nearby). Tell the emergency operator that the ambulances have arrived, including how many ambulances if you are still on the phone.

✔ When the police arrive, if you are still in touch with the emergency operator update them and hand the phone over to the police officer. He or she can tell

Terrorism

them what their name and call sign is, because they will now take over from you as command and contact point for the incident.

✔ If you have any witnesses make sure that you point them out to the police officer. They are under stress too, so make sure that they realise this person or these people are potential witnesses and have vital information. If any witnesses did leave the scene pass on their details to the police officer so that they can be tracked down and questioned before evidence is lost or forgotten.

✔ If you did all of that, congratulate yourself, whether you get one or not you earned a Knighthood today for your bravery and clear thinking. You undoubtedly saved lives, prevented further injury, protected the scene and maybe collected vital witnesses.

✔ When the emergency services are at the incident, stand back and let them do what they are trained to do. By all means offer assistance but don't get in the way.

✔ When you are no longer required, or are ordered to go, seek medical care for any injuries you may have then leave the area.

10 What Now?

Procedure

Using your knowledge of your own circumstances and skills, you should have identified the countermeasures you want to introduce.

The next step is to prioritise them, so that you do them in the order that will give you the highest benefits for your efforts.

In these circumstances most people find that they do not have the time, money or skills to introduce all of their proposed countermeasures. That leaves you with an administrative and managerial task to perform.

You must manage and administer the outstanding vulnerabilities and countermeasures, so that you don't lose track of them. You should also keep them in mind so that you can implement them as and when the opportunity presents itself.

As time passes, you must also manage that process, to ensure that you revisit and reprioritise them as your circumstances change. You must review and prioritise the outstanding vulnerabilities and countermeasures, to make sure that you concentrate your effort where you will get the greatest benefit.

Remember that an 'identified' vulnerability and a 'proposed' countermeasure are like a lock that isn't used – useless! You took the time to identify them, why not address them to make your life happier and safer?

The Real Risk

We live in the real world, so let me put your mind at rest, in case the statistics, anecdotes and discussion of crime and vulnerabilities has left you with insomnia and nightmares. Crime levels are on the increase, but you don't have to build and retreat to a crime-proof bunker in the back yard just yet.

The average person in the UK is only likely to become a target for criminals if they are careless or very unlucky.

If you use the knowledge in this book to identify risks, threats and vulnerabilities in your life, and then implement appropriate countermeasures, you are unlikely to become a victim of crime.

If you also maintain an awareness of what is going on around you, and recognise and avoid potentially hazardous situations, you are exceedingly unlikely to fall victim to crime.

Don't fool yourself into thinking that now you have reviewed your security and taken steps to improve it that you are bullet proof. A random accident can still hurt you, or an opportunist thief might still catch you off guard, no matter how unlikely that may be.

You must maintain a level of awareness, and keep your eye on the world around you. Identify new vulnerabilities, risks and threats then take appropriate action to avoid them.

When Do I Review Security Again?

When you need to. If there is a significant change in your lifestyle, you should perform a new review of your security. If there hasn't been a change in your lifestyle, but you have noticed a number of near misses or unresolved vulnerabilities, threats and risks, maybe you didn't do a very good job of your review in the first place, or maybe circumstances around you have changed more than you realise.

When you feel the need to perform a new review, do so. I suggest that you should be performing a review every 12 to 18 months anyway. Make a note of it in your diary to remind you that it is time for a new review.

I hope the collected advice and suggested countermeasures have been enlightening and helpful. Above all, I hope that you are successful in completing your review and introducing countermeasures that will keep you and your family safe.

Useful websites

The Internet makes a world of information available to everyone. Some people may think that they are excluded because they do not have a home computer or advanced computer skills, but they are wrong.

There are a wide range of places and organisations which make Internet connection services available to the general public. From coffee shops with Internet computers available for the public to use, to libraries, colleges and schools. Most make the facilities available and offer support and training to those who need it. If you want to learn how to use the Internet, ask in your local library first. Even if they don't do it, they should be able to give you a list of places that do.

If you are worried about trying to use the Internet, don't be. Most people are surprised at how easy it is. By the time the average person has had a little practice, they usually say that they don't know why they were so nervous in the first place!

I have only mentioned a few Internet sites in this book. A world of information that is specific to your own personal needs and circumstances is also available to you.

The sites I have mentioned are listed below.

Register of personal electronic equipment www.menduk.org

Visit this site to investigate the possibility of registering and recording the serial number and details of your valuable electronic equipment for free. If anything registered is stolen, tell the local police and the details will be added to a stolen property database, which will help the police to track your stolen goods and catch the offenders.

Stopping unwanted mail, fax and phone advertising

If you want to try to stop, or at least reduce, the amount of unsolicited advertising you receive by mail, fax and telephone, visit the following specific sites to register your details. It will take a while to work and isn't guaranteed to stop all junk mail, but it helps.

www.fpsonline.org.uk
Register your number and state that you do not want unsolicited fax advertising material.

www.mpsonline.org.uk
Register your number and state that you do not want unsolicited mail advertising material.

www.tpsonline.org.uk
Register your number and state that you do not want unsolicited telephone advertising material.

Domestic Violence

Victims of domestic violence have stated that The Domestic Violence Hotline telephone number was the single most important piece of information that they found to help them to resolve their problems.

The National Domestic Violence Hotline can be contacted via Freephone – 0808 2000 247 which offers a 24 hours service.
E-mail – helpline@womensaid.org.uk
Post – PO Box 391, Bristol BS99 7WS.
www.womensaid.org.uk

Rape and sexual assault

You may be looking at this information for a friend, but if you have been attacked or assaulted, please seek professional help. The first and most important thing for you to understand is that the victim is never to blame. You were attacked. You should now seek help, but there are some important things that you must know.

Go to a safe place – a hospital, police station, woman's refuge, anywhere that is well lit and has people around.

Call the police – it was a serious crime. Whether it was a 'boyfriend', somebody else you know or work with, or a total stranger. The police have specially trained female officers who will support and advise you.

Preserve evidence – don't shower or douche, allow the police to collect vital evidence, such as blood and semen. The new police suites have washing facilities that you will be encouraged to use.

Get medical care – even if you decide not to go to the police, you should seek medical care. Don't be embarrassed to describe exactly what took place, if the doctor doesn't know what happened, she can't check for injuries. You will need specialist help and support to deal with possible pregnancy, AIDS, herpes, other venereal disease, or post-traumatic physical and psychological effects.

There are a number of sites that offer advice and support. For example: www.truthaboutrape.co.uk and www.rapecrisis.org.uk

Index

abuse, children 208
advice
   to parents 215
   to victims of rape 169
alcohol
   binge drinking 109
   effects 110
   excess 108
amphetamines 229
assault 44
attacks
   on women 145
   what to do when attacked 147
awareness 46

binge drinking 109
bullying 193
   being a bully 193
   being bullied 193
   recognising the signs 194
   my child is a bully 199
   what can I do? 196

cannabis 227
car jacking 78
cars
   criminal damage 104
   getting in 96
   security 71
   theft from 83
cash cards
   theft 18

child abuse 208
child protection advice 210
children
   computers 220
   cycle helmets 224
   mobile phones 222
   signs of drug use 225
   the Internet 217
cocaine 228
computers
   children 220
conflict management 45
counterfeit money
   theft 35
credit cards
   theft 14
criminal damage
   cars 104
cycle helmets 224

date rape 165
defending yourself 43
definitions 4
domestic violence 181
driving
   the elderly 237
drug assisted sexual assault 165
drugs
   descriptions 227
   signs of use 225

ecstasy 228

Index

effects of alcohol 110
elderly
   driving 237
   vulnerability 235
ergonomics and health 60
everyone 36
excess alcohol 108
exercising
   women 143

getting into your car
   safety considerations 96

handbags 141
heroin 228

identity theft 62
IMEI number
   mobile phone 37
impact factors 51
Internet
   children 217
Internet dating 155
Internet security 54

junk mail 67

keys 38
kids
   computers 220
   cycle helmets 224
   mobile phones 222
   signs of drug use 225
   the Internet 217

lapping 99
LSD 230

men 106
methamphetamines 229
mobile phones 36
   children 222

nuisance calls 123

offenders 158
older people 235

personal space 53
phishing 64
pickpockets
   theft 27

rape
   advice to victims 169
   countermeasures 167
review method 8
review pace 10

safe dating 152
safe friend pacts 163
safety at work 173
setting boundaries 159
sexual assault 150
shopping 137
shopping
   on line 59
signs of drug use 225
spotting in car parks
   theft 100

telephone
   nuisance calls 123
Terrorism 241
   at home 243
   general 232
   travelling 246
   what to do after an attack 247
theft 14
   cash cards 18
   counterfeit money 35
   credit cards 14
   from cars 69
   identity 62
   lapping 99

pickpockets 27
  spotting in car parks 100
  valuables from a car 83
  what will they take from your car 85
  where will they steal it (cars) 87
travelling
  terrorism 246
  women 125
trusting strangers 157

useful websites 255

vehicle security review 69

women 116
  advice to rape victims 169
  at home 120
  attacks by strangers 145
  cycling 135
  domestic violence 181
  driving 132
  drug assisted sexual assault 165
  exercising 143
  handbags 141
  if attacked 147
  Internet dating 155
  jogging 143
  offenders 158
  public transport 130
  rape countermeasures 167
  riding 143
  running 143
  safe dating 152
  safe friends pacts 163
  safety at work 173
  setting boundaries 159
  sexual assault 150
  shopping 137
  travelling 125
  trusting strangers 157
  walking 127
  what men can do 188
work
  safety 173

young adults 232
young men 107